Income Volatility and Food Assistance in the United States

Dean Jolliffe
James P. Ziliak
Editors

2008

W.E. Upjohn Institute for Employment Research
Kalamazoo, Michigan

Library of Congress Cataloging-in-Publication Data

Income volatility and food assistance in the United States / Dean Jolliffe, James P. Ziliak, editors.
   p. cm.
  Includes bibliographical references and index.
  ISBN-13: 978-0-88099-335-7 (pbk. : alk. paper)
  ISBN-10: 0-88099-335-9 (pbk. : alk. paper)
  ISBN-13: 978-0-88099-336-4 (hardcover : alk. paper)
  ISBN-10: 0-88099-336-7 (hardcover : alk. paper)
  1. Food relief—United States. 2. Income—United States. 3. Food stamps—United States. 4. School children—Food—United States. 5. Elderly poor—Nutrition—United States. 6. Economic assistance, Domestic—United States. I. Jolliffe, Dean, 1963- II. Ziliak, James Patrick.

  HV696.F6I525 2008
  363.8'830973—dc22

2008037350

The facts presented in this study and the observations and viewpoints expressed are the sole responsibility of the authors. They do not necessarily represent positions of the W.E. Upjohn Institute for Employment Research.

Cover design by Alcorn Publication Design.
Index prepared by Diane Worden.
Printed in the United States of America.
Printed on recycled paper.

Contents

Part 4: Design of Food Assistance Programs

Acknowledgments

Many people provided invaluable assistance and guidance to make this book possible. We owe a special debt of gratitude to Becky Blank, Sheldon Danziger, Sarah Marsh, Pattie Rayl, and Kristin Seefeldt at the National Poverty Center and Tina Terry and Dominique Wood at the Economic Research Service (ERS) for all of their efforts in making a success of the conference "Income Volatility and Implications for Food Assistance Programs II," held November 16–17, 2006, in Washington, D.C., out of which this book grew. We also thank Katherine Smith, Susan Offutt, Betsey Kuhn, and David Smallwood at the Economic Research Service for providing generous financial support for the conference. In addition we thank the invited discussants and session chairs—Doug Besharov, Dave Betson, Bob Dalrymple, Peter Gottschalk, Steve Haider, Colleen Heflin, Joe Hotz, Julie Isaacs, Betsey Kuhn, Pam Loprest, Jim Ohls, Luigi Pistaferri, Jeff Smith, Jim Sullivan, and Lowell Taylor—for the constructive comments made on the conference papers. We also thank Kevin Hollenbeck and the staff at the Upjohn Institute for publishing the important research contained in this volume. The views and opinions expressed in this volume do not necessarily reflect the views of the Economic Research Service of the U.S. Department of Agriculture.

1
Introduction

Dean Jolliffe
Economic Research Service

James P. Ziliak
University of Kentucky

The chapters in this volume were originally papers commissioned by the National Poverty Center at the University of Michigan and by the Economic Research Service (ERS) in the U.S. Department of Agriculture. They were presented at a conference titled "Income Volatility and Implications for Food Assistance Programs II," held in November 2006 in Washington, D.C. The conference was the second in a series sponsored by ERS examining the role of income volatility on food assistance programs. As volatility continues to emerge as an important policy concern across a number of sectors of the macroeconomy—from labor markets to housing markets to financial markets—the chapters in the present volume provide a much-needed focus on the issue and an in-depth examination of the effect of income volatility on the participation in and design of food assistance programs.

The seminal paper from which this volume is derived was written by Peter Gottschalk and Robert Moffitt (1994), who documented dramatic growth in earnings volatility among white men in the 1980s. Gottschalk and Moffitt showed that rising volatility was due both to increases in the variance of so-called permanent factors, such as returns on human capital skills, and to increases in the variance of transitory factors, such as job loss from frictional unemployment. In the next chapter, Benjamin Keys updates the Gottschalk and Moffitt analysis to include the 1990s and expands the scope of the earlier work by examining volatility among other demographic groups such as black men, white and black women, and female-headed families. Because food assistance programs such as food stamps, school lunch, and WIC serve a diverse array of individuals and families, it is important to establish the basic patterns of volatility for a population that reflects the diversity of program participants. Keys also examines consumption volatility in order to test whether volatile incomes translate into variable consumption patterns, or whether families are able to smooth consumption over time in response to income changes, as predicted by Friedman's permanent income hypothesis. Friedman's hypothesis states that families make consumption decisions based on permanent income, not temporary highs or lows.

Keys finds a large increase in transitory earnings, income, and consumption over the past 30 years across all major demographic groups. Permanent volatility increased for all groups as well, except for female-headed families. Although there is evidence that families are able to smooth consumption in the face of income shocks, overall consumption volatility rose nearly one-third since the 1970s. These findings suggest that families are increasingly less able to insulate consumption from income changes, particularly among low-income households.

Understanding how this increase in volatility affects the well-being of low-income households is of particular importance for U.S. food assistance programs, whose aim is to ensure that children and needy families have access to food. Greater volatility can result in more households needing assistance to maintain an adequate level of consumption during difficult times. The U.S. Department of Agriculture supports 15 domestic food and nutrition assistance programs, and approximately one in five Americans participates in at least one of these programs during the year. Federal expenditures on these programs in 2006 totaled almost $53 billion, with the three largest of these programs (the Food Stamp Program, the National School Lunch Program, and the Special Supplemental Nutrition Program for Women, Infants, and Children, or WIC) accounting for 87 percent of the expenditures. The remaining chapters in this volume focus on these programs and examine how income volatility influences the way people participate in food assistance programs, and the way policymakers design them.

Robert Moffitt and David Ribar use data from a longitudinal survey of low-income families with children and link this to administrative records on Food Stamp Program participation. They examine whether volatility in earnings affects program participation differently depending on a household's income level. In particular, they focus on differences between households with trend incomes above and below the gross-eligibility threshold for the Food Stamp Program. Their findings suggest that earnings volatility reduces participation among low-income households but that this effect dissipates for higher-income households. One explanation for this is that for households that are initially eligible, volatility results in periods of ineligibility, but for households that are initially ineligible, increased volatility results in periods of eligibility.

David Ribar and Marilyn Edelhoch use administrative data from the state of South Carolina to identify the reasons why families with children exit the Food Stamp Program. They find that about 20 percent of exits from food stamps in South Carolina are due to income or resources exceeding eligibility limits. But this effect is dwarfed by the two-thirds of exits that are attributable to household heads failing to file the necessary paperwork for recertification (about 50 percent) or failing to provide sufficient or verifiable information (about 16 percent). These families averaged more than $230 in benefits per month before their exit, suggesting that they are leaving significant benefits on the table. Ribar and Edelhoch show that the households that failed to recertify had lower and more volatile incomes than the households determined to be income-ineligible. For both black and white households, more variable earnings histories increased the likelihood of leaving voluntarily or for other reasons. The policy implications arising from this chapter weigh heavily toward improving Food Stamp Program recertification procedures and policies for households with children, especially those with volatile earnings sources.

Brian Cadena, Sheldon Danziger, and Kristin Seefeldt use unique panel data from Michigan—the data come from the Women's Employment Study (WES)—to examine both the reasons for food stamp exits (as do Ribar and Edelhoch) and the reasons for reentry onto food stamps in the post–welfare reform world. Using competing risks, Cadena, Danziger, and Seefeldt estimate a Cox proportional hazard model of food stamp exit and entry that, coupled with the decision to work or not to work, identifies the effect of personal characteristics such as education, marital status, health status, economic conditions, and policy changes (i.e., Electronic Benefits Transfer [EBT] rollout and asset-limit expansions) on these competing decisions. They find that women living with a partner are more likely to exit, with or without work, than women not living with a partner, which suggests that marriage and cohabitation form one pathway out of the program. This finding is most likely due to the woman becoming income-ineligible once her partner's income and resources are considered in determining benefit eligibility. They also find a strong link between physical and mental health problems and the likelihood of going off food stamps. A woman with physical-health problems is about 33 percent less likely to exit with work, a woman with a mental health problem is about 30 percent less likely, and a woman with a child with learning, mental-health, or physical health problems is about 33 percent less likely. This suggests that food stamps are operating effectively as a food safety net for those suffering serious personal problems. The rollout of the EBT in Michigan and the expanded generosity of vehicle asset limits had no discernible effect on entry onto and exit from food stamps. However, women who did not understand eligibility rules for food stamps after exiting TANF were significantly more likely to exit food stamps, with or without work. The obvious policy implication here is more basic than that from Ribar and Edelhoch in that the results found by Cadena, Danziger, and Seefeldt imply the need for expanded outreach efforts to inform former welfare recipients of their ability to combine work and food stamps.

Constance Newman uses national data from the Survey of Income and Program Participation to examine the role of income volatility on eligibility for and participation in the National School Lunch Program (NSLP). The NSLP provides a critical link in the food assistance network as it offers a nutritive, free or reduced-price lunch to low-income children during the academic year (and in some communities on weekends and summer weekdays as well). A number of reports over the past decade raise concerns about the accuracy of the NSLP application and eligibility certification procedures; they variously estimate that between one in eight and one in three children receive school lunch benefits for which they are not entitled. Newman finds that households experience substantial income fluctuations, especially households that are eligible for free or reduced-price NSLP meals. Income volatility in two-thirds of lower income households causes one or more changes in their monthly NSLP eligibility during the year. An estimated 27 percent of households that are income-eligible for subsidized lunches at the beginning of the school year in August are no longer eligible for benefits by December because of monthly income changes. The fluctuations come largely from changes in labor market behavior such as changes in hours worked, and Newman argues that these changes in labor market outcomes may explain a large amount of overcertification error. However, the monthly volatility may be of less programmatic concern because Congress extended the recertification interval from one month to one year as part of the Child Nutrition and WIC Reauthorization Act of 2004. That said, eligibility for the NSLP is still based on income in the month prior to application, and fewer low-income families are estimated to be eligible based on monthly income than on annual income.

Craig Gundersen and James Ziliak use national data from the Panel Study of Income Dynamics to estimate the age gradient in Food Stamp Program participation, as well as possible interaction between income volatility and age on food stamp participation. Knowledge of how participation varies across an individual's life course is especially important to policymakers given the pending retirement of the first members of the baby boom generation. Some observers have raised concerns that food stamp participation rates tend to decline with age, particularly among the elderly, who are financially vulnerable. However, the demographic bulge caused by baby boomers may lead to higher rates of participation at older ages than in the past because this is the first generation to come of age with the modern Food Stamp Program, which began in the early 1960s. In addition, because income volatility likely varies over one's lifetime, we might expect the effect of volatility on the decision to use food stamps to vary across the age gradient. Contrary to conventional wisdom (which is based on simple descriptive statistics), Gundersen and Ziliak find evidence of a U-shaped pattern in food stamp participation by age. The probability of participation, conditional on other known risk factors, is highest when one is young or old, which is basically the mirror image of the standard inverted-U age-earnings profiles widely documented by labor economists since the late 1950s. They also find that households with above-average income volatility are more likely to participate in the Food Stamp Program than those with lower income volatility at most ranges across the age gradient. One implication of their results is that we should make efforts to enhance outreach to prime-age working individuals and those with relatively stable incomes. Because Gundersen and Ziliak find evidence of higher participation among more recent birth cohorts, Congress must be prepared for the prospect of higher Food Stamp Program participation as the baby boom generation exits the labor force and enters a potentially long period of retirement.

The last two chapters deal with the complex issues of optimal program design in the presence of volatile incomes and when households are unable to fully self-insure against income shortfalls. Robin Boadway, Katherine Cuff, and Nicolas Marceau provide a sweeping overview of the key issues in welfare program design, including identifying exogenous and endogenous sources of income volatility, possible market and government responses to volatility, and government objectives (cash versus in-kind assistance) and constraints in the face of need by individuals with low resources. The authors note the importance of timeliness in identifying and assisting those with unexpected income shortfalls. Because low-income persons typically cannot self-insure against adverse shocks, the effects of negative incentives to work and save may well be less severe in the short run than in the long run. Boadway, Cuff, and Marceau thus suggest that the response to short-term volatility should be more generous than for more long-term need, and that the issue of false positive errors in administering benefits should be given less weight. They also suggest that the trade-offs between providing timely need in the short run and the effects of negative incentives to work and save in the longer run imply the need for relatively short recertification periods as well as other measures to improve program compliance, such as monitoring and auditing.

Mark Prell examines in detail the issue of recertification duration—that is, how much time a program allows to elapse before participants must provide verification that their eligibility status has not changed. He develops a dynamic model of recertification that weighs the costs, in terms of both administrative and recipient burden, against the benefits, which include cutting down on the provision of unwarranted benefits. Prell then describes the parameters of the model using a range of parameter estimates and finds an optimal recertification duration for WIC children of between 7 and 14 months, which is longer than the actual recertification requirement of 6 months.

Although the research contained in this book expands significantly our understanding of the links between income volatility and food assistance programs, especially regarding how those links affect program participation and optimal recertification length, more research on these and related issues is warranted. We still lack an understanding of how volatility simultaneously affects participation in food assistance programs and in those programs that address other family needs, such as income assistance, subsidized housing, and health insurance. Many individuals participate in multiple transfer programs, and if volatility serves as a trigger event for eligibility in one program—say, food stamps—do current or potential recipients also change their participation in TANF, Medicaid, or Section 8? And if so, is this due to coordination failures (in cases where recipients exit programs even when still eligible) or successes (in cases where recipients sign up for multiple programs as part of one-stop shopping) across agencies of federal, state, and local governments? We are just now beginning to scratch the surface of the many and varied implications of income instability for family well-being and optimal program design, and it is our hope that the research contained in this volume will stimulate future work on income volatility and transfer programs.

Reference

Gottschalk, Peter, and Robert Moffitt. 1994. "The Growth of Earnings Instability in the U.S. Labor Market." *Brookings Papers on Economic Activity* 25(2): 217–272.

Part 1

The Relationship between Income Volatility and Program Participation

2

Trends in Income and Consumption Volatility, 1970–2000

Benjamin J. Keys
University of Michigan

A household's well-being depends not only on its level of income, but also on how much that income varies from year to year. A family with steady, predictable income finds it easier to plan, save, and anticipate future expenses such as college and retirement. On the other hand, a household with highly variable income must rely on prior savings, credit markets, or government transfers to maintain a consistent level of material comfort.

This chapter documents trends in the variability of individual earnings, family income, and household consumption in order to improve our understanding of their underlying dynamics. Trends are presented for household heads, who are classified by age, race, gender, and educational attainment. By using 30 years of data and looking beyond the earnings volatility of white men, I obtain results that extend the findings of previous studies.

Concerns about the increased risk that households face are drawing greater attention from researchers and policymakers alike (CBO 2007). Previous research finds that income volatility has significantly contributed to increased wage inequality: researchers estimate that roughly half of the overall dispersion in wages is due to temporary variation (Gottschalk and Moffitt 1994; Haider 2001; Moffitt and Gottschalk 1998).[1] Daly and Valletta (2006) attribute much of the difference between earnings inequality in the U.S. and earnings inequality in Great Britain and Germany to greater earnings instability in this country. Despite the fact that the U.S. aggregate economy has become less volatile over the past 20 years, individuals face greater income instability than ever before (Dynan, Elmendorf, and Sichel 2007).

Other aspects of economic life, such as the receipt of employer-provided pensions and health care, have also become less stable in recent years. Thirty years ago, the majority of pensions were paid out in defined benefits, which meant the amounts were certain. Today, most employers provide defined-contribution plans that have uncertain payouts that depend on how successful workers are at investing these contributions. Households are increasingly responsible for maintaining health-care benefits as well, since out-of-pocket health-care costs have grown considerably faster than earnings.

The standard economic model of life-cycle consumption, the permanent income hypothesis, predicts that households should smooth consumption across good and bad income years. However, the results below suggest that rising income volatility has even affected the stability of household food consumption. Blundell, Pistaferri, and Preston (2005) document the transmission of income shocks into consumption shocks and find that self-insurance plays only a partial role. I also present evidence that consumption volatility, while smaller in magnitude than income volatility, is substantial and has been increasing since 1970, particularly among low-income households.

In the context of the Food Stamp Program, households with highly variable incomes may be reliant on the benefits of food stamps only for a short period of time, but these households would have particular difficulty smoothing out consumption in the absence of the program. Greater volatility would suggest that middle-income households would be increasingly likely to experience negative earnings shocks large enough to make them eligible for food stamps. The result of this increased income volatility is a widening in the range of households that could potentially benefit from the Food Stamp Program and other short-term government assistance programs.

This increase in volatility has coincided with a significant improvement in the overall economic position of American households. Data from the Panel Study of Income Dynamics (PSID) show that the median earnings of all male household heads have increased by nearly $6,000 in real 1988 dollars, or about 21 percent since 1970, representing a sizable improvement in living standards.[2] Figure 2.1 presents the trends in the median and standard deviation of the annual earnings of white and black male household heads between the ages of 20 and 59 over the period from 1970 to 2000. The two solid lines, which represent

Figure 2.1 Trends in Median and Standard Deviation of Earnings for White and Black Male Heads of Household, 1970–2000

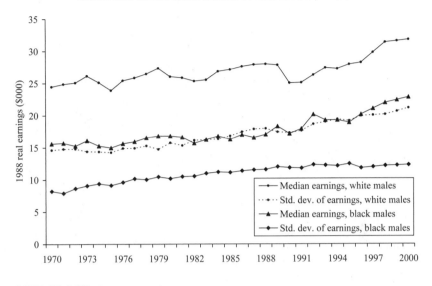

SOURCE: PSID.

the median annual earnings of white and black males, reveal the effects of business cycles (as evidenced by dips in earnings in the mid-1970s, early 1980s, and early 1990s) and the sharp increase in earnings during the economic boom of the 1990s. Over these decades, the median earnings of household heads increased by 25 percent for whites and by 45 percent for blacks.

Over the same period, the earnings distribution for men has significantly widened. The two lines of dashes in Figure 2.1 represent the standard deviation in annual earnings, which has steadily increased since roughly 1980 for white men, and which increased from 1971 to 1989 but then flattened out over the 1990s for black men. By any metric, inequality in the annual earnings distribution of adult males has grown from 1970 to 2000. Figure 2.2 presents the 90/10 ratio (the ratio of the 90th percentile to the 10th percentile) of white and black male log earnings for 1970–2000; it shows an increase in inequality between the 90th percentile and the 10th percentile in annual earnings starting in the late 1970s for both groups.

Figure 2.2 Ratio of Ninetieth to Tenth Percentile of Annual Log Earnings of Males, 1970–2000

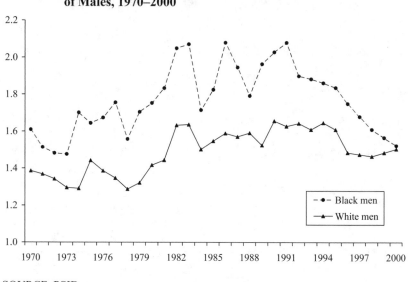

SOURCE: PSID.

The degree of inequality within the distribution of black male household heads is larger throughout the period than that of whites, though the two series converged in the late 1990s. The PSID shows a flattening in the 90/10 ratio for white men (and a dramatic downturn for black men) after 1991. Although these calculations are for annual earnings, this pattern is consistent with evidence from the Current Population Survey (CPS) on inequality in hourly wages. Autor, Katz, and Kearney (2007) document a similar leveling off of the 90/10 ratio after 1992 for all men in the CPS Outgoing Rotation Group (ORG) data.

Daly and Valletta (2006), also using the PSID and focusing on male household heads, calculate a 90/10 ratio that shows roughly the same pattern as shown in Figure 2.2: much flatter than results based on the CPS, though the trend is less noisy throughout and the downturn at the end of the series is less severe. Figure 2.2 emphasizes the value of looking beyond the earnings of white men to analyze the increases in inequality since 1970. The different experiences of black and white men in the 1990s, particularly in the decrease of the 90/10 ratio for black men and the flattening of the standard deviation in black male earnings, are overlooked when viewing aggregate trends.

Figure 2.3 presents the trends in median earnings and in standard deviation of earnings for white and black female heads of household. While the sample sizes are not large enough to draw conclusive evidence from, the trends suggest steady increases in both the median and the standard deviation of female-headed earnings.[3] In contrast to the results for men, Figure 2.4 shows that both black and white female-headed 90/10 ratios have fallen since 1970, indicative of increased labor force participation and increased real earnings for women throughout the income distribution. Again, though the small sample sizes are the likely cause of the unevenness of the series, if anything the earnings of female-headed households have become more equal over time.[4] This result is consistent with the findings of Gottschalk and Danziger (2005), who document an increasing 90/10 ratio in female hourly wages but a decreasing 90/10 ratio in annual earnings because of differences in hours worked.

These figures suggest that focusing on white men ignores much of the interesting variation in the rest of the population. Also, as is discussed below, the basic trends in the level and distribution of earnings

Figure 2.3 Trends in Median and Standard Deviation of Earnings for White Female Heads of Household, 1970–2000

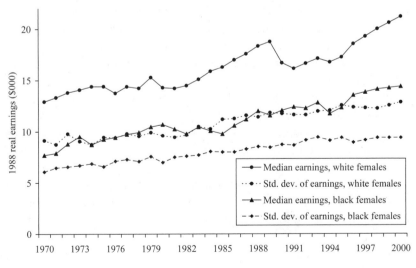

SOURCE: PSID.

Figure 2.4 Ratio of Ninetieth to Tenth Percentile of Annual Log Earnings of Female Heads of Household, 1970–2000

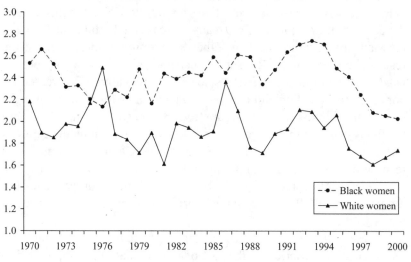

SOURCE: PSID.

mask changes in the permanent and transitory components of the variation. Studies that analyze overall population trends in inequality miss both the demographic variation and the permanent/transitory variation, which have very different implications for policymakers and researchers. If the permanent component is the sole driver of inequality, then structural inequalities in the labor market, such as educational opportunities, should be the primary focus for reform. If, instead, the transitory component dominates, then job retraining and temporary assistance programs should be emphasized to stabilize fluctuating earnings patterns. The rest of this chapter explores this dichotomy further and extends the analysis to household income and consumption. The next section describes how researchers traditionally measure volatility. The third section introduces the PSID, the data used here to document trends, and presents evidence of recent trends in income and consumption volatility. The final section offers concluding remarks.

MEASURING VOLATILITY

The change in inequality in any given year can be separated into two distinct pieces, one due to changes in the dispersion of average earnings, the other due to changes in earnings volatility for a given individual (Baker 1997; Baker and Solon 2003; Gottschalk 1997; Haider 2001). Thus, the change in the total variance of earnings is the sum of the change in lifetime earnings inequality and the change in earnings instability. When researchers and pundits discuss the growth of earnings inequality over the past several decades, these two components are usually considered jointly using a measure of inequality such as the Gini coefficient or a ratio of earnings at the ninetieth percentile to those at the tenth percentile. However, it is of great interest to researchers and policymakers to determine which component is the primary driving force behind the increased inequality.

One approach to measuring the permanent and transitory components of income inequality is to perform a variance decomposition. Let y_{it} be the log of real annual earnings of an individual i in year t, age-adjusted by regressing log earnings on a quartic in age, and using the residual as the measure of y. This age adjustment removes the effect of life-cycle patterns over each decade. The age-earnings profile differs by demographic group, which allows for age-earnings heterogeneity across age group, gender, race, education, and family structure. Thus, for each time period, I measure deviations from the age-earnings profile. In addition, the log specification removes any years with zero earnings. I follow the same restriction for consumption and family income, which are consequently referred to as "age-adjusted." Consider a permanent/transitory decomposition of earnings in any given year t for individual i:

$$(2.1) \quad y_{it} = \mu_i + v_{it},$$

where μ_i is permanent earnings and v_{it} is transitory earnings, which vary over time. These are uncorrelated by construction, so calculating the variance involves a straightforward process of addition:

$$(2.2) \quad \mathrm{var}(y_{it}) = \mathrm{var}(\mu_i) + \mathrm{var}(v_{it}).$$

The first term on the right-hand side is the permanent variance. When estimated in a population, it can be interpreted as a measure of the over-all dispersion of permanent income, or the degree of permanent income inequality. The second term represents the transitory variance and can be thought of as the instability in a given individual's earnings profile.

Empirically, we are interested in the sample mean of the variance terms in Equation (2.2). To define the variance of the transitory compo-nent, I follow the example of Gottschalk and Moffitt (1994) in selecting a time period T and computing the squared deviations from an individu-al's (age-adjusted) earnings, which cluster around his mean earnings:

$$(2.3) \quad \text{var}(v_i) = \frac{1}{T_i - 1} \sum_t^{T_i} \left(y_{it} - \overline{y}_i \right)^2 ,$$

where $\overline{y}_i$ is the mean earnings of the individual over T_i periods. Note that some individuals are not observed for all T years, so T_i varies at the individual level.

We denote the mean (across N individuals) of $\text{var}(v_i)$ as σ_v^2 .

The variance of the permanent component is thus the total variance minus the variance of the transitory component, using the following formula:

$$(2.4) \quad \sigma_\mu^2 = \frac{1}{N-1} \sum_i^N \left(\overline{y}_i - \overline{\overline{y}} \right)^2 - \left(\frac{\sigma_v^2}{\overline{T}} \right) ,$$

where $\overline{T}$ is the mean of T_i over all individuals and $\overline{\overline{y}}$ is the mean of log earnings over all individuals over all time periods.

Clearly, the unit-root decomposition used in this analysis is an over-simplification of the dynamic process of earnings, consumption, and family income. A structural decomposition of variances that exploits the auto-covariance structure of earnings, wage-growth heterogeneity, and other aspects of the labor market is a more nuanced and potentially realistic approach than the one taken here (Baker 1997; Baker and Solon 2003; Haider 2001; Moffitt and Gottschalk 1995). For instance, Baker (1997) persuasively argues that the simple permanent/transitory de-composition ignores the relationship between education and earnings.[5] In addition, estimating variances by the methods described in Equations (2.1) through (2.4) requires choosing arbitrary end points, which makes the results potentially sensitive to the choice of time period T.

Nonetheless, the structural results have aligned relatively closely with this transparent decomposition. Moffitt and Gottschalk (1998) estimate a formal ARMA(1,1) model and Haider (2001) analyzes a parametric heterogeneous growth model of earnings dynamics, but both reach conclusions that are broadly similar to the earlier work on the subject (Gottschalk and Moffitt 1994)—namely that roughly half of the increase in the variance of earnings (within education and age) can be attributed to an increase in the permanent component, and the other half to an increase in the transitory component. Moffitt and Gottschalk (1998) and Haider (2001) disagree on the timing of the increases, however. In related cross-national work, Daly and Valletta (2006) use a similar approach to that of Haider (2001) and draw analogous conclusions. In light of this evidence, the simple decomposition approach is sparingly illustrative, capturing the general trends and demographic heterogeneity relevant for this volume.

RECENT TRENDS IN VOLATILITY

To estimate trends in the permanent and transitory components of inequality in the population, longitudinal data that follows the same individuals over time is required. I use the Panel Study of Income Dynamics (PSID), a nationally representative survey that has interviewed roughly 8,000 households annually from 1968 to 1996 and biannually starting in 1997. The PSID obtains information on earnings, family income, consumption, family structure, and many other household- and individual-level attributes. I exclude all observations with zero earnings, then use a log transformation of earnings and trim the top and bottom 1 percent of the distribution to remove outliers.[6]

I follow the methodology of Gottschalk and Moffitt (1994) and further narrow my sample to nonstudent heads of household observed between the ages of 20 and 59. Thus individuals enter the sample by turning 20 and leave the sample by turning 60. Individuals are included only when they are heads of households, and two years' worth of valid information is required in each 10-year time period for inclusion in the sample. I follow the same sample restrictions for men and women, but given that the PSID is designed as a survey of "heads" and "wives," with men being designated as the default head of the household, the sample contains many more men than women.[7]

Table 2.1 presents the basic results of the above method of decomposition for the annual earnings of white males aged 20–59 for three periods: 1970–1979, 1980–1989, and 1990–2000.[8] The table presents the two components of the variance in earnings for all white males in the top row and for various demographic groups in the other rows. Below, I discuss the primary trends visible in the data.

In the first three columns, the increase in the permanent component of variance of (age-adjusted) earnings for white males across the three decades is evidence of the increase in lifetime earnings inequality. The difference from the 1970s through the 1990s represents a 31.5 percent increase in the dispersion of average annual earnings.

The nearly 38 percent growth in the transitory component of earnings, on the other hand, represents the increase in the average instability of individual earnings, which I refer to as "earnings volatility" (column 8). This is a sizable increase and is in line with earlier estimates (Gottschalk and Moffitt 1994). In addition, note that most of the growth in both the permanent and the transitory variance of earnings had occurred by the end of the 1980s; both the permanent and the transitory variances were about the same in 2000 as they were in 1989. This pattern is consistent with the evidence presented by Moffitt and Gottschalk (2002), which shows an increase in both components in the early 1990s but a decrease after 1992. Throughout the 30-year period, the permanent component is more than twice as large as the transitory component, suggesting that the majority of the overall dispersion is due to lifetime differences in earnings.

The second panel of Table 2.1 splits the sample of white male household heads by years of education. Those without a high school degree (row 1) have both larger permanent and larger transitory components of variance than the full white-male sample, and there is a similar increasing trend over the period. The most rapid increase in the permanent variance of earnings is for white male household heads with at least a college degree (row 3)—their variance increased by 76.6 percent over the 30 year period. College graduates, however, experienced the smallest increase in income volatility, at 37.4 percent, whereas volatility increased by 50.5 percent for high school graduates and by 42 percent for dropouts. The levels of both the permanent and the transitory

Table 2.1 Variances of Permanent and Transitory Real Annual Earnings, 1970–2000

	Permanent variance				Transitory variance			
	1970–1979	1980–1989	1990–2000	Percent change	1970–1979	1980–1989	1990–2000	Percent change
White males	0.28	0.36	0.37	31.5	0.11	0.16	0.16	37.7
By years of completed education								
<12 years	0.32	0.45	0.41	27.5	0.14	0.25	0.20	42.0
12+	0.23	0.32	0.31	38.3	0.10	0.14	0.15	50.5
16+	0.19	0.26	0.33	76.6	0.10	0.09	0.14	37.4
By age								
20–29	0.20	0.30	0.36	75.9	0.12	0.16	0.15	25.8
30–39	0.27	0.40	0.38	42.3	0.09	0.13	0.13	48.9
40–49	0.31	0.41	0.35	12.9	0.08	0.10	0.11	41.3
By permanent earnings								
Lowest quartile					0.26	0.36	0.31	20.4
Middle two quartiles					0.08	0.11	0.12	65.3
Top quartile					0.04	0.06	0.08	84.1
By race and gender								
White women	0.63	0.60	0.49	−22.2	0.32	0.36	0.35	9.0
Black men	0.42	0.71	0.80	88.4	0.18	0.34	0.34	90.4
Black women	0.91	0.90	0.88	−3.7	0.44	0.43	0.51	16.9

NOTE: Heads of households with positive wage and salary earnings, aged 20–59. Earnings are in logs, and observations are weighted using sample weights. "Percent change" is measured as the difference between the 1990s and the 1970s, relative to the value for the 1970s.

SOURCE: Author's calculations using the Panel Study of Income Dynamics (PSID).

components by decade for highly educated white males are for the most part smaller than for the other education groups. These patterns are reflective of the changes to low-skilled labor demand from 1970 to 2000, and of the increasing returns to skill over that time period.

Similar comparisons across age groups (third panel) and average permanent earnings (fourth panel) suggest that younger and lower-skilled white male workers are experiencing significantly greater income volatility than they did 30 years ago.[9] The instability in the highest quartile of permanent earnings is nearly 75 percent lower than the instability in the lowest quartile for the 1990s and more than 80 percent lower for the earlier decades.

The last panel of Table 2.1 presents differences across race and gender. The sample sizes for these subgroups are all significantly smaller than for white male-headed households, so the estimates should be interpreted with caution. White female heads of households have both greater permanent and greater transitory components than their male counterparts. The income volatility of white females is more than double that of white males, and this is likely an underestimate of the instability in earnings, given that this analysis excludes any years in which the household head has no earnings and that women are more likely to temporarily exit the labor force. Notably, the trend in inequality among white women is in the opposite direction from that of white men, as the permanent component of the variance has fallen by 22.2 percent, which is consistent with evidence from the 90/10 ratio shown in Figure 2.4.

The volatility of earnings of African American men and women also has increased since 1970. However, the inequality of earnings of black men has vastly increased (88 percent), while the trend in the permanent component of variance for black women is essentially flat across the three decades. The results from the fourth panel of Table 2.1 demonstrate that inequality among women (within race) has actually declined since 1970, that volatility has increased more slowly for women than for men, and that earnings are more unstable for African Americans than for white household heads across gender.

Table 2.2 investigates the similar decomposition for (age-adjusted) household consumption. The only measure of consumption available in the PSID for 30 years is food consumption. Here I use the sum of the cost of food consumed at home and of food purchased at a restaurant, not including food stamps. The consumption data is treated in an

Table 2.2 Variances of Permanent and Transitory Real Annual Food Consumption, 1970–2000

	Permanent variance			Transitory variance			
	1970–1979	1980–1989	1990–2000	Percent change	1970–1979	1980–1989	1990–2000	Percent change
White males	0.11	0.13	0.17	57.1	0.08	0.10	0.10	30.8
By years of completed education								
<12 Years	0.11	0.18	0.26	125.4	0.09	0.14	0.15	69.0
12+	0.10	0.13	0.15	54.2	0.08	0.09	0.10	26.7
16+	0.10	0.12	0.15	47.5	0.07	0.07	0.07	5.8
By age								
20–29	0.10	0.13	0.17	72.9	0.09	0.13	0.15	60.2
30–39	0.11	0.14	0.18	67.3	0.06	0.08	0.09	42.2
40–49	0.13	0.15	0.19	44.5	0.06	0.07	0.08	44.6
By permanent consumption								
Lowest quartile					0.10	0.14	0.15	39.4
Middle two quartiles					0.08	0.09	0.09	22.7
Top quartile					0.06	0.07	0.07	25.0
By race and gender								
White women	0.21	0.24	0.24	18.0	0.18	0.22	0.20	12.2
Black men	0.12	0.21	0.22	73.4	0.14	0.21	0.23	57.6
Black women	0.25	0.36	0.36	41.3	0.32	0.36	0.38	18.6

NOTE: Heads of households with positive wage and salary earnings, aged 20–59. Earnings are in logs, and observations are weighted using sample weights. "Percent change" is measured as the difference between the 1990s and the 1970s, relative to the value for the 1970s.
SOURCE: Author's calculations using the Panel Study of Income Dynamics (PSID).

identical manner to the earnings data by removing zero observations, performing a log-transformation of the data, and trimming outliers. In addition, there are a few missing years of data because of the food consumption questions not being asked.

The first row of Table 2.2 demonstrates that there is far less instability in food consumption than there is in earnings, which is consistent with households smoothing consumption across income fluctuations as predicted by the Permanent Income Hypothesis (PIH). Figure 2.5 also presents evidence that there has been little growth in either the mean or the variance of food consumption. Compared to earnings in Figure 2.6, the coefficient of variation (the mean divided by the standard deviation) of consumption is consistently below that of earnings (0.45 as compared to 0.55, on average). However, as shown in the remainder of Table 2.2, the basic demographic facts about lifetime inequality and instability hold true for consumption as well as earnings.

First, households where the head is less educated have greater lifetime inequality of consumption, as well as greater consumption instability. The instability for dropouts is nearly twice as large as the volatility for households headed by either a high-school or a college graduate

Figure 2.5 Trends in Mean and Variance of Food Consumption for White Males, 1970–2000

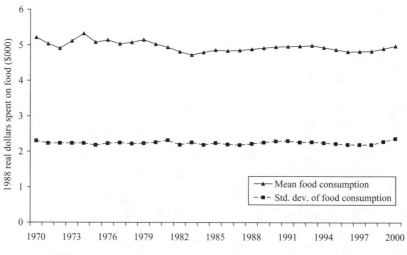

SOURCE: PSID.

**Figure 2.6   Coefficient of Variation of Earnings and Food Consumption
for White Males, 1970–2000**

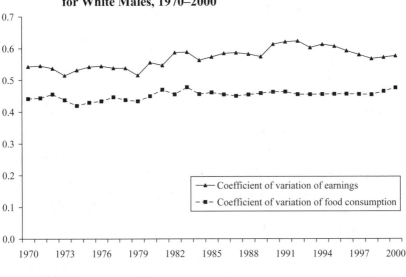

SOURCE: PSID.

in the 1990s. Second, younger households have significantly more consumption instability, a consistent trend throughout the time period. In addition, if we compare average consumption over the decade to calculate permanent consumption, we see that low permanent consumption households have much greater volatility than high permanent consumption households. Finally, households headed by white women have roughly twice the transitory variance of households headed by white men, and African American–headed households have significantly greater consumption volatility than white households (within gender).

The Food Stamp Program and other support services place a particular emphasis on aiding single mothers and a more general emphasis on helping other households with children. Tables 2.3 and 2.4 investigate instability and inequality of earnings and consumption for different household types. The second panel of Table 2.3 splits the sample of white male–headed households by whether there are children in the household and by whether the household head is married with children or unmarried with children.

White males in married households appear to have slightly lower earnings volatility than in unmarried households (both with children).

Table 2.3 Variances of Permanent and Transitory Real Annual Earnings, 1970–2000

	Permanent variance				Transitory variance			
	1970–1979	1980–1989	1990–2000	Percent change	1970–1979	1980–1989	1990–2000	Percent change
White males	0.28	0.37	0.37	31.5	0.11	0.16	0.16	37.7
White male–headed								
No children	0.30	0.41	0.36	20.0	0.11	0.17	0.17	52.2
Married w/ children	0.24	0.35	0.39	59.4	0.10	0.13	0.12	26.8
Unmarried w/ children	0.19	0.45	0.29	52.9	0.09	0.17	0.18	102.3
Black male–headed								
No children	0.52	0.95	1.10	113.6	0.19	0.41	0.38	98.9
Married w/ children	0.31	0.40	0.46	48.4	0.14	0.17	0.20	40.0
Unmarried w/ children	0.42	0.60	0.69	62.7	0.29	0.14	0.46	57.7
White female–headed								
Unmarried w/ children	0.76	0.73	0.69	−9.2	0.43	0.56	0.46	7.7
Unmarried w/o children	0.50	0.44	0.36	−27.3	0.24	0.19	0.22	−6.7
Black female–headed								
Unmarried w/ children	1.02	0.97	0.87	−14.8	0.46	0.56	0.65	40.9
Unmarried w/o children	0.55	0.52	0.90	62.2	0.30	0.23	0.25	−17.8

NOTE: Heads of households with positive wage and salary earnings, aged 20–59. Earnings are in logs, and observations are weighted using sample weights. "Percent change" is measured as the difference between the 1990s and the 1970s, relative to the value for the 1970s.
SOURCE: Author's calculations using the Panel Study of Income Dynamics (PSID).

In the third panel, the earnings of black males in married households are substantially less unstable than those of black males in unmarried households with children or those of black males in unmarried households with no children present.

For female-headed households, I present results for unmarried women without children and for the case of single mothers, as the PSID generally classifies all married couples as "male-headed." Compared to male-headed families, both married and unmarried, single mothers have much greater lifetime income inequality (permanent component of variance) and greater earnings instability. Furthermore, the transitory component is more than double that of single childless women (for whom the volatility trend is essentially flat). Thus, income inequality and volatility present a particular difficulty for the children of households headed by single mothers to overcome.

Table 2.4 shows that the headship patterns of earnings volatility also hold true for consumption volatility. Male-headed households with children have somewhat smaller consumption inequality and consumption instability than other types of male-headed households. Single mothers are again subject to the greatest instability, and this volatility has increased since 1970. Recall that I exclude any consumption from food stamps, which would smooth out consumption fluctuations, as shown in previous work by Gundersen and Ziliak (2003).

In Tables 2.5 and 2.6, I perform the same decomposition for (age-adjusted) family income (instead of individual earnings), as the consumption measure is a household measure and thus may be more comparable. If spouses' joint earnings ensure against either spouse's possible earnings fluctuations, we would expect that there would be less variability in household income. Indeed, as seen in Table 2.5, for white males the transitory component of variance is slightly smaller when measured by family income (0.135) than when measured by earnings from wages and salaries (0.157).

Comparing family income to individual earnings, we find that there is essentially no difference in inequality in the 1990s. However, in the previous two decades family income is dramatically less dispersed, and the growth of inequality in family income occurs a decade later than that of inequality in earnings. Determining why earnings inequality increased in the 1980s and then leveled out, while inequality in family income increased in both the 1980s and the 1990s, is worthy of further

Table 2.4 Variances of Permanent and Transitory Real Annual Food Consumption, 1970–2000

	Permanent variance				Transitory variance			
	1970–1979	1980–1989	1990–2000	Percent change	1970–1979	1980–1989	1990–2000	Percent change
White males	0.11	0.13	0.17	57.1	0.08	0.10	0.10	30.8
White male–headed								
No children	0.12	0.15	0.17	40.7	0.09	0.10	0.11	14.9
Married w/ children	0.08	0.11	0.13	61.7	0.05	0.07	0.07	35.3
Unmarried w/ children	0.13	0.12	0.16	20.1	0.08	0.06	0.13	50.6
Black male–headed								
No children	0.15	0.22	0.21	43.8	0.18	0.21	0.23	29.2
Married w/ children	0.08	0.18	0.16	97.6	0.09	0.15	0.15	73.0
Unmarried w/ children	0.12	0.25	0.21	81.2	0.35	0.18	0.23	−34.3
White female–headed								
Unmarried w/ children	0.19	0.32	0.31	66.1	0.17	0.25	0.26	51.7
Unmarried w/o children	0.20	0.21	0.19	−1.5	0.16	0.18	0.16	0.6
Black female–headed								
Unmarried w/ children	0.30	0.44	0.42	40.5	0.32	0.42	0.43	32.4
Unmarried w/o children	0.21	0.26	0.28	31.3	0.21	0.24	0.21	−4.2

NOTE: Heads of households with positive wage and salary earnings, aged 20–59. Earnings are in logs, and observations are weighted using sample weights. "Percent change" is measured as the difference between the 1990s and the 1970s, relative to the value for the 1970s.
SOURCE: Author's calculations using the Panel Study of Income Dynamics (PSID).

Table 2.5 Variances of Permanent and Transitory Real Annual Family Income, by Education, Age, Income, and Race and Gender, 1970–2000

	Permanent variance				Transitory variance			
	1970–1979	1980–1989	1990–2000	Percent change	1970–1979	1980–1989	1990–2000	Percent change
White males	0.20	0.28	0.37	81.2	0.08	0.10	0.14	80.0
By years of completed education								
<12 years	0.25	0.33	0.40	62.6	0.09	0.15	0.21	120.4
12+	0.16	0.24	0.32	101.9	0.07	0.09	0.12	73.9
16+	0.16	0.20	0.29	81.0	0.06	0.07	0.11	78.0
By age								
20–29	0.16	0.23	0.32	98.1	0.08	0.11	0.15	89.9
30–39	0.18	0.28	0.37	104.4	0.06	0.07	0.11	73.8
40–49	0.21	0.32	0.42	102.4	0.05	0.07	0.11	100.0
By permanent family income								
Lowest quartile					0.11	0.15	0.20	89.7
Middle two quartiles					0.07	0.09	0.12	72.9
Top quartile					0.06	0.06	0.09	65.5
By race and gender								
White women	0.28	0.39	0.44	56.9	0.18	0.20	0.26	45.9
Black men	0.36	0.66	0.89	147.9	0.13	0.29	0.41	228.0
Black women	0.31	0.52	0.63	103.9	0.17	0.24	0.36	106.4

NOTE: Heads of households with positive wage and salary earnings, aged 20–59. Earnings are in logs, and observations are weighted using sample weights. "Percent change" is measured as the difference between the 1990s and the 1970s, relative to the value for the 1970s.
SOURCE: Author's calculations using the Panel Study of Income Dynamics (PSID).

Table 2.6 Variances of Permanent and Transitory Real Annual Family Income, by Race, Gender, and Marital and Familial Status, 1970–2000

	Permanent variance				Transitory variance			
	1970–1979	1980–1989	1990–2000	Percent change	1970–1979	1980–1989	1990–2000	Percent change
White males	0.20	0.28	0.37	81.2	0.08	0.10	0.14	80.0
White male–headed								
No children	0.28	0.35	0.44	56.8	0.08	0.11	0.16	100.0
Married w/ children	0.16	0.23	0.29	86.5	0.06	0.07	0.10	61.7
Unmarried w/ children	0.27	0.26	0.34	25.3	0.07	0.12	0.14	87.7
Black male–headed								
No children	0.56	0.90	1.15	105.2	0.19	0.43	0.59	213.4
Married w/ children	0.26	0.29	0.35	35.4	0.09	0.10	0.14	58.6
Unmarried w/ children	0.28	0.46	0.48	74.5	0.14	0.09	0.62	348.9
White female–headed								
Unmarried w/ children	0.25	0.40	0.47	92.2	0.17	0.21	0.25	47.9
Unmarried w/o children	0.32	0.37	0.43	35.1	0.20	0.18	0.25	23.6
Black female–headed								
Unmarried w/ children	0.27	0.47	0.51	89.5	0.15	0.23	0.31	104.7
Unmarried w/o children	0.40	0.71	0.98	146.6	0.21	0.31	0.40	90.9

NOTE: Heads of households with positive wage and salary earnings, aged 20–59. Earnings are in logs, and observations are weighted using sample weights. "Percent change" is measured as the difference between the 1990s and the 1970s, relative to the value for the 1970s.
SOURCE: Author's calculations using the Panel Study of Income Dynamics (PSID).

research. This discrepancy is perhaps due to increases in dual-earner households or trends in assortative mating by education, and thus earnings potential, as well as to major changes in tax and social policy.

Not surprisingly, family income is no different than earnings or consumption with regard to demographic patterns, as families headed by less-educated men, younger men, and lower-income men all have much higher family income instability (Table 2.6). Households headed by white women have double the family income volatility in the 1990s as those headed by men, and measures of income instability are even larger for African American households headed by either men or women. In addition, female-headed households with children have experienced a steeper increase in transitory income volatility than female-headed households without children. This is consistent with the recent work of Bollinger and Ziliak (2007), which documents a 70 percent increase in inequality of single mothers since welfare reform in the mid-1990s. In sum, married households have experienced smaller increases in volatility in family incomes from 1970 to 2000, while the increases in both components of the variance for single mothers have been particularly acute.

CONCLUSION

This chapter has presented trends in individual earnings, family income, and household consumption volatility over 30 years for the main demographic subgroups of interest. Using the PSID, the best available panel data to study these patterns, I find a strong increase in the transitory variance of earnings, family income, and consumption over the period of 1970–2000 for all groups. This variance growth is consistent across race, gender, education, age, and family structure and is a robust result not presented elsewhere in the literature on volatility.

Focusing on the permanent component of the variance, I find that lifetime earnings inequality has increased for all demographic groups except women. However, at the household level, female-headed households have experienced an increase in the inequality of total family income. The majority of the dispersion of earnings, income, and consumption is from the permanent component, suggesting that much of the debate over inequality must address underlying fundamental determinants of lifetime earnings potential, such as health and education.

With regard to the transitory component of the variance, the earnings instability of the least-skilled, of young household heads, and of African American workers should be a preeminent policy concern. This is in part due to the sizable relative magnitude of the variance, but also because these three segments of the population are directly served by most of the government's nonretirement income assistance programs.

The trend toward increased consumption volatility since 1970 is a striking finding of this research. Consumption instability has increased 31 percent since the 1970s, an increase nearly as large as the increase in income volatility. Notably, consumption volatility is substantially smaller than earnings volatility, which suggests that households are able to smooth consumption across years by borrowing and saving accordingly. Nonetheless, the increase in fluctuations of consumption at the household level is of particular interest, given that consumption is a basic measure of well-being.

Determining the causes of these trends and demographic differences is especially challenging because of the broad secular changes that the labor force has experienced since 1970. Explanations as varied as skill-biased technical change (SBTC), secular declines in unionism, increased openness for international trade, capital complementarities, and computerization of the workforce, among others, have been offered elsewhere in the literature. In addition, the increase in the labor force participation of women has dramatically altered the demographic makeup of the workforce since 1970, making comparisons across decades difficult.

Further exploration of the underlying dynamics of earnings and consumption will broaden our understanding of the relationships between income and consumption volatility and the important way in which assistance programs such as the Food Stamp Program can serve to reduce the impact of short-term earnings fluctuations on the well-being of our nation's families.

Notes

As a PhD candidate in the Department of Economics at the University of Michigan, I am grateful for helpful comments from Rebecca Blank, Brian Cadena, Sheldon Danziger, Peter Gottschalk, Sisi Zhang, conference participants, and the editors of this volume. I thank the National Poverty Center and the Department of Education's Jacob K. Javits Fellowship for financial support. Any errors are my own.

1. Previous research disagrees on the timing of the increase in permanent income inequality and earnings volatility, however, as discussed below.
2. Median annual earnings adjusted for inflation for male household heads in the PSID increased from $21,443 to $27,254 between 1970 and 2000. The growth in mean earnings was roughly $9,000 over the same period (from $23,096 to $32,054). Throughout the paper, dollar amounts are converted to real 1988 dollars using the GDP chain-weighted deflator.
3. Sample sizes for female-headed households in the PSID range from 292 to 600 observations for whites and from 351 to 747 for blacks.
4. In addition, there has been little change in the fraction of women in the PSID who are heads of household. In 1970, 25 percent of the 3,796 age-eligible women were heads. In 1999, 27 percent of the 5,196 age-eligible women were heads.
5. I address this concern by estimating separate age-earnings profiles that differ by education group.
6. Removing outliers using this method is common practice in empirical studies of volatility because of potential measurement error and top-coding of variables.
7. Because certain questions in the PSID are only asked of household heads, individuals are in the data only as long as they are heads of households, which is not necessarily a constant status over time. Childless men and women are counted as heads if they have their own households, but not if they live with their parents.
8. Because the PSID shifted from annual surveys to biennial surveys, information on earnings and incomes are available for calendar years 1998 and 2000, but not for 1997 or 1999. For this reason, the last period appears to cover 11 years of statistics but really covers only 9.
9. To estimate permanent earnings, I calculate the average earnings over the decade and separate workers into quartiles.

References

Autor, David H., Lawrence F. Katz, and Melissa S. Kearney. 2007. "Trends in U.S. Wage Inequality: Revising the Revisionists." *Review of Economics and Statistics* 90(2): 300–323.

Baker, Michael. 1997. "Growth-Rate Heterogeneity and the Covariance Structure of Life-Cycle Earnings." *Journal of Labor Economics* 15(2): 338–375.

Baker, Michael, and Gary Solon. 2003. "Earnings Dynamics and Inequality among Canadian Men, 1976–1992: Evidence from Longitudinal Income Tax Records." *Journal of Labor Economics* 21(2): 289–321.

Blundell, Richard, Luigi Pistaferri, and Ian Preston. 2005. "Consumption Inequality and Partial Insurance." Institute for Fiscal Studies (IFS) Working Paper 04/28. London: IFS.

Bollinger, Christopher, and James P. Ziliak. 2007. "Welfare Reform and the Level, Composition, and Volatility of Income." Paper presented at the University of Kentucky Center for Poverty Research conference "Ten Years After: Evaluating the Long Term Effects of Welfare Reform on Children, Families, Welfare, and Work," held in Lexington, KY, April 12–13.

Congressional Budget Office (CBO). 2007. *Trends in Earnings Variability Over the Past 20 Years*. Washington, DC: CBO.

Daly, Mary C., and Robert G. Valletta. 2006. "Cross-National Trends in Earnings Instability and Earnings Inequality." Society for Economic Dynamics 2006 Meeting Paper No. 746. New York: Society for Economic Dynamics.

Dynan, Karen E., Douglas W. Elmendorf, and Daniel E. Sichel. 2007. *The Evolution of Household Income Volatility*. Finance and Economics Discussion Series 2007-61. Washington, DC: Federal Reserve Board.

Gottschalk, Peter. 1997. "Inequality, Income Growth, and Mobility: The Basic Facts." *Journal of Economic Perspectives* 11(2): 21–40.

Gottschalk, Peter, and Sheldon Danziger. 2005. "Inequality of Wage Rates, Earnings and Family Income in the United States, 1975–2002." *Review of Income and Wealth* 51(2): 231–254.

Gottschalk, Peter, and Robert Moffitt. 1994. "The Growth of Earnings Instability in the U.S. Labor Market." *Brookings Papers on Economic Activity* 25(2): 217–272.

Gundersen, Craig, and James P. Ziliak. 2003. "The Role of Food Stamps in Consumption Stabilization." *Journal of Human Resources* 38(Supplement): 1051–1079.

Haider, Steven J. 2001. "Earnings Instability and Earnings Inequality of Males in the United States: 1967–1991." *Journal of Labor Economics* 19(4): 799–836.

Moffitt, Robert A., and Peter Gottschalk. 1995. "Trends in the Covariance Structure of Earnings in the U.S.: 1969–1987." Institute for Research on Poverty Discussion Paper. Madison, WI: University of Wisconsin Institute for Research on Poverty.

———. 1998. "Trends in the Variances of Permanent and Transitory Earnings in the U.S. and Their Relation to Earnings Mobility." Boston College Working Papers in Economics No. 444. Boston: Boston College Department of Economics.

———. 2002. "Trends in the Transitory Variance of Earnings in the United States." *Economic Journal* 112(478): C68–C73.

3
Variable Effects of Earnings Volatility on Food Stamp Participation

Robert Moffitt
Johns Hopkins University

David C. Ribar
University of North Carolina at Greensboro

There are several sound reasons to suppose that earnings volatility plays a role in program participation behavior; however, the results from previous empirical studies have been equivocal. To the extent that researchers have considered volatility, they have mostly focused on different types and definitions of this concept, such as short-term versus long-term shocks in earnings or the overall variability of earnings histories. Researchers have not considered how associations might develop for some groups but not for others. In this paper, we examine how the effects of earnings variability on program participation are likely to differ, depending on a household's position in the income distribution. Specifically, we posit that there will be asymmetries in these effects depending on whether the household is initially above or below an eligibility threshold.

There are many reasons why asymmetric effects might appear, including a simple "mechanical" explanation. Consider a household whose long-term trend earnings place it within the eligibility guidelines of the Food Stamp Program or some other assistance program. If earnings and other characteristics are completely stable so that there is no short-term variability, the household will remain eligible for the program over time and may participate, depending on how it values the program's benefits relative to its costs of enrollment and compliance (Moffitt 1983, 2003). If we instead allow for some earnings variability, there is a chance that the household will lose eligibility from time to time, leading to a decrease in its opportunities and incentives to participate. Thus, among initially eligible households, there is a mechanical association in which greater variability reduces participation. These associations are reversed, however, when we consider households that are initially above the eligibility threshold. For these households, stable incomes lead to continuous periods of ineligibility and nonparticipation, while unstable incomes lead to temporary periods of eligibility and perhaps participation. We subsequently discuss additional conceptual reasons for the association between earnings volatility and program participation, but as this simple explanation shows, asymmetries in effects should be considered.

We examine the relationship between earnings volatility and food stamp participation using survey data from the Three-City Study that have been linked to administrative case records on program participation. The Three-City Study is a longitudinal survey of low-income families who were living in Boston, Chicago, and San Antonio. A distinct advantage of the Three-City Study for our purposes is that while it is a low-income sample and includes many food stamp recipients, it was not initially limited to program participants. Thus, the survey includes participating and nonparticipating households as well as eligible and near-eligible households. At each wave, the survey gathered information about people's work and earnings histories. These features facilitate our analyses of program participation, earnings volatility, and asymmetric effects.

Another advantage of the Three-City Study is that its survey responses have recently been linked to administrative data. Previous household-level research on participation in food assistance programs has usually relied on one or the other of these two types of data. Our approach of using combined survey and administrative data addresses some of the weaknesses of using only one or the other of these two sources. From the administrative data, we obtain more accurate and lengthy descriptions of participation histories than we could through surveys, overcoming the recall problems inherent in retrospective questionnaires. At the same time, the survey data help us to surmount some of the shortcomings of administrative data. Program records only describe behavior after people have applied to or joined a program and can only be used in limited ways to examine people's participation decisions, especially their program entry decisions. Administrative data also typically lack important explanatory variables and covariates, such as measures of disability and health status.

We use these data to compare times spent on the Food Stamp Program for households with different circumstances, including different levels and histories of earnings. Our analyses further distinguish between households that appear to be eligible and those that appear to be ineligible for food stamps based on longer-run income data. We estimate longitudinal fixed-effect regression models of the times that households spend on food stamps; these models account for additional permanent, unmeasured characteristics of households that might be conflated with their earnings histories and program outcomes. Our multivariate results indicate that short-term earnings changes and earnings variability are each negatively associated with program participation for households with low levels of permanent income. These sources of volatility appear to be less strongly associated with participation for households with higher levels of permanent income.

CONCEPTUAL ANALYSIS OF EARNINGS VOLATILITY

A gap in program research, which this and other chapters in this volume address, concerns the role of previous earnings and program experiences. While numerous studies have examined the associations between people's short-term characteristics, such as their immediate monthly incomes, and their program behavior, only a few have considered the impacts of income histories, the variability of their incomes, or other longer-term characteristics, on participation (see, e.g., Farrell et al. 2003). There are reasons to believe that earnings histories and variability might be relevant in a number of ways.

First, as mentioned in the introductory section, increased earnings variability can lead to more frequent changes in eligibility. For households that are initially eligible, these changes would take the form of brief periods of ineligibility; for households that are initially ineligible, they would take the form of brief periods of eligibility. The changes in eligibility could in turn lead to changes in participation.

A second, related consideration is that, other things being held constant, higher rates of volatility will lead to shorter continuous spells of eligibility and potential participation. Because there are fixed costs associated with entering or reentering the Food Stamp Program (such as completing the application; supplying earnings records, a birth certificate, a Social Security card, and other documentation; and attending an interview), the reduction in potential spell lengths could deter participation in the first place.

Third, the program itself may place higher compliance demands on households with variable earnings. As Ribar and Edelhoch (2008) document in this volume, some states require more frequent recertification intervals for households with earnings or with unstable incomes than for other households. Within our sample, one state, Texas, requires households to immediately report any change in work status—change in job, change in pay rate, or loss of job—while the other two states, Illinois and Massachusetts, only require households to report changes in monthly earnings of $100 or more. Higher compliance costs would again reduce the incentives for households to enter the program or to continue participating.

Fourth, while increased earnings volatility likely affects eligibility and compliance costs, it may also increase the value of food stamp participation to recipients. As a means-tested program, the Food Stamp Program provides a form of social insurance, issuing more generous benefits when incomes are low and less generous benefits when incomes are high. Thus, the Food Stamp Program helps to smooth consumption for families who lack assets or opportunities to borrow. Households with variable earnings would benefit more from this consumption-smoothing feature than would households with stable earnings, possibly contributing to a positive association between volatility and participation.

Fifth, we need to remember that households' observed earnings may not be entirely exogenous but may instead reflect behavioral elements, which may themselves be influenced by program behavior. Consider a household that receives an earnings shock in the form of a higher hourly wage rate, perhaps from an unexpected raise or a minimum wage increase. If the household's work hours remain fixed, this wage increase would translate into an earnings increase. However, if the household places a premium on its nonmarket time or just on maintaining its food stamp eligibility, it might cut back its work hours, leading to little change in earnings. In this case, we would observe that stable earnings were associated with continued participation, but earnings would not be the causal factor. In our analyses, we address possible confounding influences between earnings and program participation by estimating longitudinal fixed-effect regression models that account for permanent unobserved characteristics of households. Additionally, our analyses will examine the association between current and past earnings outcomes, on the one hand, and future program outcomes, on the other, to remove any concurrent reverse effects of participation on earnings.

DATA SOURCES AND MEASURES

The data for our analyses consist of interview data from the Three-City Study linked to administrative case records for food stamp and Temporary Assistance for Needy Families (TANF) receipt. The Three-City Study is a longitudinal survey of 2,458 children and their caregivers who were initially living in low-income neighborhoods in Boston, Chicago, and San Antonio. At the time of the first interview in 1999, the families all had incomes below 200 percent of the poverty line. Although the survey includes many public assistance recipients, it was not specifically restricted to this group. Also, by design it includes both poor and near-poor families.

After the initial interviews, follow-up interviews were conducted in 2000–2001 and 2005. Retention rates were high, as 88 percent of the original sample participated in the second round and 80 percent participated in the third round. In each wave, interviews were conducted with both the focal child and the child's caregiver.[1] In cases where the child and caregiver had separated, both were subsequently followed and interviewed. For this paper, we rely on the information provided by the current and former caregivers, as they were in the best position to describe the households' economic circumstances, demographic composition, and other characteristics.

In the most recent (third) wave of the survey, the caregivers who participated in face-to-face interviews were asked to give permission for the research team to gather administrative information about them.[2] Caregivers who agreed to this provided names and Social Security numbers, which were then used to search for food stamp and TANF records. Of the 1,980 caregivers who completed in-person interviews, 1,448 gave permission to be included in the administrative part of the study, and of this smaller number 1,286 were successfully matched to case files in Illinois, Massachusetts, or Texas.[3]

The administrative records from the state agencies cover the period from January 1997 to June 2006 and indicate the specific months in which the caregiver was a member of an assistance unit that received food stamps, TANF, or both. We use these data to form counts of the months that the caregiver received food stamp assistance in the quarter and half-year following each of the three interviews. These are the primary outcome measures for our analyses.

Besides the food stamp outcome measures, we also use the administrative data to construct measures of the number of months out of the previous 12 that a caregiver received food stamp assistance or TANF. We use the measures of prior receipt as conditioning variables in our analyses.

The interview data from the Three-City Study provide us with most of our other explanatory variables. We are especially interested in the earnings of the caregivers. To measure current earnings, we use a constructed variable (supplied with the public-use version of the survey) of the caregiver's labor earnings in her primary job during the month leading up to the interview; the measure includes her wages and salary along with possible commissions and tips.

The survey also includes retrospective questions regarding the caregiver's primary jobs for up to two years prior to each interview. From these questions, we form several summary measures of the caregiver's earnings over the preceding 12-month interval, including an indicator for whether there were any earnings during the period, the average monthly level of earnings, the maximum amount of earnings reported in any of the months, and the coefficient of variation for earnings. Because a nontrivial portion of the histories is incomplete (about 8 percent), we also include a dummy variable for whether summary measures could be formed. All of the earnings variables are adjusted for inflation using the Consumer Price Index for Urban Wage Earners (CPI-U) and expressed in 2005 values. We interpret the 12-month average of earnings as being an indicator of the long-term or persistent level of earnings, and we interpret the maximum monthly amount over this period as being an indicator of earnings capacity. The coefficient of variation is used as a measure of earnings variability. In a regression that conditions on the earnings history, the current earnings variable can be interpreted as an indicator for short-term changes in earnings.

While the retrospective earnings data are useful, there are some weaknesses in the measures. First, they only describe the earnings of the caregiver and omit other household members. Second, the data are limited to primary jobs and do not cover all sources of earnings. Finally, the measures are limited to usual earnings for a given job and only change when there is a switch in jobs or employment status; the measures do not vary within a job spell.

A unique element of our analyses is that they distinguish between households that appear to be eligible for food stamps based on their long-term incomes and households that appear to be either ineligible or marginally eligible. There are three primary tests for food stamp eligibility: 1) a household's income must be below 130 percent of the poverty threshold (the gross income test), 2) a household's income after adjusting for program deductions and exemptions must be below 100 percent of the poverty threshold (the net income test), and 3) a household's assets must be below a certain value (the asset test). Because we lack detailed information on likely deductions and exemptions and on the level of assets, we focus on the gross income test. In each wave of the Three-City Study, caregivers were asked about all of the sources of income from all household members in the previous month. The public-use version of the survey contains a measure of the income-to-needs ratio that incorporates the available information on total incomes and household composition. We fit household-specific trend lines through the 1999, 2000–2001, and 2005 income-to-needs measures and use the values along these trend lines as our indicators of long-term income-to-needs. Households whose trend values in a given wave are below 1.3 are classified as gross-income-eligible on the basis of their long-term circumstances, while households whose trend values are above 1.3 are classified as gross-income-ineligible. About 75 percent of the wave-specific observations in our analysis sample are classified as being eligible under this definition, and 90 percent of the caregivers are categorized as eligible in at least one wave.

The Three-City Study also asked caregivers about other economic circumstances of their households. We use responses to several differ-

ent questions to measure access to capital and possible financial difficulties. One direct measure of access to capital is a binary indicator for
whether anyone in the caregiver's household had a bank account, savings account, or other investment account. Another direct measure is an
indicator of whether the household had any outstanding loans, including loans from family and friends. Our analyses also include separate
indicators for whether the household owned a car or a home. Car and
home ownership would not only reveal some previous financial where-
withal but would also represent collateral against which the household
might borrow. Finally, we include an index of recent financial strains,
supplied with the public-use file, that is constructed from five questions on topics such as how frequently the household needed to borrow
money to pay bills and whether it usually ended up with any money at
the end of the month.

The interview data from the survey also provide us with demographic information about the caregiver and her household, including
the caregiver's age, race/ethnicity, education, marital status, health status, and the numbers of children and adults in the household. These
variables are routinely included in studies of benefit receipt. In all of our
multivariate analyses, we also include controls for the year and month
in which the interview took place to account for unmeasured changes in
policies and economic conditions.

We limit our analysis to caregivers who participated in all three
waves of the survey and who could be linked to administrative records.
After omitting observations with item nonresponse and dropping a
small number of separated caregivers who no longer had any children
in their households, we are left with an analysis sample of 931 caregivers and 2,793 wave-specific observations. Geographically, the observations are split nearly equally across the three cities. Means and standard
deviations for the analysis variables, calculated separately for each city,
are reported in Table 3.1.

The analysis sample is clearly made up of those who are disadvantaged, having not only been initially selected on the basis of low
incomes but also subsequently restricted to households appearing in
the assistance program records for the three states. The statistics are
consistent with this selection. On average, the households spent more
than half of each quarter or half-year following their interviews on food
stamps. Average inflation-adjusted monthly earnings just before the

interviews were $648 in Boston, $556 in Chicago, and $502 in San Antonio. Average earnings for the prior year were somewhat lower in Boston and San Antonio but somewhat higher in Chicago. More than half of the caregivers reported no earnings at all in the preceding year. Just over a third of the households had some kind of financial account, with the average incidence varying substantially across cities. Roughly half of the households reported outstanding loans. While this latter statistic might appear to be favorable, it likely reflects a lack of access to credit for many of the families. Only about one out of eight of the households owned the homes they lived in, and just over half of the caregivers were without a car. Few of the caregivers were married, and less than two-thirds had completed or gone beyond high school. Most of the caregivers were black or Hispanic (98 percent in San Antonio). About one-sixth reported disabilities severe enough to interfere with work. Lastly, the average number of children was high, at just under three per household.

Descriptive Analysis

Food stamp and TANF receipt in the two cities were strongly associated with several economic characteristics of the caregivers. Table 3.2 shows the average months of each type of program receipt in the year following the interview, calculated separately for some of these characteristics. From top to bottom, the table is divided into three sections: the first section reports estimates for the general sample of households, the second section reports estimates for households with trend incomes below the gross-eligibility threshold, and the third section reports estimates for households with trend incomes above the gross-eligibility cutoff. From left to right, results are listed separately for Boston, Chicago, and San Antonio.

Near the top of the table, the estimates show the anticipated result that the months of subsequent food stamp participation generally fall with the level of current earnings. Among the caregivers from Boston, the gradient was especially steep, as the participation rates for caregivers without earnings was more than four times higher than the participation rates for caregivers with $1,000 in monthly earnings. Moffitt and Winder (2003) and Frogner, Moffitt, and Ribar (2007) similarly found

Table 3.1 Characteristics of Analysis Sample

	Boston		Chicago		San Antonio	
	Mean	Std. dev.	Mean	Std. dev.	Mean	Std. dev.
Months on food stamps in next 3	1.57	(1.47)	1.64	(1.45)	1.92	(1.38)
Months on food stamps in next 6	3.13	(2.85)	3.24	(2.82)	3.81	(2.64)
Earnings in interview month ($)	648.47	(878.46)	555.83	(747.09)	502.03	(677.20)
Any earnings in last year (0/1)	0.56	(0.50)	0.61	(0.49)	0.59	(0.49)
Average earnings in last year ($)	614.39	(792.75)	579.44	(718.72)	494.35	(643.47)
Coefficient of variation for earnings in last year	0.39	(0.78)	0.42	(0.77)	0.46	(0.81)
Maximum earnings in last year ($)	840.99	(936.03)	793.53	(849.55)	693.20	(761.58)
Prior year's earnings information missing (0/1)	0.09	(0.29)	0.07	(0.25)	0.09	(0.28)
Household income-to-needs	1.09	(0.70)	1.02	(0.63)	0.91	(0.57)
Bank, savings, or financial account (0/1)	0.52	(0.50)	0.29	(0.46)	0.35	(0.48)
Outstanding loans (0/1)	0.47	(0.50)	0.44	(0.50)	0.52	(0.50)
Owns home (0/1)	0.04	(0.19)	0.15	(0.36)	0.19	(0.39)
Owns vehicle (0/1)	0.38	(0.49)	0.37	(0.48)	0.57	(0.50)
Financial strain index	0.05	(0.73)	0.03	(0.73)	−0.01	(0.72)
Months on food stamps in last year	6.61	(5.43)	6.69	(5.31)	8.09	(4.87)
Months on TANF in last year	4.49	(5.35)	3.78	(5.16)	2.78	(4.42)
Non-Hispanic black (0/1)	0.32	(0.47)	0.55	(0.50)	0.39	(0.49)
Hispanic (0/1)	0.50	(0.50)	0.35	(0.48)	0.59	(0.49)
Age	35.07	(9.11)	33.76	(9.68)	31.80	(8.99)
Completed high school or GED (0/1)	0.47	(0.50)	0.33	(0.47)	0.35	(0.48)
Completed college (0/1)	0.22	(0.41)	0.22	(0.41)	0.22	(0.42)

Disability that prevents work (0/1)	0.23	(0.42)	0.16	(0.37)	0.17	(0.38)
Number of minors in household	2.50	(1.26)	2.88	(1.42)	2.72	(1.37)
Married, spouse present (0/1)	0.08	(0.28)	0.16	(0.37)	0.18	(0.38)
Number of adults in household	1.56	(0.80)	1.85	(0.96)	1.71	(0.82)
Number of caregivers	308		300		323	
Number of observations	924		900		969	

NOTE: Amounts in rows labeled as "(0/1)" represent binary variables.

SOURCE: Authors' calculations, using interview data from the Three-City Study matched to administrative records.

Table 3.2 Months of Food Stamp Assistance Following the Interview for Different Types of Households

Characteristic	Boston			Chicago			San Antonio		
		Average months on food stamps in next...			Average months on food stamps in next...			Average months on food stamps in next...	
	N	3 months	6 months	N	3 months	6 months	N	3 months	6 months
All caregiver observations	924	1.6	3.1	900	1.6	3.2	969	1.9	3.8
Earnings in interview month[a]									
None	456	2.1	4.2	441	1.8	3.5	450	2.3	4.6
$1,000 or less	140	1.7	3.5	172	1.8	3.7	225	2.0	3.8
More than $1,000	245	0.5	1.0	225	1.1	2.2	210	1.0	1.9
Average earnings in last year[a]									
None	321	2.2	4.3	293	1.7	3.3	311	2.5	4.9
$1,000 or less	269	1.9	3.8	314	2.0	4.0	374	2.0	4.0
More than $1,000	251	0.5	1.0	231	1.0	2.0	200	0.8	1.7
Coefficient of variation of earnings in last year[a,b]									
Less than 0.5	325	0.9	1.8	332	1.3	2.6	318	1.3	2.6
0.5 or higher	195	1.8	3.5	213	1.9	3.9	256	1.9	3.9
Observations with trend income below gross eligibility threshold	671	1.8	3.7	702	1.9	3.7	795	2.2	4.3
Earnings in interview month[a]									
None	392	2.2	4.3	378	1.9	3.7	419	2.4	4.7
$1,000 or less	119	1.8	3.6	151	2.0	3.9	198	2.1	4.1
More than $1,000	104	0.6	1.3	120	1.5	3.0	103	1.5	2.8
Average earnings in last year[a]									
None	274	2.2	4.5	262	1.7	3.4	291	2.5	5.0

$1,000 or less	227	2.0	4.0	261	2.2	4.3	319	2.1	4.2
More than $1,000	114	0.6	1.2	126	1.4	2.7	110	1.3	2.6
Coefficient of variation of earnings in last year[a,b]									
Less than 0.5	187	1.1	2.3	210	1.7	3.4	209	1.8	3.5
0.5 or higher	154	2.0	3.9	177	2.1	4.2	220	2.1	4.1
Observations with trend income above gross eligibility threshold[a]	253	0.9	1.7	198	0.9	1.7	174	0.8	1.6
Earnings in interview month[a]									
None	64	1.8	3.4	63	1.2	2.3	31	1.6	3.4
$1,000 or less	21	1.3	2.6	21	1.1	2.2	27	0.8	1.3
More than $1,000	141	0.4	0.8	105	0.6	1.2	107	0.5	1.0
Average earnings in last year[a]									
None	47	1.8	3.4	31	1.2	2.4	20	1.5	3.2
$1,000 or less	42	1.4	2.7	53	1.1	2.2	55	1.3	2.5
More than $1,000	137	0.4	0.8	105	0.6	1.2	90	0.3	0.6
Coefficient of variation of earnings in last year[a,b]									
Less than 0.5	138	0.5	1.0	122	0.7	1.3	109	0.4	0.9
0.5 or higher	41	1.1	2.0	36	1.1	2.3	36	1.3	2.6

SOURCE: Authors' calculations, using interview data from the Three-City Study matched to administrative records.
[a] Excludes observations with missing earnings information.
[b] Excludes observations with zero earnings.

that earnings and program receipt were negatively related when they examined self-reports of program participation in these data.

When we move to the next three rows of results, we see that average earnings over the preceding year are also negatively associated with food stamp participation. Although it is not entirely clear from the table, the association is slightly stronger for 12-month average earnings than for the current month's earnings. This result is consistent, since the 12-month figure is a longer-term measure.

The next two rows report 1) participation levels for households with positive earnings whose coefficient of variation was positive but below one-half and 2) participation levels for households with more variable earnings. In all three cities, more variable incomes were associated with higher levels of participation.

Households with trend incomes below the food stamp gross eligibility threshold have participation rates that are more than twice as high as households with larger trend incomes. Though the participation rates for the high-trend-income households are much smaller in relative terms, they are still appreciable. Differences in actual versus trend incomes account for much of the residual participation; differences in the timing of the income and participation reports also account for some of the residual.

Multivariate Analyses

The simple conditional means reported in Table 3.2 show gross associations and do not account for confounding influences from other variables. For example, the bivariate cross-program associations between caregivers' earnings variability and their subsequent food stamp participation may be an artifact of mutual correlations between these measures and the level of earnings. Alternatively, the association may reflect correlations with some other variable. To address these possible sources of mutual correlation, we estimate longitudinal fixed-effect regression models of the characteristics associated with the caregivers' food stamp receipt. The estimates from these models represent partial associations that hold the other observed characteristics constant.

Coefficient estimates and standard errors for the models of program receipt are reported in Table 3.3. The first two columns of Table 3.3 list results from models of food stamp participation in the quarter and the half-year following the caregivers' interviews. In these models we constrain the effects of the earnings history variables so that they are the same for households with trend incomes above and below the gross eligibility threshold. The next two columns list results from models that allow the coefficients for the earnings history variables to differ depending on trend income. Explanatory variables are listed in the rows of the table. In addition to the variables found in the table, each of the models also includes an intercept and controls for age, education, missing earnings effects, and piecewise-linear trends, or linear splines, for the year and month of the interview. Each of the models in Table 3.3 pools data across the three cities.

As with the bivariate analyses, the regression results from the first two columns indicate that earnings in the month prior to the interview are negatively related to subsequent food stamp participation. The sizes of these associations, however, are modest. A $1,000 increase in current earnings, holding all else constant, is estimated to reduce food stamp participation in the subsequent three months by just over a week. Recall that the fixed-effects regression controls for permanent characteristics of the households, such as their permanent incomes. So, the coefficient on current earnings must be interpreted as a change in this variable, holding permanent income and the other observed characteristics constant. In other words, the coefficient represents the association between food stamp receipt and a temporary (and permanent-income compensated) change in earnings.

In contrast to the bivariate estimates, the results from the first two models indicate that more variable earnings are negatively, albeit modestly, associated with subsequent food stamp participation. Again, these are estimates that hold permanent characteristics constant, including permanent incomes and permanent income variability. Thus, temporary positive earnings shocks and increased medium-term earnings variability both appear to modestly reduce food stamp receipt.

The estimates from the first two columns indicate that the association between prior and subsequent food stamp receipt is statistically and substantively large. For example, being on food stamps for the entire year before the interview increases the expected participation in the following quarter by 2.1 months and increases the expected participation in the follow half-year by 3.6 months.

Table 3.3 Fixed-Effects Regression Models of Food Stamp Receipt Following the Interview

	Models with uniform effects of earnings history—months receiving food stamps out of next...		Models with variable effects of earnings history—months receiving food stamps out of next...	
	3 months	6 months	3 months	6 months
Earnings ($000) in interview month	−0.282**	−0.516**	−0.361**	−0.675**
	(0.048)	(0.092)	(0.060)	(0.115)
Any earnings in last year	0.100	0.133	0.217**	0.388*
	(0.091)	(0.175)	(0.106)	(0.204)
Average earnings ($000) in last year	−0.019	−0.116	−0.025	−0.276
	(0.102)	(0.196)	(0.136)	(0.261)
Coefficient of variation for earnings in last year	−0.098**	−0.194**	−0.115**	−0.263**
	(0.044)	(0.084)	(0.051)	(0.097)
Maximum earnings ($000) last year	0.051	0.132	−0.003	0.141
	(0.085)	(0.163)	(0.106)	(0.204)
Trend HH inc. > gross elig. × earnings in interview month[a]			0.119	0.258
			(0.092)	(0.176)
Trend HH inc. > gross elig. × any earnings in last year			−0.274	−0.671*
			(0.179)	(0.343)
Trend HH inc. > gross elig. × average earnings in last year			−0.035	0.305
			(0.208)	(0.399)
Trend HH inc. > gross elig. × c.v. earnings in last year			0.009	0.147
			(0.111)	(0.213)

Trend HH inc. > gross elig. × maximum earnings last year			0.166 (0.181)	0.025 (0.348)
Trend HH income-to-needs	0.035 (0.079)	−0.032 (0.152)	0.006 (0.084)	−0.071 (0.162)
Household income-to-needs	0.043 (0.063)	0.088 (0.122)	0.047 (0.063)	0.093 (0.122)
Months on food stamps in last year	0.172** (0.006)	0.299** (0.011)	0.172** (0.006)	0.300** (0.011)
Months on TANF in last year	0.004 (0.006)	0.013 (0.011)	0.003 (0.006)	0.011 (0.011)
Bank, savings, or financial account	−0.057 (0.053)	−0.116 (0.103)	−0.062 (0.053)	−0.129 (0.103)
Outstanding loans	0.034 (0.050)	0.054 (0.097)	0.035 (0.050)	0.054 (0.097)
Own home	0.010 (0.084)	−0.004 (0.162)	0.008 (0.085)	−0.011 (0.163)
Own vehicle	0.008 (0.056)	0.096 (0.107)	0.014 (0.056)	0.110 (0.108)
Financial strain index	0.031 (0.036)	0.108 (0.070)	0.031 (0.036)	0.107 (0.070)
Disability that limits work	0.098 (0.080)	0.119 (0.154)	0.092 (0.080)	0.104 (0.154)

(continued)

Table 3.3 (continued)

	Models with uniform effects of earnings history—months receiving food stamps out of next...		Models with variable effects of earnings history—months receiving food stamps out of next...	
	3 months	6 months	3 months	6 months
Number of minors in household	0.025	0.018	0.027	0.023
	(0.025)	(0.048)	(0.025)	(0.048)
Married, spouse present	0.040	−0.023	0.049	−0.006
	(0.080)	(0.155)	(0.081)	(0.155)
Number of adults in household	−0.065**	−0.104*	−0.063**	−0.102*
	(0.029)	(0.056)	(0.029)	(0.056)
R^2	0.60	0.66	0.61	0.66

NOTE: Longitudinal fixed-effect regression models estimated using interview data from the Three-City Study matched to administrative records. Models also include intercepts, controls for age, education, missing earnings histories, and calendar time. Standard errors appear in parentheses. * significant at the 0.10 level (two-tailed test); ** significant at the 0.05 level (two-tailed test).

[a] Trend household income being above the gross eligibility threshold is interacted (×) with the current monthly earnings variable.

SOURCE: Authors' estimations.

Increases in the number of adults are estimated to be negatively associated with food stamp receipt. None of the other estimated coefficients in the first two columns is statistically significant.

The next two columns in Table 3.3 report results from fixed-effect models that include interactions of the indicator for having a trend income above 130 percent of the poverty threshold and each of the earnings history measures. Except for these interactions, all of the other explanatory variables are identical to those in the previous two specifications.

The added interactions are jointly marginally significant (the p-values for joint significance for the three- and six-month outcome models are 0.17 and 0.12, respectively).[4] Including the interactions does alter several of the uninteracted coefficients. In particular, the coefficient on the uninteracted current earnings variable becomes approximately one-third larger in magnitude compared to the previous specifications. The absolute value of the uninteracted earnings variability measure becomes 10 percent larger in the three-month model and one-third larger in the six-month model. Also, the uninteracted coefficient on having any earnings during the past year becomes significantly positive. The changes indicate that the program behavior of households with trend incomes below the gross income threshold is more sensitive to changes in earnings histories than that of higher-income households.

We reestimated each of the interacted models separately for each of the three cities. Recall from the discussion of conceptual issues that some states have policies that effectively increase the compliance costs for households with volatile incomes. By estimating separate models we can see whether our results come from a particular state or a particular policy environment. Results from the state-specific fixed-effects models are listed in Table 3.4.

From the table, we see that current earnings are consistently negatively related to food stamp participation among low-income households. In the three-month models, the point estimates indicate that a $1,000 increase in earnings is associated with one to two fewer weeks of food stamp participation. In the six-month models, the effect size is on the order of two to three fewer weeks. The modest associations in each of the states are again consistent with the coefficients capturing temporary changes in earnings.

Table 3.4 Fixed-Effects Regression Models of Food Stamp Receipt Following Interview by City

	Boston		Chicago		San Antonio	
	Months receiving food stamps out of next...		Months receiving food stamps out of next...		Months receiving food stamps out of next...	
	3 months	6 months	3 months	6 months	3 months	6 months
Earnings ($000) in interview month	−0.440**	−0.765**	−0.298**	−0.561**	−0.260**	−0.500**
	(0.096)	(0.189)	(0.108)	(0.207)	(0.110)	(0.204)
Any earnings in last year	0.226	0.601	0.336*	0.575	0.111	0.080
	(0.205)	(0.403)	(0.190)	(0.363)	(0.172)	(0.321)
Average earnings ($000) in last year	0.185	0.294	−0.351	−0.851*	0.083	−0.268
	(0.232)	(0.455)	(0.232)	(0.443)	(0.256)	(0.478)
Coefficient of variation for earnings in last year	−0.151	−0.360**	−0.155*	−0.314*	−0.036	−0.088
	(0.092)	(0.181)	(0.089)	(0.170)	(0.085)	(0.159)
Maximum earnings ($000) last year	0.023	−0.118	0.127	0.449	−0.197	−0.053
	(0.189)	(0.371)	(0.188)	(0.359)	(0.181)	(0.338)
Trend HH inc. > gross elig. × earnings in interview month[a]	0.074	0.120	0.042	0.086	0.253	0.555
	(0.141)	(0.276)	(0.167)	(0.320)	(0.191)	(0.357)
Trend HH inc. > gross elig. × any earnings in last year	−0.213	−0.789	−0.226	−0.243	−0.650**	−1.372**
	(0.332)	(0.653)	(0.308)	(0.587)	(0.315)	(0.587)
Trend HH inc. > gross elig. × average earnings in last year	−0.146	−0.017	0.322	0.740	−0.157	0.295
	(0.341)	(0.671)	(0.369)	(0.704)	(0.394)	(0.735)
Trend HH inc. > gross elig. × c.v. earnings in last year	0.089	0.409	−0.096	−0.218	0.124	0.341
	(0.188)	(0.370)	(0.208)	(0.397)	(0.188)	(0.350)

55

	(1)	(2)	(3)	(4)	(5)	(6)
Trend HH inc. > gross elig. × maximum earnings last year	0.251 (0.293)	0.466 (0.576)	−0.051 (0.333)	−0.352 (0.636)	0.279 (0.335)	0.002 (0.625)
Trend HH income-to-needs	−0.119 (0.133)	−0.272 (0.260)	0.163 (0.159)	0.257 (0.304)	−0.033 (0.156)	−0.286 (0.290)
Household income-to-needs	0.037 (0.105)	0.049 (0.206)	0.069 (0.111)	0.143 (0.212)	0.093 (0.116)	0.216 (0.217)
Months on food stamps in last year	0.167** (0.011)	0.280** (0.021)	0.182** (0.010)	0.327** (0.020)	0.169** (0.010)	0.293** (0.019)
Months on TANF in last year	0.004 (0.011)	0.020 (0.022)	−0.013 (0.011)	−0.021 (0.021)	−0.0001 (0.011)	−0.004 (0.020)
Bank, savings, or financial account	0.005 (0.088)	0.189 (0.172)	−0.333** (0.116)	−0.639** (0.221)	0.071 (0.084)	−0.013 (0.157)
Outstanding loans	−0.130 (0.091)	−0.219 (0.179)	0.083 (0.090)	0.074 (0.171)	0.116 (0.085)	0.189 (0.159)
Own home	−0.120 (0.229)	−0.134 (0.450)	0.037 (0.141)	0.024 (0.268)	0.045 (0.122)	0.017 (0.228)
Own vehicle	0.143 (0.093)	0.293 (0.183)	−0.061 (0.110)	0.078 (0.209)	−0.089 (0.095)	−0.128 (0.177)
Financial strain index	0.095 (0.065)	0.233* (0.128)	0.058 (0.072)	0.125 (0.137)	−0.013 (0.057)	0.043 (0.107)
Disability that limits work	−0.023 (0.141)	−0.247 (0.276)	0.020 (0.158)	0.044 (0.301)	0.254** (0.126)	0.444* (0.236)
Number of minors in household	−0.119** (0.048)	−0.319** (0.094)	0.057 (0.044)	0.118 (0.084)	0.090** (0.041)	0.158** (0.076)

Table 3.4 (continued)

	Boston		Chicago		San Antonio	
	Months receiving Food Stamps out of next...		Months receiving Food Stamps out of next...		Months receiving Food Stamps out of next...	
	3 months	6 months	3 months	6 months	3 months	6 months
Married, spouse present	−0.019	−0.026	0.041	−0.005	0.115	0.046
	(0.156)	(0.306)	(0.144)	(0.275)	(0.130)	(0.242)
Number of adults in household	−0.124**	−0.202*	−0.036	−0.086	−0.035	−0.034
	(0.053)	(0.105)	(0.047)	(0.090)	(0.052)	(0.096)
R^2	0.15	0.11	0.51	0.61	0.11	0.20

NOTE: Longitudinal fixed-effect regression models estimated using interview data from the Three-City Study matched to administrative records. Models also include intercepts, controls for age, education, missing earnings histories, and calendar time. Standard errors appear in parentheses. * significant at the 0.10 level (two-tailed test); ** significant at the 0.05 level. (two-tailed test).

[a] Trend household income being above the gross eligibility threshold is interacted (×) with the current monthly earnings variable.

SOURCE: Authors' estimations.

Earnings variability among low-income households is also consistently negatively associated with food stamp participation; however, only three of the six coefficients are statistically significant. The significant negative associations between earnings variability and participation appear for Massachusetts and Illinois, but not for Texas. One difference in policies that could lead to greater sensitivity to income changes in the former two states is that they both have program waivers that allow them to change benefits within certification periods based on changes reported to other programs such as Medicaid; Texas does not coordinate in the same way. Texas, however, has more stringent income reporting requirements for its Food Stamp Program than do the other two states (Rosenbaum 2000), so we might have expected stronger associations there.

Among low-income households, food stamp participation is higher if the caregiver had any earnings at all during the preceding year, although only one of these associations is statistically significant. The positive associations could reflect the different treatment of work income in the benefit and eligibility formulas; specifically, low levels of earnings are not counted against the benefit formula, while earnings above the exemption amount are "taxed" at a lower rate than other income.

Among the other coefficients, prior food stamp receipt is consistently positively associated with subsequent food stamp receipt. Increases in financial assets are negatively associated with food stamp receipt in Illinois but not in the other two states. Disability is positively associated with food stamp receipt in Texas. Adding an adult or a child to the household is significantly negatively associated with food stamp receipt in Massachusetts; adding a child to a household is positively associated with food stamp receipt in Texas.

CONCLUSION

This chapter examines the relationship between earnings histories and program participation in a sample that matches administrative data on program outcomes with longitudinal survey information from the Three-City Study about earnings and other household characteristics. We conduct multivariate analyses, employing fixed-effect regression models that account for time-invariant characteristics of households, such as their permanent incomes. A unique aspect of our analyses is that we separately consider households with long-term trend incomes that make them more or less likely to be eligible for food stamps.

The chapter finds strong evidence that higher levels of current monthly earnings reduce program participation. This result is expected, as increased earnings reduce the need for assistance and also affect the eligibility and benefits associated with food stamps. What may be more surprising is that the magnitudes of the estimated associations are all relatively modest. The small sizes of the associations are likely due to our use of longitudinal fixed-effect controls and numerous other economic controls. With these controls, the identifying variation in current earnings comes from temporary changes.

We also find evidence that medium-term earnings variability, measured by the coefficient of variation for the preceding year's earnings, is negatively associated with food stamp participation, at least among low-income households. There are several potential explanations for these results. For households that are initially below the eligibility threshold, variable earnings could lead to occasional periods of ineligibility and shorter eligibility spells. Program compliance costs may also increase with earnings variability. Other possible explanations for the negative association are that participation affects earnings, reducing variability, or that some other characteristic affects both earnings and variability. While we cannot rule out these other explanations, our empirical methodology, which controls for permanent unobserved characteristics and which relates past earnings variability to subsequent program participation, makes them less likely.

Additionally, the estimation results provide modest evidence that program behavior in households with low long-term incomes is more sensitive to changes in their earnings and earnings variability than behavior in households with higher long-term incomes. When interactions of the earnings-history variables and the long-term income indicator are included in our models, the estimated coefficients for the earnings and earnings-variability measures for the low-income segment of our sample each increase. The changes in the coefficients are consistent with earnings volatility reducing eligibility among low-income households but not among higher-income households.

Notes

This chapter originally appeared as a paper for the National Poverty Center and Economic Research Service conference "Income Volatility and Implications for Food Assistance Programs II," November 16–17, 2006, in Washington, D.C. The authors gratefully acknowledge financial assistance from the National Institute of Child Health and Human Development under grant numbers R01 HD36093 and R01 HD050370 and from the Economic Research Service of the U.S. Department of Agriculture under cooperative agreement number 43-3AEM-4-80116. They thank Paula Fomby and Bianca Frogner for their help preparing the survey data; Robert Goerge, Daniel Shroeder, and Jesse Valente for their help preparing the administrative data; and Rich Depolt and Irene Navarrete for valuable research assistance. They also thank Dean Jolliffe, Doug Besharov, and Jim Ziliak for helpful comments. The views expressed in this chapter are those of the authors and are not necessarily shared by the supporting agencies.

1. A single child in each family was followed through all three interviews.
2. Of the 2,056 current and former caregivers who participated in the third wave, 1,980 were interviewed in person and were asked for their permission to obtain administrative records.
3. Robert Goerge from the Chapin Hall Center at the University of Chicago supplied the records for Illinois, Daniel Shroeder from the Ray Marshall Center at the University of Texas supplied the records for Texas, and Jesse Valente from the Massachusetts Department of Transitional Assistance provided the records for that state.
4. Evidence of differences in behavior is considerably stronger in alternative specifications that omit the maximum earnings variable and in random effect specifications.

References

Farrell, Mary, Michael Fishman, Matthew Langley, and David Stapleton. 2003. *The Relationship of Earnings and Income to Food Stamp Participation: A Longitudinal Analysis.* E-FAN Report No. 03-011. Washington, DC: U.S. Department of Agriculture.

Frogner, Bianca, Robert Moffitt, and David Ribar. 2007. "How Families Are Doing Nine Years after Welfare Reform: 2005 Evidence from the Three-City Study." Paper presented at the University of Kentucky Center for Poverty Research conference "Ten Years After: Evaluating the Long-Term Effects of Welfare Reform on Work, Welfare, Children and Families," held in Lexington, KY, April 12–13.

Moffitt, Robert. 1983. "An Economic Model of Welfare Stigma." *American Economic Review* 73(5): 1023–1035.

————. 2003. "The Role of Nonfinancial Factors in Exit and Entry in the TANF Program." *Journal of Human Resources* 38(Supplement): 1221–1254.

Moffitt, Robert, and Katie Winder. 2003. "The Correlates and Consequences of Welfare Exit and Entry: Evidence from the Three-City Study." Working Paper 03-01, from *Welfare, Children, and Families: A Three-City Study*. Baltimore: Johns Hopkins University.

Ribar, David C., and Marilyn Edelhoch. 2008. "Earnings Volatility and the Reasons for Leaving the Food Stamp Program." In *Income Volatility and Food Assistance in the United States*, Dean Jolliffe and James P. Ziliak, eds. Kalamazoo, MI: W.E. Upjohn Institute for Employment Research, pp. 63–102.

Rosenbaum, Dorothy. 2000. *Improving Access to Food Stamps: New Reporting Options Can Reduce Administrative Burdens and Error Rates*. Washington, DC: Center on Budget and Policy Priorities.

Part 2

Income Volatility, Welfare Reform, and Use of the Food Stamp Program

4

Earnings Volatility and the Reasons for Leaving the Food Stamp Program

David C. Ribar
University of North Carolina at Greensboro

Marilyn Edelhoch
South Carolina Department of Social Services

The primary goal of the Food Stamp Program is to improve the well-being of low-income households by increasing their food purchasing power and helping them obtain more nutritious diets than they could otherwise afford. To maximize well-being, program administrators want benefits to reach as many poor households as possible. Through means testing, the program also acts to stabilize consumption and provide a degree of social insurance. Beyond these assistance objectives, the Food Stamp Program also has other goals. As a publicly financed program, it must be a good steward of taxpayer dollars and maintain program integrity by ensuring that benefits are directed toward truly needy households. More recently, the Food Stamp Program has also sought to promote economic self-sufficiency.

In some cases, these goals conflict with each other. For instance, it is well-known that the benefit formula, which reduces a household's allotment of food stamps as its income rises, creates work disincentives that undermine the self-sufficiency goal. Less understood is how administrative procedures, intended mostly to help maintain program integrity, affect household well-being and self-sufficiency.

The federal and state governments are partners in the Food Stamp Program, with the federal government setting general rules for the program and paying the entire cost of benefits and the states administering the program. In their role as administrators, states have considerable latitude in a number of areas, including establishing and running food

63

stamp offices, developing and reviewing initial applications, and setting recertification intervals. This latitude increased with the passage of the 2002 Farm Bill. States may also obtain waivers from the federal government to alter other features of their programs.

Researchers have only recently begun to quantify the impacts of these policies and procedures. For example, Ribar, Edelhoch, and Liu (2006a,b) found that exits from the Food Stamp Program in South Carolina occur mainly at recertification periods and that more frequent recertifications hasten exits and decrease the caseload. Staveley, Stevens, and Wilde (2002) uncovered similar patterns in administrative data from Maryland, and Currie and Grogger (2001), Kabbani and Wilde (2003), Kornfield (2002), and Ratcliffe, McKernan, and Finegold (2007) have documented negative associations between recertification frequency and food stamp caseloads. While this research has identified general impacts associated with policies and procedures, it has not yet explained why certain effects appear. With respect to recertification frequency, shorter intervals could increase the detection of ineligible households, deter ineligible households from continuing their participation, or discourage eligible households by increasing the costs of program compliance.

In this chapter, we use administrative records from South Carolina on over 30,000 food stamp spells for cases with children that began between the second half of 1997 and the beginning of 2005. We use descriptive and multivariate event-history methods to look generally at the characteristics of households that contribute to exits from the Food Stamp Program and more specifically at the reasons why households leave the program. A focus of our investigation is on how earnings histories and especially previous earnings volatility are associated with different types of exits. The data from South Carolina are very helpful in this regard.

First, South Carolina's administrative records are extremely rich and detailed. The records not only contain the start and stop dates of Food Stamp Program participation—information needed to construct spells—but also contain demographic information about the participating households and the specific reason why each household stopped receiving benefits. The records are also linked to quarterly earnings records from the state's Unemployment Insurance (UI) system, allowing us to construct earnings histories.

Second, some of South Carolina's food stamp policies are particularly easy to measure. This paper concentrates on the state's recertification policies, which are directly relevant to the issue of earnings volatility because they expressly condition on it. The policies changed over the period that we study. Prior to October 2002, the state required most households with earnings and other fluctuating sources of income to recertify quarterly and most other households with stable unearned incomes to recertify annually. In October 2002, the state lengthened the recertification interval for households with fluctuating incomes from three to six months. Because the recertification dates are set relative to the beginning of a spell, they can be distinguished from regular calendar effects. The changes in policy over time provide an additional source of longitudinal variation, and the differences in their applicability across groups provide additional cross-sectional variation.

The centrality of the recertification process is confirmed when we analyze the reasons why participation spells end. These analyses reveal that *half* of the food stamp households in South Carolina with children that leave the program do so by letting their certification periods lapse and not filing the necessary paperwork for recertification. Households with earnings at the start of their certification periods are especially likely to leave for this reason. A further sixth of caseload exits occur because people either fail to provide sufficient information or they give information that cannot be verified. Just over a fifth of exits occur because people either report or are discovered to have incomes or resources that are too high. For white households, more variable earnings histories are negatively associated with exits for income ineligibility. For both black and white households, more variable earnings histories increase the odds of leaving voluntarily or for other reasons.

THE FOOD STAMP PROGRAM IN SOUTH CAROLINA

General description. As mentioned, the Food Stamp Program is administered by the U.S. Department of Agriculture and operated by the states to help low-income individuals and families obtain more nutritious diets. The federal government pays the cost of food stamp benefits and also pays half of the states' administrative costs. Set by the federal government, the monthly benefit formula is the same for all states in the contiguous United States. In FY 2005, the maximum benefit for a household of three was $399.

Benefits are provided to households, and to qualify, households have to meet income and resource tests (unless all members are receiving benefits from the Temporary Assistance for Needy Families, [TANF] or Supplemental Security Income [SSI] programs, which makes the household "categorically eligible"). The federal government sets eligibility standards at 130 percent of the poverty line based on gross monthly income, and at 100 percent of the poverty line based on net income. Most households must meet both the gross and the net income tests, but a household with an elderly or disabled person only has to meet the net income test.[1]

Application procedures. In South Carolina, applicants may complete an application form for food stamps at the local Department of Social Services (DSS) office, or may download the form from the agency Web site and deliver, mail, or fax the application to the local DSS office. Applications are considered filed on the date they are received by the county offices. An interview with the applicant is required for approval, either in person or on the telephone, and information regarding identity, residency, income, and expenses must be verified.

Local DSS offices must approve applications within 27 days after receipt in the county office, and benefits must be accessible within 30 days.[2] Actual processing time from application to receipt of benefits averages 16 days statewide. In cases where an application is denied, the notification must reach the household by the thirtieth day after receipt.

Income reporting. Clients are required to report and verify all sources of income, including earnings, at initial certification, with pay stubs or an official employer's statement being needed to verify earnings. For clients receiving other government benefits, the agency can verify these sources by accessing automated records on-line.

Food stamp eligibility and benefits are determined on a monthly basis; however, rules for reporting income changes depend on the clients' circumstances. Households in which all members are elderly or disabled must report changes to the local DSS office within 10 days. All other households must report changes when the household's gross income exceeds 130 percent of poverty or when the household moves out of the state. Recipients are also allowed to report decreases in income, as these would allow them to increase their food stamp benefits.

Recertification. In addition to these reporting requirements, recipients are required to complete paperwork or interviews to recertify their eligibility on a periodic basis. Recipients on fixed incomes, such as disability income, are required to recertify less often than those recipients with variable incomes.

As we said above, prior to October 2002, South Carolina required most food stamp recipients with earnings and other fluctuating sources of income to recertify their eligibility quarterly and most recipients with fixed incomes to recertify annually. For those with fluctuating incomes, face-to-face interviews were only required once a year and mail-in recertifications were required each quarter. After October 2002, the recertification interval for recipients with fluctuating incomes increased from three to six months. In addition, a larger number of recertification interviews were conducted over the phone, and income verification procedures were relaxed.[3]

Case closures. Cases are certified for the intervals listed in Table 4.1. If a household fails to recertify its eligibility, its case is automatically closed at the end of the certification period. Cases may also be closed at recertification if their paperwork is incomplete, if households fail to participate in interviews, or if their incomes cannot be verified. Cases are also closed at recertification or at other times if a reported change in income or resources brings them above the applicable thresholds. Prior to March 2004, some cases could be closed for failure to participate in required employment and training activities.[4] In addition, cases are closed if the client cannot be located or moves out of state, as well as under some other circumstances.

Once one of these issues arises, the household is sent a notice telling it that eligibility will be terminated in 10 days. Recertifications are due in the first half of the last month of certification; people who miss this deadline are sent their notices near the middle of the month and have their cases terminated at the end of the month. If a client reports an earnings change that puts her over 130 percent of the poverty line, the 10-day timely notice period begins the first day of the next month.

Table 4.1 Food Stamp Certification Intervals in South Carolina for Households with Children

Characteristics of case	Before October 2002	October 2002– February 2005
Unstable circumstances (e.g., no income), migrant worker	1–2 months	1–2 months
Fluctuating income (e.g., earnings)	3 months	6 months
Fixed income	12 months	12 months

For example, if the change occurs on June 15, the report must be received by July 10 in order for the client not to have to repay overages in benefits. If the client reports in the last 10 days of the month, her case cannot be closed until the first of the following month. So, for example, if a client reports an earnings change between September 21 and September 30 that renders her ineligible, her case cannot be closed until November 1.

Clients are required to verify wages at certification and reverify at recertification. Unless clients report increases in income during the three- or six-month certification period, ineligibles are not identified until the end of that period. If a UI wage match shows a discrepancy at either certification or recertification, clients are asked to verify wages again. However, if a wage match shows a discrepancy during the intervening period, claims workers ignore the information until recertification. If the client has collected food stamp benefits to which she was not entitled, the claims worker in the county seeks reimbursement from the client by establishing a repayment agreement. If that does not work, the case is sent to "tax intercept" and future tax refunds are garnished to repay the overage.

Caseload trends. Food stamp caseloads plummeted during the late 1990s in South Carolina and elsewhere. The state's food stamp caseload declined from 143,000 families in 1996 to 120,000 in 2000. Since 2000, the food stamp caseload has increased dramatically, climbing to more than 226,000 families by the end of 2005.

PREVIOUS RESEARCH

Conceptual framework. The conceptual framework that we use to examine the different reasons for food stamp exits is Moffitt's (2003) model of program compliance. In Moffitt's model, households receive and value different levels of income, which vary depending on their participation in assistance programs, such as the Food Stamp Program. Households also care about other things, such as stigma (Moffitt 1983), household production, and leisure; these things all vary with program participation.

To remain on a program, households must exert effort to comply with the program's rules by completing their recertification paperwork and interviews. Higher levels of compliance increase the chances—but do not guarantee—that a household will remain in good standing with a program and continue receiving benefits. The chance element is important because even if a household complies with the rules, it may be randomly terminated—paperwork can be lost, information can be mistyped into computers, etc. Increased efforts by households to comply, of course, also raise the effective costs of program participation to those households.

Households in this model rationally choose their compliance efforts to balance the anticipated monetary and other benefits of program participation against the costs of compliance, and this choice has some straightforward implications for program behavior. On the one hand, policies (such as longer recertification intervals) that unambiguously reduce compliance costs should lead to higher levels of compliance and hence to higher levels of participation. On the other hand, larger incomes or smaller benefits, which lower the relative gains to program participation, should reduce compliance and participation.

The impacts of other changes are more difficult to predict—income volatility is a case in point. Variable incomes, especially in households with few assets and limited access to credit markets, increase the utility of food stamps and other social insurance programs (Gundersen and Ziliak 2003). At the same time, more volatile incomes increase compliance costs. In South Carolina, food stamp households with fluctuating incomes are required to recertify more frequently than other households. Even if this were not the case, income volatility would increase the probability that a participating household would become ineligible in a given month. It would also raise documentation costs, for instance, by increasing the sources of income that would have to be reported and verified. Because volatility increases the benefits and costs of program participation and also affects eligibility itself, the net impacts are ambiguous and a matter for empirical investigation.

The foregoing discussion treats compliance as if it were a unidimensional concept, but of course with multiple program rules there are many possible dimensions of compliance. The discussion also overlooks the important issue of purposeful underreporting. The various rules and additional eligibility considerations give rise to the multiple reasons for program exits, which we subsequently examine.

Empirical studies. There have been numerous studies of the food stamp caseload and food stamp participation. Many of these have simply examined the incidence of food stamp participation, either by modeling the aggregate number of people or households receiving benefits (Currie and Grogger 2001; Danielson and Klerman 2006; Kabbani and Wilde 2003; Kornfeld 2002; Wallace and Blank 1999; Wilde et al. 2000; Ziliak, Gundersen, and Figlio 2003) or by modeling receipt among individual households (Currie and Grogger 2001; Farrell et al. 2003; Fraker and Moffitt 1988; Haider, Jacknowitz, and Schoeni 2003; Keane and Moffitt 1998; Ratcliffe, McKernan, and Finegold 2007). Some other studies break individual participation decisions into separate entry and exit decisions but examine these as simple bivariate outcomes (Blank and Ruggles 1996; Gleason, Schochet, and Moffit 1998; Hofferth 2003; Mills et al. 2001; Ribar, Edelhoch, and Liu 2006a,b; Staveley, Stevens, and Wilde 2002). To our knowledge, previous food stamp studies have not modeled different types of exit outcomes.[5]

There has been less research on food stamp policies, other than benefit levels. Many studies fail to include measures of policies and procedures at all. Several other studies include broad and imprecise measures like the average recertification interval or the distribution of intervals in a state (Currie and Grogger 2001; Hofferth 2003; Kabbani and Wilde 2003; Kornfeld 2002; Ratcliffe, McKernan, and Finegold 2007); these studies have tended to generate weak and sometimes contradictory findings. Stronger results are found in a few studies that have been more careful in measuring policies and procedures. For instance,

Bartlett, Burstein, and Hamilton (2004) gather detailed information on administrative policies, such as outreach efforts and operating hours, and on administrator and staff attitudes across food stamp offices in different localities. They find that these administrative characteristics influence participation behavior. Ribar, Edelhoch, and Liu (2006a,b) use administrative data from South Carolina and look in a detailed way at the timing of exits from individual food stamp spells; they find that exits coincided with the expected timing of recertifications. In an analysis of administrative data from Maryland, Staveley, Stevens, and Wilde (2002) also find that the timing of food stamp exits was clustered at recertification dates.

The role of income volatility in food stamp participation has been largely overlooked in previous research. One exception, however, is a study by Farrell et al. (2003), which compares the income histories of food stamp participants and nonparticipants at different points in time. The authors find that participants have lower and less volatile incomes than eligible nonparticipants.

DATA

Food stamp spells. The data for the empirical analyses of food stamp exits come from electronic case management records from South Carolina covering the period from July 1997 until January 2005. The records, which are maintained by the Office of Research and Statistics (ORS) of the South Carolina State Budget and Control Board, cover the universe of households that applied to and participated in the state's Food Stamp Program over the period. The records contain a wealth of household- and client-level information, including the starting and ending dates of participation spells, demographic characteristics of households, geographic identifiers, and benefit and reported income amounts during each month of program receipt.

Because of the large number of food stamp cases in South Carolina, we reduced the analysis extract by using a 1-in-11 random sample of longitudinal cases. We then further reduced the analysis sample by only considering records associated with approved applications, records with complete information about the processes involved in continuing a spell of program receipt, and records describing food stamp cases with adults and children present.

The units of analysis for our investigation are food stamp spells. Food stamp spells can begin anytime during a month. However, once a spell begins, benefits are only paid once a month. Also, when a case is terminated, the official closing date almost always occurs at the end of the month. Because of the timing of payments and case closings, we treat the spell data as a series of discrete, monthly observations, with the initial and terminal observations for each spell corresponding to the first and last months of benefit receipt. We only consider spells that began during our observation window and accordingly drop ongoing, or left-censored, spells. Also, we ignore short breaks in spells (breaks that last one month or less) and instead treat the two adjoining spells as a single spell of participation.[6]

For each month that a case continues, the records indicate the benefits that the household received as well as all of the economic information that enters into the benefit calculation, including gross reported earned and unearned income amounts, deductions and exemptions, and net incomes. We use several of these income and expense variables in our descriptive and multivariate analyses, adjusting all dollar amounts to 2005 levels using the Consumer Price Index for All Urban Consumers (CPI-U).

From the information on demographic characteristics, we construct measures of the number and age composition of the case members. We also construct indicators for the age, sex, race, educational attainment, and marital status of the household member heading the case.

The records indicate the county of residence for the household, which allows us to link the administrative data to measures of the county unemployment rate to control for local economic conditions. It also allows us to link the data to measures of the population density to control for the level of urbanization. We further include controls for whether the county is on the state border.

Once the programmatic, demographic, and geographic information is processed, we make one final set of exclusions to the data. First, we limit the analysis to households in which the adult in charge was between the ages of 18 and 59 and no other adults were over the age of 59. Second, we restrict the analysis to households in which the head of the case was white or black. Only 5 percent of cases were identified as being of another race or ethnicity, leaving us with too few cases to examine these groups. Third, we drop a small number of observations with missing or incomplete information. Our final analysis data set contains 398,586 monthly observations from 30,569 spells of food stamp receipt.

Reasons for exit. For every case that is closed, the administrative records give a reason for closure. There are 33 detailed codes that are used at least once in our records. We grouped the codes into five broad categories: cases that ended because the household

1) missed its recertification,

2) lost eligibility because its income or assets were too high,

3) lost eligibility because it failed to provide information or provide reliable information,

4) lost eligibility because of some other reason, or

5) voluntarily quit.

The detailed codes, our categorizations, and the relevant frequencies are reported in Table 4.2.

The tabulations of the reasons for exit reveal that 50 percent of cases headed by blacks and 51 percent of cases headed by whites ended because the clients let their certification periods lapse without submitting any paperwork for a new certification. This confirms the findings from earlier studies by Ribar, Edelhoch, and Liu (2006a,b) that recertification is an important element in food stamp exits. The tabulations also indicate that just over one-fifth of the exits—23 percent among cases headed by blacks and 17 percent among cases headed by whites—occurred because the households either reported or were found to have a change in income or resources that made them ineligible. Approximately one-sixth of cases ended because the households failed to provide sufficient or reliable information. Nine percent of cases lost their eligibility for some other reason, most typically because the households moved or could not be located, and 3 to 4 percent withdrew voluntarily.

UI earnings data. For each client in the food stamp case management records, the ORS has obtained quarterly earnings records, if any exist, from the state's UI system. The UI database contains earnings

Table 4.2 Detailed Reasons for Food Stamp Exits by Race of Case Head

Reason for exit	Black Number	Black Percent	White Number	White Percent
Missed recertification	6,458	50.36	5,049	50.88
MR: Failed to file mandatory recertification	4,316	33.66	3,398	34.24
CE: Closed–certification ended (S-Gen)[a]	2,142	16.70	1,651	16.64
Income or assets too high	2,906	22.66	1,699	17.12
IN: Income (net) meets/exceeds req.	2,119	16.52	1,252	12.62
IE: Increase–earned income	602	4.69	321	3.23
IU: Unearned income exceeds limits	111	0.87	70	0.71
RE: Resources	72	0.56	56	0.56
LS: Lump sum ineligibility	2	0.02	0	0.00
Failed to provide reliable information	2,075	16.18	1,796	18.10
FI: Failed to furnish information	1,398	10.90	1,272	12.82
FP: Failed to provide info. (S-Gen)	438	3.42	274	2.76
VR: Verification—failed to provide	153	1.19	198	2.00
FC: Failed to complete interview (S-Gen)	52	0.41	30	0.30
IM: Incompletely verified MR	34	0.27	22	0.22
Other loss of eligibility	990	7.72	972	9.80
NR: Nonresident	483	3.77	516	5.20
CL: Cannot locate	231	1.80	297	2.99
HH: No eligible household members	102	0.80	69	0.70
AE: Application opened in error	32	0.25	24	0.24
ET: Failure to comply with E&T req.	28	0.22	15	0.15
DE: Death	24	0.19	13	0.13
SH: Not separate FS household	24	0.19	11	0.11
WR: Work req.—refused/failed to comply	24	0.19	3	0.03
CC: Opened/closed case with claim	15	0.12	9	0.09
AB: ABAWD time limit expired[b]	12	0.09	4	0.04
QC: Refused to cooperate with QC[c]	7	0.05	2	0.02
CH: Change in law/policy	4	0.03	0	0.00
FE: Fail to accept reim. comp.—FS E&T	1	0.01	4	0.04
CD: Drug conviction	0	0.00	2	0.02
DR: Disqualified—misrep. residency/ID	0	0.00	2	0.02
DF: HH disqualified for fraud	1	0.01	0	0.00
FF: Fleeing felon—probation parole[d]	1	0.01	0	0.00
RJ: Refused to accept a job	0	0.00	1	0.01
SS: SSN—refused/failed to furnish or apply	1	0.01	0	0.00
Voluntary exit	394	3.07	407	4.10
VW: Voluntary withdrawal	362	2.82	390	3.93
VQ: Voluntary quit	32	0.25	17	0.17

Table 4.2 (continued)

[a] "S-Gen" stands for "system-generated," as opposed to being entered by a caseworker.
[b] "ABAWD" stands for "able-bodied adults without dependents."
[c] "QC" stands for "quality control audit."
[d] "Fleeing felon—probation parole" means that the person was declared ineligible because he or she either has a felony arrest warrant or is in violation of probation or parole restrictions.
SOURCE: Authors' calculations from South Carolina food stamp administrative records.

information for most private, nonagricultural employers. However, it overlooks government employment and some types of private-sector jobs, such as agricultural and domestic work. It also misses employment by people who commute out of the state to work.

We construct measures of the total amount of earnings for all clients in the food stamp household for the current quarter of a given spell observation, for the previous quarter, and for the previous year. We adjust these amounts using the CPI-U and express them as monthly equivalents to make them comparable to the reported earnings and income figures. To measure earnings volatility, we calculate the coefficient of variation for the household's covered earnings for the previous year. We also create an indicator for the maximum quarterly earnings during the previous year and an indicator for having no reported earnings during that period.

DESCRIPTIVE ANALYSIS

Tables 4.3 and 4.4 list statistics describing the characteristics of food stamp cases from South Carolina in the months in which the cases closed. The characteristics were measured as of the start of the month, and the cases generally closed at the end of the month, so the characteristics reflect conditions immediately preceding the closures. Table 4.3 lists statistics for cases in households headed by blacks, while Table 4.4 lists statistics for whites. In each table, averages of the characteristics are calculated according to one of five conditions, depending on the reason why the cases closed.

The rows at the top of each table describe economic conditions of the cases, including the level of food stamp benefits, reported levels

Table 4.3 Characteristics at Spell Exits by Reason of Exit: Cases Headed by Blacks

	Missed recertification	Income/assets too high	Failed to provide information	Other loss of eligibility	Voluntary exit
Case income and benefits[a]					
Benefits	224.3	200.1	272.3	293.0	238.8
Reported earned income	646.4	731.8	332.3	249.0	424.6
Reported unearned income	275.1	358.9	288.2	285.2	363.5
Countable income	568.8	683.8	375.7	298.1	496.2
Any earnings start of spell (%)	57.1	60.0	39.3	28.0	43.4
No income start of spell (%)	13.7	9.9	26.5	30.7	17.5
UI earnings current quarter	912.2	1,235.3	776.1	261.7	839.7
UI earnings last quarter	781.9	1,104.8	625.4	305.8	742.6
Average UI earnings last year	752.4	1,150.4	631.4	336.4	720.2
C.V. UI earnings last year	0.579	0.497	0.662	0.650	0.595
Maximum UI earnings last year	1,121.7	1,608.6	1,004.9	594.3	1,110.4
No UI earnings last year (%)	18.9	14.1	23.6	41.8	25.9
Spell length (months)	11.5	10.4	11.9	11.8	11.6
PI characteristics[b]					
Female (%)	95.8	94.0	93.9	95.7	93.9
Age	31.6	34.5	30.7	30.5	34.4
Education[c]	11.8	11.9	11.7	11.5	11.8
Currently married (%)	12.3	21.6	11.2	8.2	17.3
Formerly married (%)	26.8	28.5	25.4	29.3	34.0

Case composition					
Number in case	3.1	3.3	3.1	3.0	3.0
Number of children 0–2	0.4	0.3	0.4	0.5	0.4
Number of children 3–5	0.4	0.3	0.4	0.4	0.3
Number of children 6–11	0.7	0.6	0.6	0.6	0.6
Number of children 12–14	0.3	0.3	0.2	0.2	0.3
Number of children 15–17	0.2	0.3	0.2	0.2	0.2
Number of adults	1.2	1.4	1.2	1.2	1.3
Geographic characteristics					
County unemployment rate	5.6	6.1	5.9	6.0	6.4
County population density[d]	202.2	186.7	211.4	190.9	180.5
Border county (%)[e]	36.3	34.2	39.2	38.2	37.8
Number of exits	6,458	2,906	2,075	990	394

NOTE: Dollar amounts are expressed in 2005 dollars; UI earnings amounts are expressed in monthly equivalents.

[a] All categories of "Case income and benefits" are in $ unless otherwise specified, except for "C.V. UI earnings last year," which gives the coefficient of variation for unemployment insurance earnings.

[b] "PI" stands for "primary informant," the head of the case.

[c] Values for "Education" measure average years in school.

[d] Measured as people per square mile in county.

[e] "Border county" is a 0/1 indicator for whether a person lives in a county that borders on another state; the statistic reflects the percentage of people living in such counties.

SOURCE: Authors' calculations from South Carolina food stamp administrative records.

Table 4.4 Characteristics at Spell Exits by Reason of Exit: Cases Headed by Whites

	Missed recertification	Income/assets too high	Failed to provide info.	Other loss of eligibility	Voluntary exit
Case income and benefits[a]					
Benefits	254.9	233.3	302.5	303.3	288.3
Reported earned income	645.4	721.1	301.2	280.0	336.7
Reported unearned income	250.3	320.9	256.4	236.2	354.4
Countable income	523.0	623.5	308.0	281.6	396.7
Any earnings start of spell (%)	56.0	57.6	35.6	30.3	39.8
No income start of spell (%)	17.7	14.2	32.9	35.2	23.3
UI earnings current quarter	812.3	1,207.2	719.9	300.9	741.8
UI earnings last quarter	700.4	1,051.1	584.9	361.3	615.7
Average UI earnings last year	698.7	1,097.0	602.6	377.5	684.6
C.V. UI earnings last year	0.670	0.548	0.741	0.666	0.584
Maximum UI earnings last year	1,097.2	1,605.2	1,031.0	664.1	1,087.3
No UI earnings last year (%)	23.1	19.1	26.6	42.4	36.1
Spell length (months)	9.8	8.6	8.9	9.0	8.7
PI characteristics[b]					
Female (%)	89.1	87.6	89.4	92.4	88.2
Age	31.5	33.2	30.8	30.2	33.2
Education[c]	11.2	11.5	11.2	11.1	11.4
Currently married (%)	35.5	46.1	29.3	25.0	36.9
Formerly married (%)	41.7	34.4	44.6	42.0	46.4

Case composition					
Number in case	3.3	3.4	3.2	3.1	3.3
Number of children 0–2	0.4	0.4	0.4	0.5	0.4
Number of children 3–5	0.4	0.3	0.4	0.4	0.3
Number of children 6–11	0.6	0.6	0.6	0.6	0.7
Number of children 12–14	0.3	0.3	0.2	0.2	0.3
Number of children 15–17	0.2	0.2	0.2	0.1	0.2
Number of adults	1.4	1.6	1.4	1.3	1.4
Geographic characteristics					
County unemployment rate	5.3	5.7	5.6	5.6	5.8
County population density[d]	205.2	200.4	210.2	202.4	203.8
Border county (%)[e]	57.1	59.2	60.9	61.3	58.0
Number of exits	5,049	1,699	1,796	972	407

NOTE: Dollar amounts are expressed in 2005 dollars; UI earnings amounts are expressed in monthly equivalents.
[a] All categories of "Case income and benefits" are in $ unless otherwise specified.
[b] "PI" stands for "primary informant," the head of the case.
[c] Values for "Education" measure average years in school.
[d] Measured as people per square mile in county.
[e] "Border county" is a 0/1 indicator for whether a person lives in a county that borders on another state; the statistic reflects the percentage of people living in such counties.
SOURCE: Authors' calculations from South Carolina food stamp administrative records.

of income, and the earnings history reported into the state UI system. It is immediately evident that the economic conditions of cases differ substantially depending on clients' reasons for exit. Cases in which the recipients lost their eligibility for reasons of income or resources tend to have the lowest level of benefits. Cases whose recipients failed to recertify also have relatively low benefits, which is consistent with such recipients having reduced incentives for complying with program rules. Cases that ended because the recipients failed to provide necessary or reliable information and cases where the recipients lost eligibility for other reasons had the highest benefits on average, while cases that ended voluntarily fell in between these extremes. These associations apply to both black- and white-headed households.

While the average monthly benefits for households that missed their recertifications were low in a relative sense, they were still substantial—$224 for blacks and $255 for whites—on an absolute basis. To the extent that clients remained eligible, their willingness to give up such large sums when letting their certifications lapse suggests that the effective costs of program compliance are high.

The differences among cases whose clients had different reasons for exit were even more pronounced when it came to incomes and earnings. As might be expected, households that lost eligibility for income and resource reasons tended to be the most economically advantaged, with the highest reported earnings and countable incomes and the strongest and least volatile histories of UI-covered earnings. At the other end of the spectrum were households in our residual category, whose clients lost their eligibility for reasons other than high incomes, missed recertifications, or failures to provide information.

Relative to cases that ended for income reasons, the cases in the residual category were roughly three times as likely to have begun their food stamp participation spells with no reported income whatsoever. On average, the residual case clients had countable incomes that were less than half the size of cases that ended for income reasons and covered earnings that were less than a third the size of this group. The differences in covered earnings were starkest in the quarters in which the cases actually ended, indicating possible continuing disadvantage after the clients left the Food Stamp Program.[7] Cases that failed to get recertified had economic resources that were below those of income-ineligibles but above those of the other groups. Cases that ended voluntarily came next, followed by cases that ended because of clients' failure to provide information. Cases that ended for information reasons had the highest levels of covered-earnings volatility.

Cases that lost eligibility for income reasons also tended to have the shortest durations, while cases that missed their recertifications tended to last more than a month longer. Among blacks, cases that ended for information reasons, other reasons, and voluntarily were slightly longer on average than cases that ended because of missed recertifications. Among whites, the opposite was true.

The demographic patterns are generally consistent with the income and earnings patterns: cases that lost eligibility for income and resource reasons had higher average levels of education and marriage and fewer children than other cases. Cases in our residual category had the lowest rates of marriage, lowest levels of education, and the most young children.

Although many of the patterns of food stamp use among households headed by blacks and whites are similar, there are some differences worth noting. Average spell lengths are two to three months longer for blacks than for whites, even though average benefits are slightly lower for blacks than for whites. The longer spells for blacks are consistent with national data from Wolkwitz (2007) that indicate higher rates of participation for blacks conditional on their eligibility. Black food stamp households are less likely to be headed by men than white households. Also, substantially fewer black household heads are currently or were formerly married compared to white household heads.

MULTIVARIATE ANALYSIS

For our multivariate analyses we estimate discrete-time competing-risk hazard models of different types of food stamp exits (see Allison 1982 for a thorough discussion of discrete-time models). The hazard rate, which refers to the probability that a spell of remaining in one situation ends at a given point in time, conditional on the spell having lasted up to that time, is a standard tool for analyzing program behavior. Hazard models are especially useful in this regard because they account for the fact that some spells of program participation are not observed to their ends: they either continue past the analyst's observation window (in this case past January 2005) or are missing information at some point during their duration. The competing-risk framework further accounts for the fact that there are several reasons why a spell might end but that only one of those reasons is actually observed. For example, a spell that ended because of a missed recertification might have soon ended anyway for eligibility reasons.

The discrete-time version of the competing-risk model is easy to apply. Estimation can be carried out with a multinomial logit model in which the different reasons for exit in any month are the outcomes. We model exits for four reasons: 1) missed recertifications, 2) losses of eligibility for income or resource reasons, 3) failures to provide information, and 4) all other reasons. The last category combines voluntary exits and other eligibility losses from our descriptive analyses. This collapsing was necessary because of the relatively small number of exits in each category; however, it may make the results for the combined category hard to interpret.

Another advantage of the discrete-time model is that it is a straightforward way to incorporate controls for duration dependence in spells. Our models include 36 monthly dummy variables that cover the first three years of a spell duration and four semiannual dummy variables that cover the next two years; thus, we essentially adopt a semiparametric specification for the spell duration, which is akin to a Cox proportional hazard model. The models also include quarterly, semiannual, and annual duration indicators corresponding to the likely ends of certification periods.

Besides the duration controls, all of our models also include controls for the fiscal year of the observation to account for unmeasured statewide changes in policies, program formulas, economic conditions, and attitudes. For brevity's sake, we do not report the estimation results for the duration or time-series controls, though the complete results are available upon request. The models were estimated separately for households headed by blacks and whites.

Analyses of all exits. We first report marginal effects and standard errors of the hazard of making any type of food stamp exit. These effects were calculated from the competing-risk model and represent the sum of the marginal effects for each of the four specific types of exit.

The results, which are reported separately for black- and white-headed cases, are listed in Table 4.5. Because they describe exits generally, the marginal effects in Table 4.5 are broadly comparable to results previously reported by Ribar, Edelhoch, and Liu (2006a) and by other researchers. However, unlike most previous specifications, the models include detailed controls for earnings histories.

At the top of the table are marginal effects for benefits, reported earned incomes, and reported unearned incomes. For blacks and whites the marginal effects have the anticipated signs: higher benefits reduce the probability of leaving the Food Stamp Program, and higher incomes increase the probability. For blacks, all three effects are statistically significant, though not especially large. A $100 increase in monthly benefits is estimated to lower the probability of exit, which is about 5 percent on average, by 0.19 percent. A $100 increase in earnings raises the probability of exit by 0.05 percent, while a $100 increase in unearned income raises the probability of exit by 0.09 percent. For whites, the estimated marginal effects are smaller, and only the estimated effect for unearned income is significant.

More surprising are the next two sets of results, which indicate that households that start their food stamp spells without any income have higher exit rates than other households, while households that start either their spells or their subsequent certification periods with some positive earnings have substantially lower exit rates than other households. Though the results seem counterintuitive when viewed from the perspective of household resources, there is a policy basis for the findings. South Carolina instructs its caseworkers to grant short certification periods to transient households and households without any stable means of support. South Carolina also requires nonworking households to report changes in their employment within 10 days, whereas working households only need to make immediate reports if their income changes bring them above the gross income threshold. In addition to these explanations, households with children but without earnings, and especially those without income, are likely to be unstable.

As expected, higher levels of UI-covered earnings in the preceding quarter are associated with faster exits from the Food Stamp Program. Given that the models already control for current earned income, the estimates for previous quarter's UI earnings most likely reflect a recent history of job-holding and attachment to the labor force. Black house-

Table 4.5 Estimated Marginal Effects for the Probability of Exiting the Food Stamp Program for Any Reason, Reported Separately by the Race of the Case Head

	Black		White	
	Coefficient	(Std. error)	Coefficient	(Std. error)
Benefits (/100)[a]	−0.188***	(0.047)	−0.101	(0.070)
Reported earned income (/100)	0.047***	(0.011)	0.030	(0.017)
Reported unearned income (/100)	0.091***	(0.014)	0.066***	(0.021)
No income at start of spell	0.467***	(0.081)	0.852***	(0.130)
Any earnings start of cert. period	−0.690***	(0.082)	−1.072***	(0.137)
UI earnings last quarter (/300)	0.052***	(0.005)	0.063***	(0.008)
Avg. UI earnings last year (/300)	−0.015	(0.013)	−0.081***	(0.017)
C.V. UI earnings last year	0.289***	(0.070)	0.109	(0.100)
Max. UI earnings last year (/300)	0.030***	(0.007)	0.056***	(0.010)
No UI earnings last year	0.227	(0.122)	0.166	(0.167)
Female	−0.900***	(0.152)	−0.317**	(0.144)
Age spline, 18–21 years	0.090	(0.068)	−0.247**	(0.102)
Age spline, 22–40 years	−0.018***	(0.006)	−0.044***	(0.010)
Age spline, 41+ years	−0.047***	(0.009)	−0.089***	(0.018)
Education spline, 0–12 years	−0.044	(0.030)	−0.035	(0.040)
Education spline, 12+ years	0.204***	(0.045)	0.217**	(0.088)
Completed high school or GED	0.317***	(0.080)	0.376***	(0.126)
Completed college	−0.357	(0.247)	−0.548	(0.471)
Currently married	0.411***	(0.099)	0.442***	(0.131)
Formerly married	0.339***	(0.068)	0.549***	(0.116)

Number of children 0–2	−0.473***	(0.067)	−0.602***	(0.107)
Number of children 3–5	−0.512***	(0.067)	−0.657***	(0.105)
Number of children 6–11	−0.475***	(0.056)	−0.481***	(0.089)
Number of children 12–14	−0.446***	(0.067)	−0.524***	(0.110)
Number of children 15–17	−0.531***	(0.072)	−0.367***	(0.122)
Number of adults	0.106	(0.071)	0.169	(0.111)
County unemployment rate	−0.030**	(0.013)	−0.037	(0.026)
County population density	−0.015	(0.021)	−0.002	(0.037)
Border county	0.177***	(0.050)	0.197**	(0.080)
Spell quarter (before 10/02)	2.973***	(0.370)	5.300***	(0.763)
Spell 6 months (after 10/02)	1.432***	(0.324)	1.647***	(0.504)
Spell year (before 10/02)	0.437	(0.573)	1.312	(2.220)
Spell year (after 10/02)	2.190***	(0.758)	3.955	(2.137)
AE x spell quarter (bef. 10/02)[b]	1.357***	(0.186)	2.433***	(0.344)
AE x spell 6 mo. (after 10/02)	5.270***	(0.675)	9.945***	(1.373)
AE x spell year (before 10/02)	0.011	(0.288)	−0.752	(0.528)
AE x spell year (after 10/02)	−0.640**	(0.326)	−0.348	(0.681)
Log likelihood	−56,171.88		−40,012.18	
Monthly observations / spells	256,406 / 17,686		142,180 / 12,883	

NOTE: The columns report estimated marginal effects (in percentage terms) of the probability of exiting the Food Stamp Program for any reason. The estimates are derived from multinomial logit competing-risks models of food stamp exits for four different reasons. In addition to the listed controls, the model includes controls for fiscal year and spell duration. Estimated standard errors appear in parentheses. ** significant at the 0.05 level (two-tailed test); *** significant at the 0.01 level (two-tailed test).

[a] The designation "/100" means that the number has been divided by 100 to help make the coefficients roughly comparable. Similarly, "/300" means divided by 300. This is done because the figures come from quarterly rather than monthly data. Dividing by 300 makes the quarterly figures comparable to the monthly amounts.

[b] AE stands for "any earnings at the start of the certification period."

SOURCE: Authors' calculations.

holds with more variable UI earnings also have higher probabilities of exit. As later results for specific reasons of exit will reveal, variable earnings appear to be more indicative of unstable household circumstances generally than of extra compliance costs or frequent income eligibility changes. The maximum level of UI earnings in the previous year is also positively associated with exits, which seems consistent with maximum earnings acting as a proxy for earnings capacity.

The results for the demographic variables fit with findings from previous studies. Being female, being older, having more children, and living in a high unemployment area are all negatively associated with food stamp exits. Completing high school or a GED, completing more postsecondary schooling, and being currently or formerly married are positively associated with exits.

The last eight rows of estimates in the table are from dummy variable controls for likely recertification months and for interactions of those dummy variables with the household's earnings status at the beginning of its certification period. As with Ribar, Edelhoch, and Liu (2006a), the estimates in the last eight rows indicate that households were substantially more likely to leave the Food Stamp Program in recertification months than in other months, with households that reported incomes being even more likely to leave at the quarterly or semiannual dates than other households.

Analyses of exits for specific reasons. Estimated marginal effects from the same competing-risk models, but this time calculated separately for each of the specific reasons of exit, are reported in Tables 4.6 and 4.7. The estimates in the tables indicate that higher levels of food stamp benefits are associated with a lower probability of missing recertifications. For black-headed households, higher benefits are also significantly negatively associated with failing to provide information; for white-headed households, the association is negative but insignificant. Each of these results is consistent with higher benefits incentivizing efforts to stay on the program. Higher benefits are positively associated with exits for income ineligibility, though neither of the estimates is statistically significant. Higher benefits are also positively associated with other losses in eligibility and voluntary withdrawals among black-headed households.

Higher reported incomes are positively associated with exits for missed recertifications and income ineligibility but negatively associated with exits for information reasons. The first two results are expected, while the results for income ineligibility may reflect difficulties in obtaining documentation for low-paying jobs or reflect misreported earnings amounts being detected. As with the results for earned incomes, reported unearned incomes are positively associated with exits for income ineligibility and negatively associated with exits for information reasons.

Households that report no income at the start of their food stamp spells are at substantially higher risk of losing eligibility for information reasons or exiting through the residual category. The first result is consistent with misreporting, while the second result is consistent with no-income households having unsustainable living circumstances that make it hard for them to remain intact, independent, or living in the same place. For white-headed households, starting a spell without any income is also positively associated with missed recertifications. Results for the any-earnings indicator are even stronger. Black- and white-headed households that begin a spell or certification interval without any earnings are at substantially increased risk of exiting the Food Stamp Program for all four reasons.

The amount of covered earnings in the previous quarter is significantly positively associated with exits for all four reasons. These results are consistent with expectations. Higher maximum-covered earnings in the previous year are also significantly positively associated with missed recertifications and information problems for black-headed households and with missed recertifications, income ineligibility, and information problems for white-headed households. The absence of any covered earnings in the previous year is associated with substantially more exits for voluntary reasons and other types of ineligibility.

The positive association between covered-earnings volatility and food stamp exits appears to be limited to the residual category. Again, this would be consistent with other evidence that households in this group have highly unstable circumstances. Covered-earnings volatility is significantly negatively associated with exits for income ineligibility among white-headed households but essentially uncorrelated with these types of exits for black-headed households.

Table 4.6 Results from Discrete-Time Competing-Risk Hazard Models of Food Stamp Exits for Specific Reasons: Cases Headed by Blacks

	Missed recertification	Income/assets too high	Failed to provide information	Other ineligible/ voluntary exit
Benefits	-0.155***	0.021	-0.129***	0.075***
Reported earned income	0.013***	0.066***	-0.044***	0.012**
Reported unearned income	0.006	0.085***	-0.023***	0.023***
No income at start of spell	0.007	-0.014	0.268***	0.205***
Any earnings, start of cert. period	-0.116***	-0.249***	-0.193***	-0.132***
UI earnings last quarter	0.019***	0.009***	0.017***	0.007***
Avg. UI earnings last year	-0.025***	0.018***	-0.008	0.0005
C.V. UI earnings last year	0.007	0.036	0.042	0.203***
Max. UI earnings last year	0.015***	0.004	0.009**	0.002
No UI earnings last year	-0.078**	-0.067	-0.087	0.458***
Female	-0.244***	-0.120	-0.487***	-0.050
Age spline, 18–21 years	-0.014	0.180***	-0.020	-0.057**
Age spline, 22–40 years	-0.009***	0.006**	-0.016***	0.001
Age spline, 41+ years	-0.016***	-0.003	-0.018***	-0.009**
Education spline, 0–12 years	-0.007	-0.034**	-0.001	-0.003
Education spline, 12+ years	0.066***	0.088***	0.021	0.029
Completed high school or GED	0.071**	0.203***	0.062	-0.020
Completed college	-0.049	-0.133	-0.224	0.048
Currently married	0.039	0.173***	0.073	0.125***
Formerly married	0.057**	0.022	0.104***	0.156***

Number of children 0–2	-0.073***	-0.314***	0.047	-0.134***
Number of children 3–5	-0.057**	-0.337***	0.026	-0.144***
Number of children 6–11	-0.042**	-0.354***	0.042	-0.122***
Number of children 12–14	-0.060**	-0.270***	0.042	-0.159***
Number of children 15–17	-0.027	-0.347***	0.035	-0.192***
Number of adults	0.040	-0.069**	0.211***	-0.076**
County unemployment rate	-0.015***	-0.001	-0.009	-0.005
County population density	0.012	-0.024***	0.025**	-0.027***
Border county	0.043**	0.007	0.088***	0.039
Spell quarter (before 10/02)	2.650***	0.249***	-0.066	0.140
Spell 6 months (after 10/02)	1.053***	0.184	0.033	0.162
Spell year (before 10/02)	-0.042	-0.196	0.627	0.049
Spell year (after 10/02)	1.502***	0.360	0.351	-0.022
AE x spell quarter (bef. 10/02)[a]	0.411***	0.695***	0.187	0.064
AE x spell 6 mo. (after 10/02)	3.206***	1.629***	0.370	0.066
AE x spell year (before 10/02)	-0.317***	-0.156	0.422**	0.061
AE x spell year (after 10/02)	-0.534***	-0.391***	0.275	0.010

NOTE: The columns report estimated marginal effects (in percentage terms) from a multinomial logit competing-risk hazard specification of the probability of the listed type of food stamp exit. In addition to the listed controls, the model includes controls for fiscal year and spell duration. It was estimated with 256,406 monthly observations and had a log likelihood of −56,171.88. ** significant at the 0.05 level (two-tailed test); *** significant at the 0.01 level (two-tailed test).

[a] "AE" stands for "any earnings at the start of the certification period."

SOURCE: Authors' calculations.

Table 4.7 Results from Discrete-Time Competing-Risk Hazard Models of Food Stamp Exits for Specific Reasons: Cases Headed by Whites

	Missed recertification	Income/assets too high	Failed to provide information	Other ineligible/ voluntary exit
Benefits	−0.123***	0.047	−0.034	0.009
Reported earned income	0.019***	0.071***	−0.047***	−0.013
Reported unearned income	0.003	0.087***	−0.019	−0.005
No income at start of spell	0.078**	0.067	0.438***	0.270***
Any earnings start of cert. period	−0.295***	−0.283***	−0.295***	−0.199***
UI earnings last quarter	0.016***	0.013***	0.022***	0.012***
Avg. UI earnings last year	−0.020***	−0.020***	−0.043***	0.001
C.V. UI earnings last year	0.060	−0.226***	0.013	0.262***
Max. UI earnings last year	0.009***	0.020***	0.027***	0.001
No UI earnings last year	−0.052	−0.310***	−0.168	0.695***
Female	−0.163***	0.031	−0.231**	0.045
Age spline, 18–21 years	−0.084***	−0.014	−0.127**	−0.021
Age spline, 22–40 years	−0.018***	0.008	−0.022***	−0.012**
Age spline, 41+ years	−0.022***	−0.006	−0.043***	−0.018
Education spline, 0–12 years	0.007	−0.031	0.014	−0.025
Education spline, 12+ years	0.041	0.123***	−0.008	0.060
Completed high school or GED	−0.009	0.278***	−0.006	0.113
Completed college	0.090	0.036	−0.609***	−0.065
Currently married	0.159***	0.197***	0.055	0.031
Formerly married	0.175***	−0.001	0.303***	0.073

Number of children 0–2	-0.199***	-0.315***	-0.017	-0.072
Number of children 3–5	-0.073**	-0.395***	-0.052	-0.137**
Number of children 6–11	-0.070**	-0.313***	-0.027	-0.071
Number of children 12–14	-0.010	-0.343***	-0.079	-0.091
Number of children 15–17	0.050	-0.373***	0.040	-0.084
Number of adults	0.034	-0.043	0.156**	0.022
County unemployment rate	-0.025***	0.007	-0.017	-0.002
County population density	0.008	-0.018	0.014	-0.006
Border county	-0.033	0.048	0.109**	0.074
Spell quarter (before 10/02)	4.845***	0.373**	-0.059	0.142
Spell 6 months (after 10/02)	1.422***	-0.113	0.056	0.281
Spell year (before 10/02)	-0.191	-0.358	2.527	-0.665***
Spell year (after 10/02)	2.291**	0.353	1.897	-0.586**
AE x spell quarter (bef. 10/02)[a]	0.817***	0.808***	0.621***	0.187
AE x spell 6 mo. (after 10/02)	6.769***	2.725***	0.258	0.194
AE x spell year (before 10/02)	-0.329***	-0.280	0.003	-0.146
AE x spell year (after 10/02)	-0.687***	-0.424***	0.544	0.220

NOTE: The columns report estimated marginal effects (in percentage terms) from a multinomial logit competing-risk hazard specification of the probability of the listed type of food stamp exit. In addition to the listed controls, the model includes controls for fiscal year and spell duration. It was estimated with 142,180 monthly observations and had a log likelihood of –40,012.18. ** significant at the 0.05 level (two-tailed test); *** significant at the 0.01 level (two-tailed test).

[a] "AE" stands for "any earnings at the start of the certification period."

SOURCE: Authors' calculations.

Among the demographic results, households headed by females are less likely than households headed by males to exit food stamps for missed recertifications and information problems. Being older is also negatively associated with exits for missed recertifications and information problems. Being currently or formerly married is generally positively associated with different types of exits. The number of children is most strongly associated with exits for income ineligibility and is hardly associated at all with exits for information problems. At the same time, the number of adults in the household is significantly positively associated with exits for information problems, possibly reflecting problems documenting sources of income for multiple adults.

Not surprisingly, the indicators for recertification intervals have their strongest association with exits for missed recertifications. The indicators are also significantly associated with exits for income ineligibility, which is consistent with some high incomes being detected during the recertification process. Fewer large or significant coefficients for the recertification indicators exist for the information and residual exit categories.

Analyses without controls for benefits and reported incomes. There are three analytical concerns with including month-by-month measures of benefits and reported incomes in the event-history models. The first is that these amounts may be endogenous, even though they are measured roughly one month *prior* to the continuation or exit outcome that we observe. A second, related concern for the two income variables is that they may be systematically and strategically misreported, especially in the middle of certification periods. A third concern is that the benefit and reported income variables may be overcontrolling for economic circumstances and not allowing us to see the gross impact of the earnings history variables. To address these concerns we reestimated all of the event history models, dropping the controls for benefits and reported earned and unearned incomes. The results for the covered-earnings history (including the volatility measure), demographic, and recertification interval variables were not substantially changed by this respecification.

Competing-risk counterfactuals. One especially useful feature of the competing-risks framework is that it can be used to conduct a counterfactual analysis of what else might have happened to a food stamp household if it had not terminated its participation for the stated reason. In particular, we can apply the estimated coefficients from the model to the observed characteristics of the cases and predict the probabilities of each of the alternative reasons for exit. For example, we can examine cases of households that terminated for lapsed certifications and estimate the probabilities that the clients would have been found to be financially ineligible, would have failed to furnish appropriate information, or would have stopped receiving food stamps for some other reason. Similarly, we can examine the probabilities of different types of exits conditional on other circumstances. Tables 4.8 and 4.9 report distributions of conditional predicted probabilities along these lines.

The first five rows of each table report conditional predicted probabilities of households letting their certifications lapse separately for actual households that either continued their spells, let their certifications lapse, were found to be financially ineligible, failed to provide appropriate information, or left for some other reason. The second five rows report similar conditional predicted probabilities of exiting for financial eligibility reasons, the third five rows report conditional probabilities of failing to provide appropriate information, and the last five rows report conditional probabilities of leaving for other reasons.

On average, households that left the Food Stamp Program for one reason were at increased risk of leaving for *each* of the other reasons. For example, households that let their certifications lapse faced a risk of being found to be ineligible that was nearly as high as the risk for the households that were actually found to be ineligible. Households that let their certifications lapse also faced a hazard of failing to provide appropriate information that was nearly as high as that for households that actually left for this reason.

Similarly, households that exited for financial eligibility reasons simultaneously faced substantially elevated risks of missing their recertifications and slightly elevated risks of failing to provide appropriate information or leaving for other reasons.

While the risks of all types of exits were relatively higher in the months that the households actually exited, the models predict that there also are still large probabilities of remaining in the program. For instance, among black households that let their certifications lapse, the average predicted hazard of leaving for recertification reasons is only

Table 4.8 Predicted Hazard Probabilities of Specific FS Exits Conditioned on Observed Spell Transitions for Cases Headed by Blacks (%)

		Percentile				
	Mean	10th	25th	50th	75th	90th
Prob(miss recertification)						
Continued spell	2.20	0.11	0.25	0.54	1.42	7.27
Missed recertification	11.72	1.06	4.98	10.79	17.26	23.41
Income/assets too high	6.87	0.21	0.57	1.71	12.14	20.29
Failed to provide info.	4.65	0.18	0.38	0.96	6.63	15.14
Other inelig./vol. exit	3.14	0.17	0.34	0.76	2.83	10.37
Prob(income/assets too high)						
Continued spell	1.05	0.15	0.28	0.57	1.20	2.37
Missed recertification	3.04	0.45	0.91	1.99	3.94	6.66
Income/assets too high	3.66	0.52	1.00	2.18	4.70	8.45
Failed to provide info.	1.49	0.20	0.36	0.76	1.69	3.42
Other inelig./vol. exit	1.29	0.18	0.32	0.64	1.37	2.95
Prob(fail to provide info.)						
Continued spell	0.78	0.23	0.36	0.60	0.95	1.47
Missed recertification	1.45	0.44	0.62	0.91	1.58	3.45
Income/assets too high	1.03	0.33	0.51	0.79	1.16	1.93
Failed to provide info.	1.47	0.43	0.67	1.06	1.72	3.12
Other inelig./vol. exit	1.04	0.32	0.52	0.82	1.27	1.91
Prob(other/voluntary exit)						
Continued spell	0.53	0.16	0.26	0.43	0.70	1.05
Missed recertification	0.63	0.25	0.37	0.53	0.79	1.12
Income/assets too high	0.57	0.20	0.32	0.48	0.72	1.02
Failed to provide info.	0.67	0.24	0.37	0.57	0.86	1.22
Other inelig./vol. exit	0.84	0.28	0.44	0.70	1.09	1.58

NOTE: The table reports means and percentile values of predicted probabilities that are computed using estimated coefficients from the discrete-time competing-risk models presented in Table 4.5, applied to observed characteristics from the study's sample of South Carolina food stamp administrative records. The probabilities are computed conditional on the observed type of transition: either a continuation of a spell or an exit for the listed reason.
SOURCE: Authors' calculations.

Table 4.9 Predicted Hazard Probabilities of Specific FS Exits Conditioned on Observed Spell Transitions for Cases Headed by Whites (%)

		Percentile				
	Mean	10th	25th	50th	75th	90th
Prob(miss recertification)						
Continued spell	2.92	0.10	0.33	0.62	1.32	10.62
Missed recertification	17.47	1.26	9.44	17.06	25.32	32.20
Income/assets too high	8.69	0.21	0.52	1.23	16.85	26.99
Failed to provide info.	5.64	0.19	0.43	0.88	8.30	20.18
Other inelig./vol. exit	3.87	0.25	0.43	0.78	2.28	14.56
Prob(income/assets too high)						
Continued spell	1.11	0.21	0.38	0.70	1.33	2.40
Missed recertification	2.87	0.57	1.04	2.06	3.83	6.34
Income/assets too high	2.95	0.58	0.98	1.89	3.94	6.91
Failed to provide info.	1.34	0.29	0.46	0.83	1.53	2.91
Other inelig./vol. exit	1.23	0.27	0.45	0.77	1.34	2.43
Prob(fail to provide info.)						
Continued spell	1.22	0.33	0.58	0.98	1.56	2.36
Missed recertification	1.94	0.60	0.90	1.41	2.38	4.09
Income/assets too high	1.40	0.45	0.70	1.09	1.69	2.63
Failed to provide info.	2.07	0.70	1.09	1.69	2.58	3.79
Other inelig./vol. exit	1.58	0.56	0.89	1.35	1.98	2.77
Prob(other/voluntary exit)						
Continued spell	0.96	0.23	0.44	0.81	1.32	1.90
Missed recertification	1.03	0.31	0.56	0.88	1.34	1.92
Income/assets too high	0.97	0.28	0.51	0.84	1.28	1.79
Failed to provide info.	1.22	0.34	0.63	1.05	1.65	2.34
Other inelig./vol. exit	1.45	0.52	0.86	1.33	1.90	2.59

NOTE: The table reports means and percentile values of predicted probabilities that are computed using estimated coefficients from the discrete-time competing-risk models presented in Table 4.6, applied to observed characteristics from the study's sample of South Carolina food stamp administrative records. The probabilities are computed conditional on the observed type of transition: either a continuation of a spell or an exit for the listed reason.

SOURCE: Authors' calculations.

11.7 percent, the average predicted hazard of leaving for any other reason is 5.1 percent, and the average predicted probability of continuing is 83.2 percent. Among white households that let their certifications lapse, the corresponding estimates are 17.5, 5.8, and 76.3 percent.

CONCLUSION

In this chapter, we have used electronic case records from South Carolina and event-history methods to examine the characteristics of households with children that are associated with faster exits from the Food Stamp Program. Our investigation is distinctive because it not only examines general exit behavior but also measures and analyzes specific programmatic reasons for exit, including exits for missed recertifications, income ineligibility, failure to provide sufficient or reliable information, other types of ineligibility, and voluntary reasons. As such, the chapter adds to a growing body of research that carefully considers the impact of administrative features of assistance programs. Our analysis also includes controls for earnings histories, allowing us to examine how earnings volatility interacts with these administrative features.

A principal finding from the chapter is that households with children in South Carolina are far more likely to leave the Food Stamp Program for administrative reasons of failing to submit their recertification paperwork and failing to provide sufficient or reliable information than for other eligibility reasons, including income eligibility. Half of the food stamp case terminations that we examined, involving nearly identical percentages for blacks and whites, occurred because households had let their certification periods lapse. A further one-sixth of terminations, again with nearly identical percentages for blacks and whites, occurred when the households failed to provide information, failed to attend required interviews, or could not document their economic circumstances.

In contrast to the two-thirds of the exits that occurred for these paperwork reasons, only about one-fifth of exits occurred because households were formally determined to be ineligible on the basis of income or resources. A further 9 percent of exits occurred through some other loss of eligibility, usually related to the household moving or the client being a nonresident, and about 3 percent of exits occurred voluntarily.

There are several potential explanations for why food stamp recipients might let their eligibilities lapse or run into paperwork problems, each with different implications for the well-being of exiting households. On the one hand, households with increases in income or resources may realize that they are soon likely to be found ineligible and may therefore lose the incentive to complete paperwork. On the other hand, the documentation requirements for continued participation may be unduly burdensome in some circumstances, leading to a number of otherwise eligible households being dropped from the program. The documentation may be especially hard to provide when there is low-wage employment, when there are many members of the household or changes in household composition, or when the members frequently change jobs.

We find evidence for both types of explanations. In the descriptive analyses, the households that fail to recertify have better economic circumstances on average—higher and more stable incomes—than households that voluntarily withdraw or lose their eligibility for nonfinancial reasons, and they have only slightly worse economic circumstances than households that are determined to be financially ineligible. Results from the multivariate analysis further indicate that households that let their certifications lapse were facing relatively higher risks of leaving for financial eligibility and other reasons. At the same time, the descriptive analyses indicated that substantial proportions of the households that missed their recertifications were lacking financial resources just before they exited. Also, households that failed to recertify were receiving an average of $224 to $255 in monthly benefits at the time of their exits, and predictions from the multivariate models revealed that there were high probabilities that they might have continued to receive benefits.

Compared with households that miss their recertifications or lose eligibility for financial reasons, the households that run into information and documentation problems appear to be especially disadvantaged, suggesting that their unstable circumstances may be interfering with their ability to get needed assistance.

There is evidence that households respond to the incentives associated with higher food stamp benefits. Households with higher benefits are significantly less likely than other households to let their certifications lapse. Among black-headed households, higher benefits are also significantly negatively associated with information failures.

One feature of South Carolina's food stamp policy is that it requires households with earnings to recertify their eligibility more frequently than households with fixed incomes. As one would expect, the length of the certification period is strongly associated with food stamp exits. Besides the purely mechanical issue of whether there is a recertification to miss, our multivariate analyses also indicate that recertifications lead to determinations of income ineligibility. The multivariate analyses confirm that households with earnings are more likely to leave for missed recertifications and for income ineligibility at shorter intervals than other households.

More variable earnings histories are also associated with food stamp exits, but in different ways for different types of exits. Among white-headed households, more variable earnings are significantly negatively related to exits for income ineligibility but positively related to exits in our "other" category. Among black-headed households, more volatile earnings are also significantly positively related to exits in our residual category.

State policymakers face an unenviable (and as our research has shown consequential) trade-off in setting their food stamp recertification policies. Shorter intervals improve program integrity; however, they also raise compliance costs and reduce participation among at least some otherwise eligible households. Simpler recertification forms that only request information about changes in relevant circumstances might help to reduce the paperwork burden for families. State policymakers might also consider better coordination across public assistance programs and possibly even with the state tax departments.

Notes

This chapter was originally prepared for the National Poverty Center and Economic Research Service conference on "Income Volatility and Implications for Food Assistance Programs II," November 16–17, 2006, in Washington, DC. It was also presented at the Association for Public Policy Analysis and Management Annual Research Conference, November 2–4, 2006, in Madison, Wisconsin, and the Southern Economic Association Annual Meetings, November 18–21, 2006, in Charleston, South Carolina. The authors acknowledge funding from the Economic Research Service of the U.S. Department of Agriculture under cooperative agreement number 43-3AEM-5-80097. They thank Ellen Rodilo-Fowler and David Patterson for their help in preparing the administrative data, Sandy Allen and Julie Taylor for descriptions of South Carolina's food stamp policies, and Molly Jacobs and Irene Valerio Navarette for research assistance. They also thank Dean Jolliffe, Tom Mroz, Lowell Taylor, and Jim Ziliak for helpful comments. The views expressed in this report are the authors' own and do not necessarily reflect those of the U.S. Department of Agriculture or the South Carolina Department of Social Services.

1. In terms of federally defined resource limits, households may have $2,000 in countable resources, such as a bank account, and may have $3,000 if at least one person is aged 60 or older, or is disabled. Certain resources are not counted, such as a home and in some cases a vehicle. However, in April 2001, South Carolina opted to expand "categorical eligibility" under federal regulatory authority, which allows states to exclude consideration of assets if income is at or below 180 percent of federal poverty guidelines and the household is receiving services from the state's TANF program.

2. If the application is expedited for an emergency situation, the application must be dated within four days and benefits must be accessible by the seventh day.

3. Procedures for households consisting entirely of elderly or disabled clients living on fixed incomes are different. These households are certified for two years but receive an interim contact annually.

4. In 1985, legislation was passed establishing the Food Stamp Employment and Training (E&T) program, designed to assist able-bodied recipients in gaining employment skills. Only about 10 percent of food stamp recipients were subject to these requirements. South Carolina obtained a statewide waiver to exempt able bodied adults without dependents from time limit provisions in March 2004. This made voluntary participation in the E&T program practical for food stamp recipients. Although the program is no longer mandatory, more than 3,000 clients in South Carolina elected to participate in E&T activities in 2005.

5. Some studies of welfare participation (e.g., Harris 1993) have distinguished among losses of eligibility for different reasons, and Moffitt (2003) has recently examined nonfinancial reasons for welfare exits.

6. Food stamp households in South Carolina that miss their recertifications and have their cases closed have one month to submit their paperwork and have it treated as a recertification. After a month, any paperwork is treated as a new application.

7. Some of the differences in covered earnings at the time of exit are undoubtedly the result of clients in the residual cases moving out of state and in a few cases dying. However, evidence of disadvantage precedes the exits and is seen in other indicators such as low levels of education and marriage.

References

Allison, Paul D. 1982. "Discrete-Time Methods for the Analysis of Event Histories." *Sociological Methodology* 13(1982): 61–98.

Bartlett, Susan, Nancy Burstein, and William Hamilton. 2004. *Food Stamp Program Access Study: Final Report*. E-FAN Report No. 03-013-3. Washington, DC: U.S. Department of Agriculture, Economic Research Service.

Blank, Rebecca M., and Patricia Ruggles. 1996. "When Do Women Use Aid to Families with Dependent Children and Food Stamps? The Dynamics of Eligibility versus Participation." *Journal of Human Resources* 31(1): 57–89.

Currie, Janet M., and Jeff Grogger. 2001. "Explaining Recent Declines in Food Stamp Program Participation." In *Brookings-Wharton Papers on Urban Affairs*, William G. Gale and Janet Rothenberg Pack, eds. Washington, DC: Brookings Institution Press, pp. 203–244.

Danielson, Caroline, and Jacob Alex Klerman. 2006. "Why Did the Food Stamp Caseload Decline (and Rise)? Effects of Policies on the Economy." Institute for Research on Poverty Discussion Paper No. 131*-06. RAND Labor and Population Working Paper Series. RAND: Santa Monica, CA.

Farrell, Mary, Michael Fishman, Matthew Langley, and David Stapleton. 2003. *The Relationship of Earnings and Income to Food Stamp Participation: A Longitudinal Analysis*. E-FAN Report No. 03-011. Washington, DC: U.S. Department of Agriculture, Economic Research Service.

Fraker, Thomas, and Robert Moffitt. 1988. "The Effect of Food Stamps on Labor Supply: A Bivariate Selection Model." *Journal of Public Economics* 35(1): 25–56.

Gleason, Philip, Peter Schochet, and Robert Moffitt. 1998. *The Dynamics of Food Stamp Program Participation in the Early 1990s*. Report to the U.S. Department of Agriculture, Food and Nutrition Service. Princeton, NJ: Mathematica Policy Research.

Gundersen, Craig, and James P. Ziliak. 2003. "The Role of Food Stamps in Consumption Stabilization." *Journal of Human Resources* 38(Supplement): 1051–1079.

Haider, Steven J., Alison Jacknowitz, and Robert F. Schoeni. 2003. "Food Stamps and the Elderly: Why Is Participation So Low?" *Journal of Human Resources* 38(Supplement): 1080–1111.

Harris, Kathleen Mullan. 1993. "Work and Welfare among Single Mothers in Poverty." *American Journal of Sociology* 99(2): 317–352.

Hofferth, Sandra. 2003. "Public Policy, the Economy, and Food Stamp Participation Dynamics, 1989–2003." Unpublished manuscript, University of Maryland.

Kabbani, Nader S., and Parke E. Wilde. 2003. "Short Recertification Periods in the U.S. Food Stamp Program." *Journal of Human Resources* 38(Supplement): 1112–1138.

Keane, Michael, and Robert Moffitt. 1998. "A Structural Model of Multiple Welfare Program Participation and Labor Supply." *International Economic Review* 39(3): 553–589.

Kornfeld, Robert. 2002. *Explaining Recent Trends in Food Stamp Program Caseloads*. E-FAN Report No. 02-008. Washington, DC: U.S. Department of Agriculture, Economic Research Service.

Mills, Bradford, Sundar Dorai-Raj, Everett Peterson, and Jeffrey Alwang. 2001. "Determinants of Food Stamp Program Exits." *Social Service Review* 75(4): 539–558.

Moffitt, Robert 1983. "An Economic Model of Welfare Stigma." *American Economic Review* 73(5): 1023–1035.

———. 2003. "The Role of Nonfinancial Factors in Exit and Entry in the TANF Program." *Journal of Human Resources* 38(Supplement), 1221–1254.

Ratcliffe, Caroline, Signe-Mary McKernan, and Kenneth Finegold. 2007. *The Effect of State Food Stamp and TANF Policies on Food Stamp Program Participation*. Washington, DC: Urban Institute.

Ribar, David C., Marilyn Edelhoch, and Qiduan Liu. 2006a. *South Carolina Food Stamp and Well-Being Study: Transitions in Food Stamp and TANF Participation and Employment among Families with Children*. Food Assistance and Nutrition Research Program, Contractor and Cooperator Report No. 17. Washington, DC: U.S. Department of Agriculture, Economic Research Service.

———. 2006b. *South Carolina Food Stamp and Well-Being Study: Transitions in Food Stamp Participation and Employment among Adult-Only Households*. Food Assistance and Nutrition Research Program, Contractor and Cooperator Report No. 18. Washington, DC: U.S. Department of Agriculture, Economic Research Service.

Staveley, Jane, David Stevens, and Parke Wilde. 2002. "The Dynamics of Food Stamp Program Entry and Exit in Maryland." Paper presented at the annual meeting of the National Association for Welfare Research and Statistics, held in Albuquerque, NM, August 25–28.

Wallace, Geoffrey, and Rebecca M. Blank. 1999. "What Goes Up Must Come Down? Explaining Recent Changes in Public Assistance Caseloads." In *Economic Conditions and Welfare Reform*, Sheldon H. Danziger, ed. Kalamazoo, MI: W.E. Upjohn Institute for Employment Research, pp. 49–89.

Wilde, Parke, Peggy Cook, Craig Gundersen, Mark Nord, and Laura Tiehen. 2000. *The Decline in Food Stamp Program Participation in the 1990's*. Food Assistance and Nutrition Research Report No. 7. Washington, DC:

U.S. Department of Agriculture, Economic Research Service.

Wolkwitz, Kari. 2007. *Trends in Food Stamp Program Participation Rates: 1999 to 2005*. Current Perspectives on Food Stamp Program Participation Series. Washington, DC: U.S. Department of Agriculture, Food and Nutrition Service.

Ziliak, James P., Craig Gundersen, and David N. Figlio. 2003. "Food Stamp Caseloads over the Business Cycle." *Southern Economic Journal* 69(4): 903–919.

5

The Dynamics of Food Stamp Receipt after Welfare Reform among Current and Former Welfare Recipients

Brian Cadena
University of Colorado

Sheldon Danziger
Kristin Seefeldt
University of Michigan

In the decade following passage of the Personal Responsibility and Work Opportunity Reconciliation Act of 1996 (PRWORA, or welfare reform), numerous studies examined the correlates of leaving, returning to, and remaining on cash assistance. However, fewer have analyzed food stamp dynamics after welfare reform. Income limits for the Food Stamp Program are set higher than for the Temporary Assistance for Needy Families (TANF) program, under the assumption that low-income working families not eligible for cash assistance should continue to receive food assistance. Declines in the food stamp caseload after welfare reform, although smaller than TANF declines, were greater than some observers thought were warranted. These observers point out that many eligible families were not receiving benefits to which they were entitled (FRAC 2000). Since the recession of 2001, food stamp caseloads have increased substantially, whereas TANF caseloads have hardly changed.

In this paper, we analyze data from the Women's Employment Study (WES), a panel study conducted in one county in Michigan from 1997 to 2003. WES includes monthly data on benefit receipt that allow us to examine several questions related to food stamp dynamics among current and former welfare recipients. The questions include the following:

- What characteristics are associated with a higher probability of exiting from food stamp receipt versus remaining on the rolls after the 1996 welfare reform?

- What characteristics are associated with a higher probability of returning to food stamps after a postwelfare reform exit from the rolls?

- What impact, if any, did two state policy changes—the switch to an Electronic Benefit Transfer (EBT) system and changes in eligibility rules concerning assets—have on food stamp receipt?

The paper is organized as follows. First, we briefly summarize previous relevant studies. Next, we describe welfare policy changes in Michigan, particularly as they relate to the Food Stamp Program. We then describe our panel data, our analytic strategy, and the measures we use. Then, we present empirical results and conclude with a discussion of policy implications.

PRIOR RESEARCH ON FOOD STAMP DYNAMICS

While a large literature has examined the correlates of entry and exit from the cash welfare roles, both before and after welfare reform (e.g., Blank and Ruggles 1996; Grogger and Michalopoulos 2003), fewer studies have focused on food stamp dynamics. While we do not review all studies here, we highlight several that examine the role that individual factors, public policies, and the macroeconomy play in food stamp dynamics.

Zedlewski and Gruber (2001) and Zedlewski (2004) analyze data from the National Survey of America's Families (NSAF) and find that poor households that recently received cash welfare are more likely to use food stamps than are poor households that have no prior welfare receipt. However, the two studies find few differences in the personal characteristics of food stamp users versus nonusers: those with less education and African Americans were more likely to remain on the rolls, but other characteristics, such as poor physical or mental health, were not significantly different between food stamp participants and nonparticipants (Zedlewski 2004).

McKernan and Ratcliffe (2003) use data from the Survey of Income and Program Participation (SIPP) to examine the correlates of food stamp participation among low-income working households. They find that those working traditional daytime hours, holding multiple jobs, and working more hours are less likely to participate. However, this relationship between employment and participation was stronger in the early 1990s than in the late 1990s, suggesting that program efforts to decrease barriers to participation may have become more successful.

The study most closely related to ours is that of Heflin (2004), who examines food stamp exits and returns using the Women's Employment Study. She finds that women who move into work are more likely to leave both cash assistance and the Food Stamp Program. Those who are married, have other adults in the household, and meet the diagnostic screening criteria for drug dependence are more likely to exit, while those who are older, have less education, a shorter welfare history, more children, lack access to a car, and have less knowledge of eligibility rules are less likely to exit. Heflin uses the first four waves of WES data, whereas we use all five waves. Heflin limits her sample to women whose incomes were below 130 percent of the poverty line, roughly the eligibility limit for the Food Stamp Program. However, her method for calculating household income is not exactly the same as the one that the welfare agency uses to determine program eligibility. Also, WES collected detailed household income for the month of the survey, not for every month.

Our analyses build upon and extend Heflin's work by using all five survey waves and including all respondents. Most importantly, Heflin estimates the hazard of exiting from food stamps, whereas we distinguish between recipients who exit from food stamps while working and those who exit without a job, and, as discussed below, find that many individual characteristics have differential effects on these exit types.

Other studies examine how program policies and the economy affect food stamp usage. Danielson and Klerman (2006) find that welfare reform and an improving economy explain food stamp caseload declines during the late 1990s, while policies aimed at increasing program access and the weakening economy explain about half of the caseload increase in the early 2000s.

Ratcliffe, McKernan, and Finegold (2007) combine data from SIPP and state-level policy data to test the effects of various welfare, food stamp, minimum wage, and Earned Income Tax Credit (EITC) policies on food stamp receipt. They find that in states with more lenient vehicle exemption policies, longer periods between eligibility recertification, and expanded categorical eligibility (e.g., deeming families receiving services funded through TANF automatically eligible for food stamps), food stamp receipt increases. On the other hand, biometric technology (such as fingerprint imaging) reduces food stamp receipt. Simplified reporting and implementation of the EBT program, which moved food stamps from coupons to an electronic swipe card, increase food stamp receipt.

Ribar, Edelhoch, and Liu (2008) use state administrative data from South Carolina and find that exits from the Food Stamp Program are five to six times higher in months in which families have to recertify their eligibility than in other months. Once South Carolina increased the length of time between eligibility recertification, median spell lengths of food stamp receipt increased by nearly three months for households with earnings.

Our analyses build on these previous studies. Before describing our model, we review the policy context in Michigan.

THE POLICY CONTEXT IN MICHIGAN, 1997–2003

The Food Stamp and TANF programs have different eligibility limits, treatment of earnings, definition of the family unit, and so on, but the rules in one may affect use of the other. Michigan began adopting a work-first approach to welfare in 1994, requiring some recipients to participate in activities designed to move them into employment quickly (Seefeldt, Danziger, and Danziger 2003). Once PRWORA passed, all but a small number of recipients (for example, those with disabilities or those caring for children or other family members with disabilities) were required to participate in job search activities immediately after applying for cash assistance. Failure to comply with these or other requirements could result in loss of benefits, either immediately (for new applicants) or gradually (for those who were already recipients).

Michigan is one of 16 states that link receipt of food stamp benefits to compliance with TANF or other means-tested program rules (USDA 2004). A mother not complying with TANF rules could face reduction or loss of TANF cash benefits for her entire family along with elimination of her individual food stamp allotment. In other states, food stamp benefits may not increase when TANF benefits are reduced by sanctioning, but the noncompliant adult may not lose her food stamp benefits (Zedlewski, Holcomb, and Duke 1998).

As of April 1997, Michigan recipients on TANF for fewer than 60 days and not complying with work requirements could be terminated immediately from TANF and be hit with a reduction in food stamp benefits. Those receiving TANF for at least 60 days prior to noncompliance faced a 25 percent reduction in both TANF and food stamp benefits, and their TANF case would be closed if noncompliance continued for four months.[1]

Recipients who followed the new rules could combine work, cash welfare, and food stamps, or just work and food stamps, depending on their monthly earnings. Like most states, Michigan changed its earned income disregard to encourage work; it allowed TANF recipients to keep the first $200 of monthly earnings and 20 percent of the remainder. In 1997, a single mother with two children earning $6 an hour for 20 hours of work a week could receive about $200 a month in TANF and about $310 in food stamps. If she worked 35 hours a week, she would lose all TANF benefits but would still receive about $300 in food stamps.[2]

The PRWORA implemented a lifetime limit on receipt of cash assistance: adults could receive TANF for no more than 60 months cumulatively in their lifetime, or fewer months if the states where they lived chose a shorter time limit. All states must abide by the prohibition against using federal TANF funds for families exceeding this 60-month limit. However, Michigan is one of two states that did not put time limits on cash assistance.[3] Instead, the state uses its own funds to provide cash assistance to recipients who reach the federal limit and are in compliance with program rules.

Several analysts (Blank and Schmidt 2001; Pavetti and Bloom 2001; Zedlewski, Holcomb, and Duke 1998) developed post-PRWORA classifications of the stringency of state policy regimes. Most labeled Michigan's policies as "moderate" or "mixed." Policies such as the requirement to engage immediately in work activities (the federal requirement at the time was, within 24 months, to start looking for work or to participate in activities geared toward finding a job) and the possibility of full-family sanctions were strict. Others, such as the lack of a time limit, were lenient. The state's cash benefit in the late 1990s was higher than average—$459 a month for a family of three with no other income, compared to $379 for the median state. However, the earned income disregard policy was not especially generous, and only part-time and low-wage workers could combine welfare and work. As noted above, a single mother with two children who worked 35 hours a week at a job paying $6 an hour was not eligible for cash assistance; in 24 other states, she would be eligible.

Even though Michigan's policies were moderate relative to those of other states, its TANF caseload declined at a rate similar to the national average. Between 1996 and 2003, cash assistance cases declined by about 56 percent nationwide and by about 58 percent in Michigan (authors' tabulations). Food stamp caseloads declined less. Over the same years, the average number of food stamp recipients declined by only 10 percent in Michigan and by only 17 percent nationwide. Food stamp caseloads in Michigan fell by 36 percent between 1996 and 2000 but then rose because of the 2001 recession. The average monthly caseload in Michigan climbed from 603,000 to 838,000 between 2000 and 2003 (HHS 2005). In Michigan, the food stamp participation rate among eligible families is estimated to be 65 percent, well above the 56 percent national average (Castner and Schirm 2005). It is unclear the extent to which this higher participation rate is related to particular state practices, to the state's distressed economy, or to some combination of the two.

As noted, Michigan families who are sanctioned for noncompliance with TANF rules can also lose their food stamps. Sanctioned families are more likely to be disadvantaged than nonsanctioned recipients on measures such as low education or poor health (Cherlin et al. 2002; Kalil, Seefeldt, and Wang 2002). If these disadvantages also make it less likely that sanctioned adults find jobs, then they might be more likely to reapply for TANF, food stamps, or both. On the other hand, if these disadvantages make it difficult for sanctioned adults to understand program rules about why they were sanctioned or how they might become eligible again, then they might be less likely to reapply.

Michigan's choice about how frequently to require food stamp recipients to recertify their eligibility affects participation, as shorter recertification periods are associated with lower program use (Kabbani and Wilde 2003). Federal policy requires that all cases with working adults be redetermined for eligibility at least once every 12 months. Before passage of the 2002 Farm Bill, states could choose periods as short as six months for working recipients in an effort to lower program error rates. In Michigan, TANF recipients are subject to the federal 12-month recertification period; those not on TANF must be recertified every six months if they have earnings (USDA 2003). Frequent recertifications might reduce participation, particularly among working TANF leavers, as more frequent updating of eligibility raises participation costs.

Michigan simplified reporting requirements for TANF and food stamp recipients, which may ease administrative burdens. Typically, families must report any changes in employment, earnings, or income, along with other changes that could affect eligibility. For adults whose earnings or employment status changes frequently, this reporting requirement might be burdensome. With simplified reporting for the Food Stamp Program, families must report changes in earned income only when they exceed 130 percent of usual monthly earnings (USDA 2003).

Other policy changes might have affected participation over our study period. First, between 1996 and 2000, Michigan faced federal penalties for having food stamp overpayment of benefits by rates of 11 to 16 percent, which was above the national 9 percent rate (Seefeldt, Danziger, and Danziger 2003). In an effort to achieve compliance, the state devoted extra resources during 2000 and 2001 to monitoring the Food Stamp Program. Increased monitoring might have deterred some working families from applying and caused others to be deemed ineligible.

Second, in 2001, because of federal program changes, Michigan adopted an Electronic Benefit Transfer program (EBT) to distribute both TANF and food stamp benefits. Instead of receiving food coupons, recipients are issued a "Bridge Card," which functions like a debit card. Proponents argue that this reduces the stigma associated with food stamps, as shoppers using the Bridge Card appear no different than debit-card users at checkout counters. If stigma kept some recipients from using food stamps, then EBT might encourage a return to the rolls.

Michigan also changed how it treated assets in eligibility determination over the study period. Prior to 1997, Michigan received a federal waiver to exempt one vehicle from a client's assets. Because it was thought that car ownership would facilitate the transition from welfare to work, the state allowed recipients who owned cars to maintain eligibility for food stamps. In September of 1999, the waiver expired, and for about one year vehicles were included in the asset test for eligibility determination. Through a creative categorical eligibility policy, the state eventually exempted all vehicles from consideration.

Finally, changes in Michigan's economic climate are likely to have affected participation over time. In the first few years following the 1996 reform, Michigan's economy was booming, and its unemployment rate was below the national average. However, the recession of 2001 and the continuing loss of manufacturing jobs led the unemployment rate to increase and remain above the national average. In 2003, the national unemployment rate was 6 percent, but in Michigan the rate was more than 7 percent.

DATA SOURCES

We analyze panel data from the Women's Employment Study (WES), conducted by the Program on Poverty and Social Welfare Policy at the University of Michigan. Respondents were chosen randomly from a list of white and African American women who received cash assistance as single-parent cases in February 1997 in one urban county in Michigan. Respondents were interviewed five times over a six-year period (Fall 1997, Fall 1998, Fall 1999, Fall 2001, Fall 2003). Response rates for the five waves were high: 86, 92, 91, 91, and 93 percent, respectively. There were 753 respondents in the first wave. Because there is little evidence that attrition from the sample was nonrandom, sample weights are not used (see Cadena and Pape [2006] for an analysis).

Information was gathered on factors known to affect welfare and food stamp usage, including employment, marriage and cohabitation, household size, race, and education. WES also gathered information on factors that are not usually available, including physical health and mental health status, experiences of domestic violence, child behavior, and health problems. WES also contains monthly administrative data on food stamp and TANF participation provided by the Michigan Family Independence Agency.[4]

We combined survey and administrative data to create a panel data set with variables measured at the monthly level. We have measures of employment (self-reported) and TANF and food stamp receipt (administrative data) at this frequency. Most variables from the five interviews were not measured on a monthly basis. We used retrospective relationship questions asked at each wave to create a monthly marriage and cohabitation history for each woman.[5] Most other questions refer to the respondent's experiences during the interval between surveys. We apply the values of these variables backwards in time for all months between interviews. For example, suppose that in the wave 3 interview (1999) a woman reports having experienced severe domestic abuse since the last interview but that she did not report abuse at the wave 2 interview (1998). We code her as experiencing abuse in each month between the wave 2 and the wave 3 interview, but as not experiencing abuse in any month between waves 1 and 2. This methodology is imperfect and introduces some measurement error.

TRENDS IN RECEIPT OF BENEFITS

Figure 5.1 shows monthly patterns of employment, cash welfare usage, and food stamp receipt. All respondents received TANF in February 1997, as benefit receipt was the key study selection criterion. TANF receipt fell from February 1997 until early 2001, when it leveled off at about 20 percent and remained there until the study period ended. Almost all women received food stamps in February 1997. Receipt fell to about 45 percent by early 2000, stayed at this rate for about 18 months, and then increased to about 50 percent in spring 2002, where it remained for the duration of the study. The monthly employment rate increased from about 40 percent in February 1997 to about 75 percent in mid-2000; it then fell during and after the 2001 recession; so that it was just under 70 percent at the final WES survey (Fall 2003).

As employment fell after 2000, food stamp participation increased but TANF participation did not. These simple trends suggest that, after

Figure 5.1 Employment, Cash Welfare Usage, and Food Stamp Receipt, February 1997 to August 2004 (%)

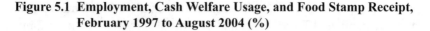
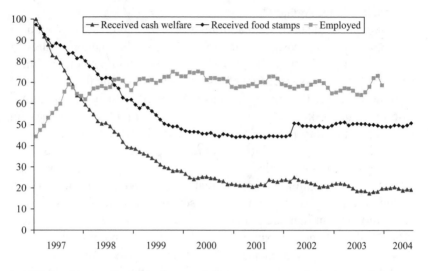

NOTE: Employment line ends January 2004.
SOURCE: Authors' calculations from the Women's Employment Study. The data include all available observations.

welfare reform, women were more likely to use food stamps than TANF in order to smooth temporary fluctuations in earnings. We document this in Figure 5.2.

We select a sample of all spells of nonemployment preceded by a month in which the woman was working and received neither food stamps nor cash welfare. This sample includes women who have successfully transitioned from welfare to work but who then experience at least one month of nonemployment. The Kaplan-Meier failure functions in Figure 5.2 show the unconditional probability (i.e., not adjusted for covariates) that a woman will have returned to benefit receipt after the number of months given on the x-axis. Women are more likely to return to food stamps than to cash assistance when work ends. After three months of nonemployment, 24 percent of women have returned to food stamps (Figure 5.2, Panel A) compared to 15 percent who have returned to cash welfare (Figure 5.2, Panel B). By nine months of nonemployment, the return rates are 42 and 23 percent, respectively.

Figure 5.2 Kaplan-Meier Estimates for Returning to Food Stamps within an Unemployment Spell (%)

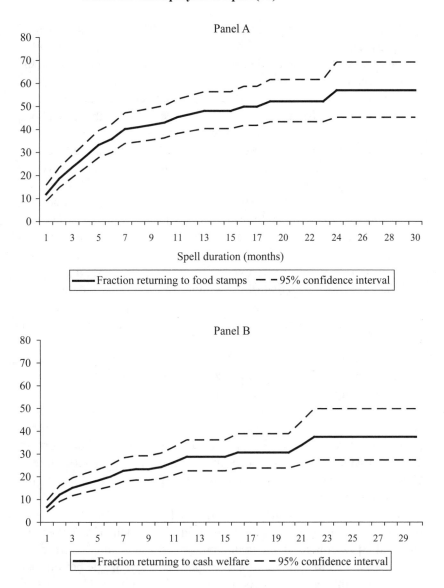

NOTE: The sample includes all spells of unemployment preceded by a month of employment with no food stamps or cash welfare.
SOURCE: Authors' calculations from the Women's Employment Study.

MULTIVARIATE ANALYSES—DEPENDENT VARIABLES

Our multivariate analyses examine three different aspects of food stamp dynamics. The first examines factors that are associated with a recipient's exit from the food stamp spell that was in progress when the sample was drawn. At that time, the typical respondent had received welfare and food stamps for about 7.5 years since she reached age 18 and was in the midst of a 33-month spell. We consider the initial spell (first exit) to be completed when she does not receive food stamps for two consecutive months. We treat spells that are ongoing at the date of the final interview or that are ongoing when respondents leave the sample because of attrition as right-censored. We classify the initial exits into two types: 1) spells ending in a month in which the woman was employed and 2) spells ending in a month in which she was not employed. Because we do not know monthly earnings, we cannot directly measure whether a spell ended because a woman's income exceeded program limits. We consider exits with work as proxies for exits due to higher income. Exits that occur without work are likely the result of sanctions, family status changes like marriage or a child's becoming an adult, or situations in which eligible recipients fail to comply with program rules.

Because the WES sampling frame selected women receiving cash welfare benefits in February 1997 (spells-in-progress), it oversamples longtime recipients. Fortunately, our administrative data contain the date the current cash welfare spell began. We assume that the food stamp spell also began on this date. Thus, there is measurement error to the extent that the food stamp spell began at another time. For February 1997 we assign to each respondent the duration of the spell-in-progress. Our analysis of returns to food stamps after an exit is not subject to the length-bias problem.

Figure 5.3 displays the percentage of food stamp spells that end by a given month following the beginning of the spell. The darker line shows the percentage of spells that end when a woman exits from her food stamp spell in a month in which she is employed. The bottom line shows spells that end without employment. For example, 24 months after the spell began, 32 percent of women had left the rolls in a month in which they were employed, and 13 percent had left in a month in which

Figure 5.3 Cumulative Incidence Estimates of Exiting the Initial Food Stamp Spell (%)

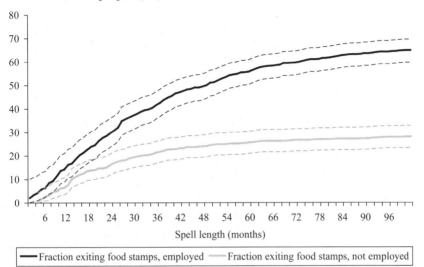

Spell length (months)

━ Fraction exiting food stamps, employed   ━ Fraction exiting food stamps, not employed

NOTE: 95% confidence intervals shown as dashed lines.
SOURCE: Authors' calculations from Women's Employment Study.

they were without work. The remaining 55 percent of spells were still in progress.[6]

The second analysis includes respondents who made a first exit after April 1997 (the third month of the panel) and analyzes factors associated with their first return to food stamp receipt. Each respondent contributes only one spell to each of the first two samples. Figure 5.4 displays this probability of returning. For example, at 24 months after their first exit from food stamps, 61 percent of women had returned to the caseload. The third analysis focuses on returns to food stamps after spells of nonemployment. This dependent variable was shown in Figure 5.2, Panel A.

Thus, food stamp participation is particularly dynamic. Most respondents exit the program at least once during the study period, and most women who exit their initial spell return.

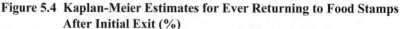

Figure 5.4 Kaplan-Meier Estimates for Ever Returning to Food Stamps After Initial Exit (%)

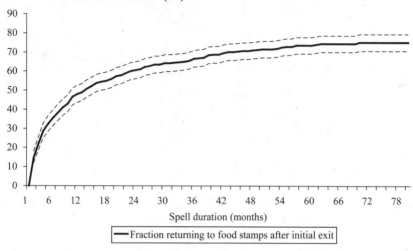

Spell duration (months)

Fraction returning to food stamps after initial exit

NOTE: 95% confidence intervals shown as dashed lines.
SOURCE: Authors' calculations from Women's Employment Study.

REGRESSION MODELS

We estimate regression models that address several questions about food stamp dynamics. First, which characteristics are associated with a higher probability of leaving the food stamp spell that was in progress when the WES study began (first exit)? Do these covariates have different associations for work-based versus nonwork exits? Then, which characteristics are associated with a higher probability of returning to food stamps after exiting from the caseload (first return)? Finally, which characteristics are associated with reentry to food stamps conditional on experiencing a transition from work to nonemployment?

We estimate the semiparametric proportional hazards model outlined in Cox (1972).[7] The parameter of interest is the hazard rate $\lambda(t)$—the probability that a spell ends in month t given that it has lasted until t. Cox's model consists of two parts: 1) a baseline hazard that depends only on t ($\lambda_0[t]$) and 2) a portion that depends on covariates. This specification does not require parametric assumptions about the baseline hazard; the time pattern can take any form as long as it is common across spells. We model the portion that depends on covariates using an exponential functional form. The complete hazard rate, conditional on covariates x and coefficients β, is therefore

$$\lambda(t \mid x, \beta) = \lambda_0(t)\exp(x'\beta).$$

To estimate β, we assume that different covariate values lead to equal proportional changes in the likelihood that a spell ends in any month, regardless of the baseline probability. Our approach provides estimates that are robust to any form of time dependence in the baseline hazard. However, this approach does not allow us to test the nature of time dependence in the data.

As a robustness check, we include dummy variables for calendar years to control for unobserved differences in policies and state enforcement efforts over the study period. We report hazard ratios (exponentiated coefficients) and delta method–based standard errors. The coefficients can be interpreted as the proportional effect of a one-unit increase in the covariate on the probability of the spell ending in a given month. A hazard ratio equal to one means that women have an equal probability of exit for all values of the covariate. Ratios greater than one imply that an increase in the covariate increases the hazard rate; ratios less than one imply the opposite.

REGRESSION RESULTS

We first analyze exits from the initial food stamp spell, treating exits accompanied by employment and exits without employment as independent competing risks. The baseline hazard and the effect of each covariate can vary by type of exit. The hazard function we estimate is thus

$$\lambda(t \mid x, \beta) = \lambda_0(t)\exp(x'\beta_0) + \lambda_1(t)\exp(x'\beta_1) \ ,$$

with 0 representing employment-based exits and 1 representing non-employment-based exits. This specification is equivalent to estimating separate models for each exit type (treating observations that end with the other exit type as censored). By estimating a model that allows for both types of exits simultaneously, we can test whether the covariates have the same proportional effect for both exit types.[8]

Table 5.1 defines the variables we use and presents their means and standard deviations, the number of observations, and the frequency with which the observations are measured. For example, age, education, and race are measured at the first wave in Fall 1997. On the other hand, as mentioned above, we have monthly information on employment and receipt of TANF and food stamps. The typical respondent was about 30 years old in 1997. About one-third of respondents had completed some education beyond high school, 37 percent had graduated from high school or completed a GED, and 31 percent had not finished high school. Over the course of the study period, a typical respondent worked for 67 percent of the months, received food stamps for 62 percent of the months, and received TANF for 40 percent of the months.

At a typical wave, many respondents reported physical and mental health problems; one advantage of WES over other welfare-reform data sets is the extent of this information. About one quarter of respondents reported physical limitations that placed them in the bottom quartile of functioning for their age and reported their overall health as fair or poor. About one-third met the diagnostic screening criteria for one of several psychiatric disorders measured in the WES instrument. Six percent had serious substance abuse problems, and 13 percent had experienced severe domestic abuse in the 12 months before the survey. These personal attributes, as documented elsewhere (Seefeldt and Orzol 2005; Turner, Danziger, and Seefeldt 2006), are associated with reduced work and increased TANF receipt among WES respondents.

Table 5.2 presents the results for the exit from the food stamp spell that was in progress in February 1997. In each of the three specifications, the first column reports hazard ratios for employment-based exits and the second column gives hazard ratios for exits without work; the final column (denoted as "Diff") reports whether the proportional effect of the covariate on the hazard rate is significantly different for the two exit types. The first specification includes only characteristics of women and their households that are fixed at their 1997 values. Women with at least a high school degree are more likely to leave food stamps with a job in any given month than those who have not finished high school (the omitted category). There are no significant effects of education on the likelihood of exiting without work. With or without work, African Americans are less likely than whites to exit from food stamps.

The coefficients on the fixed attributes are attenuated in size and fall in significance when we include the rich set of time-varying variables in the second specification. This suggests that race and education are correlated with some of the variables included in the expanded model. Women living with a partner are more likely to exit with or without work than women not living with a partner: married women are 1.86 times as likely to exit with work—and cohabiting women 1.27 times as likely—as women who do not live with partners. A husband's financial resources are more likely to raise a woman's family income above the food stamp eligibility cutoff. Those who cohabit with an employed partner may have less financial need and hence be less likely to go through the recertification process.

For a given level of income, women with larger families are eligible for larger food stamp benefits, making them less likely to lose their eligibility when working. The analysis supports this hypothesis: each additional person in the household reduces the likelihood of exit with work by about 12 percent.

Women with significant problems with their physical or mental health or personal lives are less likely to find and keep a job and hence less likely to exit food stamps with work. The evidence supports this hypothesis. For example, a woman with health problems is about 33 percent less likely to exit with work, a woman with a mental health problem about 30 percent less likely, and one with a child with learning, mental health, or health problems about 36 percent less likely. Some women whose children have persistent problems may have been exempted from the TANF work requirement (Seefeldt and Orzol 2005).

Some critics of welfare reform expected that some recipients with many personal problems would fall through all the safety nets once reform was implemented (Edelman 1997). The fact that there is no significant relationship between personal problems and food stamp exits without work (hazard ratios near one in the second column of the second specification) suggests that the most disadvantaged are no more likely than others to exit food stamps without work. On the other hand, other work with the WES (Turner, Danziger, and Seefeldt 2006) has shown that a small but growing proportion of women lose jobs and do

Table 5.1 Variable Descriptions and Descriptive Statistics—Women's Employment Survey

Variable label	Variable definition	Mean	Std. Dev.	N	Frequency
Age in 1997	Respondent's age in years, measured at the time of first interview	29.75	7.40	753	Fixed
Age squared/100	Age in 1997 squared, divided by 100	9.40	4.82	753	Fixed
High school diploma or GED	1 if respondent has exactly a high school degree or equivalent; 0 otherwise	0.37	0.48	753	Fixed
More than high school	1 if respondent has more education than a high school degree; 0 otherwise	0.32	0.47	753	Fixed
Race dummy: 1 if African American	1 if African-American; 0 otherwise	0.56	0.50	753	Fixed
Worked during this month	1 if respondent reports working at least one hour this month; 0 otherwise	0.67	0.47	49,428	Month
Received food stamps during this month	1 if administrative data show food stamp receipt for this month; 0 otherwise	0.62	0.49	49,428	Month
Received TANF during this month	1 if administrative data show TANF receipt for this month; 0 otherwise	0.40	0.49	49,428	Month
Married	1 if married; 0 otherwise	0.17	0.38	49,381	Month[a]
Cohabiting, not married	1 if living with a male partner, but not married; 0 otherwise	0.28	0.45	49,417	Month[a]
Lagged unemployment rate in survey county	Monthly unemployment rate for the survey county, lagged one month	6.68	1.97	49,428	Month
Age-specific physical limitation & fair/poor health	1 if respondent has an age-specific physical limitation & reports fair or poor health; 0 otherwise	0.23	0.42	49,169	Wave

Any mental health barrier	1 if respondent has any mental health problem (PTSD, general anxiety disorder, social phobia, depression); 0 otherwise	0.34	0.47	49,428	Wave
Caregiven child has learning/mental/physical health problem	1 if respondent is responsible for a child with special needs (learning disability, mental health or physical health problems); 0 otherwise	0.17	0.37	49,301	Wave
Any substance dependence or hard drug use	1 if respondent meets DSM-IV criteria for alcohol or drug dependence or uses "hard" drugs; 0 otherwise	0.06	0.23	49,305	Wave
Severe domestic abuse in past year	1 if respondent reports severe physical violence from an intimate partner; 0 otherwise	0.13	0.34	49,255	Wave
Owns a vehicle	1 if owns or has reliable access to a vehicle; 0 otherwise	0.79	0.41	49,418	Wave
Assets used to determine eligibility	1 if calendar date between 10/1999 and 9/2000; 0 otherwise	0.12	0.35	49,428	Month
Assets used × owns a car	Interaction between "Owns a car" and "Assets used to determine eligibility"	0.35	0.32	49,418	Month
After EBT rollout	1 if after March 2001; 0 otherwise	0.14	0.48	49,428	Month
Knows still eligible for food stamps if working	1 if respondent answers "no" to the question "Once anyone receiving cash assistance gets a job, do the rules say they will stop receiving food stamps?"; 0 otherwise	0.67	0.47	630	Wave 3 (Once)

NOTE: The number of observations for variables measured at the month or wave level is the number of valid person-months. Variables measured only at the wave level are assigned to individual months using the procedure described in the text.

[a] Although the marriage and cohabitation questions are only asked at each wave, they contain sufficient detail to create an accurate monthly history.

SOURCE: Authors' calculations from the Women's Employment Survey.

Table 5.2 Hazard Ratios from Competing-Risks Cox Proportional Hazard Models for First Exit from Food Stamps

	(1)			(2)			(3)		
	Working	Not working	Diff.	Working	Not working	Diff.	Working	Not working	Diff.
Age in 1997	0.947	1.088		0.994	1.068		1.000	1.110	
	(0.049)	(0.096)		(0.053)	(0.096)		(0.056)	(0.107)	
Age squared /100	1.073	0.884		1.016	0.909		1.002	0.863	
	(0.085)	(0.119)		(0.081)	(0.125)		(0.085)	(0.125)	
High school diploma or GED	1.548***	0.845	**	1.367**	0.906		1.465***	0.948	*
	(0.210)	(0.174)		(0.190)	(0.194)		(0.213)	(0.209)	
More than high school	1.723***	0.798	***	1.488***	0.870	**	1.566***	0.807	**
	(0.237)	(0.175)		(0.213)	(0.200)		(0.234)	(0.194)	
Race dummy: 1 if African American	0.756***	0.627***		0.832	0.671**		0.807*	0.657**	
	(0.082)	(0.110)		(0.095)	(0.125)		(0.096)	(0.129)	
Married				1.859***	2.078***		1.883***	1.943**	
				(0.310)	(0.528)		(0.324)	(0.516)	
Cohabiting, not married				1.273**	1.150		1.274*	1.123	
				(0.156)	(0.240)		(0.162)	(0.245)	
Number of people in household				0.876***	1.000	*	0.876***	1.014	**
				(0.034)	(0.056)		(0.035)	(0.058)	
Age-specific physical limitation & fair/poor health				0.673***	1.137	**	0.680**	1.149	**
				(0.102)	(0.241)		(0.106)	(0.251)	
Any mental health barrier				0.714***	1.199	**	0.711**	1.287	**
				(0.093)	(0.235)		(0.096)	(0.261)	
Caregiven child has learning/mental/ physical health problem				0.634***	0.845		0.584***	0.818	
				(0.107)	(0.195)		(0.104)	(0.194)	

	Exit w/ employment	Exit w/o employment	Diff.	Exit w/ employment	Exit w/o employment	Diff.
Any substance dependence or hard drug use	0.790 (0.217)	1.001 (0.356)		0.808 (0.230)	1.102 (0.395)	
Severe abuse in past year	0.837 (0.148)	0.940 (0.237)		0.912 (0.167)	0.869 (0.235)	
Owns a vehicle	1.264 (0.190)	0.788 (0.171)	*	1.367* (0.222)	0.745 (0.167)	*
Lagged unemployment rate in survey county	0.949 (0.042)	1.015 (0.061)		0.956 (0.043)	1.011 (0.065)	
After EBT rollout	1.271 (0.713)	1.532 (1.676)		1.255 (0.705)	1.501 (1.643)	
Assets used to determine eligibility	0.762 (0.379)	1.172 (0.663)		0.831 (0.417)	1.117 (0.634)	
Assets used × Owns a car	1.356 (0.682)	0.483 (0.297)		1.234 (0.627)	0.519 (0.320)	
Knows still eligible for food stamps if working				0.786** (0.092)	0.715* (0.138)	
N spells	679	679		570	570	
N exits	369	135		342	125	

NOTE: The models also include dummy variables for each calendar year. The first column in each specification gives the hazard ratio for exit from food stamps accompanied by employment. The second column gives the hazard ratio for exit from food stamps without employment. The third column reports the significance level on a test of equal proportionate effects on both types of exit. Exact partial likelihood method used for ties. * = p < 0.10; ** = p < 0.05; *** = p < 0.01. Standard errors in parentheses. "Diff." stands for "difference."
SOURCE: Authors' calculations from the Women's Employment Survey.

not return to welfare; however, many of them continue to receive food stamps.

We also evaluate two policy changes implemented by Michigan. As noted, in 2001, the state adopted an Electronic Benefit Transfer system designed both to reduce fraud and to reduce the stigma of purchasing food by eliminating government coupons. Our analysis does not reveal any significant change in the probability of food stamp exit following EBT implementation, perhaps because these two effects tend to offset each other. Because we have only time series variation in the EBT variable, concurrent changes such as the rising unemployment rate might reduce our ability to identify an EBT effect.

We also examine how changes in the state's treatment of assets affected exit from the initial spell. For about one year in the middle of the study period, the state could not exclude the value of a car from the food stamp asset test. We include a dummy variable for the months in which an asset test was in place and an interaction with this variable and the vehicle ownership variable.[9] We find no evidence that asset testing affected the probability of exit, whether or not a woman owned a vehicle.

The third specification includes an indicator for knowledge about program rules. In Fall 1999, respondents were asked, "Once anyone receiving cash assistance gets a job, do the rules say they will stop receiving food stamps?" About a third did not know that "no" is the correct answer. Those answering correctly are about one quarter less likely to leave food stamps than women who answered incorrectly or were unsure. This suggests that some women who exited from TANF may have left food stamps by mistake, thinking that they were no longer eligible.

Table 5.3 presents our analysis of the probability of reentering the food stamp rolls following an exit of at least two months. Many of the same attributes associated with a lower exit probability in Table 5.2 are associated with a higher return probability here. For example, African Americans are more likely to return than whites, and those with more education than a high school degree are less likely to return (all columns, Table 5.3). Similarly, women who are married or cohabiting are much less likely to return to food stamps than women who do not live with partners (columns 2 and 3). Women who are not working are about 1.7 times as likely as working women to return to food stamps; this is not surprising since nonworkers will have lower monthly incomes than workers. Additionally, when the county unemployment rate increases by one percentage point, women are 1.13 times as likely to return to food stamps. High unemployment rates likely translate into less job security and worse employment prospects for those looking for work and hence encourage women to return to food stamp receipt.

Women who own cars are about 30 percent less likely to return to food stamps than those who do not. Car ownership may be a proxy for greater economic stability, indicating that the woman has and expects to continue to have stable employment. Alternatively, women may be misinformed about the treatment of assets and, thinking that the car makes them ineligible, may not reapply. Any of these mechanisms could explain why car owners are less likely to return.

Women who experienced severe domestic violence in the year before the survey are about 50 percent more likely than others to return to food stamps. Some women may leave a violent relationship suddenly and unexpectedly and then seek public assistance. It represents a policy success when battered women return to food stamps as part of their coping strategy.

Knowledge of the food stamp eligibility rule concerning combining work and benefits does not predict with any statistical significance who returns to the rolls (Table 5.3, column 3). This conflicts with the data in Table 5.2 showing that program knowledge reduced the probability of an exit. The lack of relationship between knowledge and food stamp returns could be due to heterogeneity in the types of women who exited and are thus eligible to return. Some women may exit when they earn enough to make them ineligible for benefits. Their correct knowledge of the ability to combine work and food stamps cannot affect their likelihood of return since they are ineligible. Other women are eligible to combine employment and food stamp benefits but may be disproportionately likely to believe incorrectly that they are ineligible. The women who knew they were eligible may have never left the caseload. This differential selection can explain the insignificant results for the knowledge indicator in the return specification.

Women were much less likely to return to food stamps after coupons were replaced by the Bridge Card in 2001. This result does not support the hypothesis that EBT removed a stigma that was keeping women from participating. We do not consider this a definitive test of the effect of EBT on participation because the policy changes only once

Table 5.3 Hazard Ratios from Cox Proportional Hazard Models for First Return to Food Stamps

	(1)	(2)	(3)
Age in 1997	0.937	0.921	0.914
	(0.057)	(0.060)	(0.061)
Age squared /100	1.079	1.102	1.109
	(0.104)	(0.113)	(0.117)
High school diploma or GED	0.798	0.901	0.920
	(0.110)	(0.129)	(0.135)
More than high school	0.567***	0.704**	0.722**
	(0.084)	(0.110)	(0.116)
Race dummy: 1 if African American	1.802***	1.638***	1.637***
	(0.214)	(0.207)	(0.212)
Unemployed		1.738***	1.805***
		(0.221)	(0.234)
Married		0.577***	0.584***
		(0.102)	(0.106)
Cohabiting, not married		0.666***	0.696**
		(0.094)	(0.100)
Owns a vehicle		0.700**	0.711**
		(0.117)	(0.123)
Number of people in household		0.974	0.976
		(0.038)	(0.039)
Age-specific physical limitation & fair/poor health		1.182	1.201
		(0.178)	(0.183)
Any mental health barrier		1.053	1.039
		(0.148)	(0.149)
Caregiven child has learning/mental/ physical health prob		1.188	1.141
		(0.205)	(0.204)
Any substance dependence or hard drug use		1.117	1.170
		(0.308)	(0.325)
Severe abuse in past year		1.520**	1.521**
		(0.260)	(0.266)
Lagged unemployment rate in survey county		1.129***	1.125***
		(0.041)	(0.043)
After EBT rollout		0.313***	0.353**
		(0.132)	(0.153)

Table 5.3 (continued)

	(1)	(2)	(3)
Assets used to determine eligibility		1.172	1.179
		(0.386)	(0.390)
Assets used × owns a car		1.268	1.252
		(0.424)	(0.422)
Knows still eligible for food stamps			0.959
if working			(0.120)
N spells	527	527	490
N returns	341	341	324

NOTE: The models also include dummy variables for each calendar year. Exact partial likelihood method used for ties. $* = p < 0.10$; $** = p < 0.05$; $*** = p < 0.01$. Standard errors in parentheses.
SOURCE: Authors' calculations from the Women's Employment Survey.

over the sample period and could easily be confounded with other factors changing at a similar time.

The specification in Table 5.4 is similar to that in Table 5.3, except the sample is restricted only to those who have exited a food stamp spell and who have experienced a transition from work to nonwork. The results are quite similar to those in Table 5.3, with the exception that women who have mental health problems are about 50 percent more likely to return to food stamps during a spell of unemployment than those who do not have mental health problems.

POLICY IMPLICATIONS

Our empirical results provide some good news from a policy perspective. First, food stamp participation among WES respondents was more sensitive to employment variability than was TANF receipt. Second, those with health and mental problems are less likely to exit food stamps with work, but they are not more likely to exit without work. Women in larger households are less likely than similar women in smaller households to exit, probably because their earnings are farther below the food stamp eligibility cutoff, which increases with household size. Similarly,

Table 5.4 Hazard Ratios from Cox Proportional Hazard Models for Return to Food Stamps during an Unemployment Spell

	(1)	(2)	(3)
Age in 1997	0.700***	0.649***	0.658***
	(0.068)	(0.071)	(0.075)
Age squared /100	1.727***	1.934***	1.904***
	(0.262)	(0.341)	(0.347)
High school diploma or GED	0.559**	0.623*	0.583**
	(0.128)	(0.154)	(0.150)
More than high school	0.437***	0.463**	0.427***
	(0.122)	(0.141)	(0.134)
Race dummy: 1 if African American	1.891***	1.671**	1.798**
	(0.393)	(0.398)	(0.438)
Married		0.413***	0.431***
		(0.122)	(0.129)
Cohabiting, not married		0.666	0.669
		(0.177)	(0.185)
Owns a vehicle		1.492	1.692
		(0.486)	(0.576)
Number of people in household		0.951	0.960
		(0.072)	(0.073)
Age-specific physical limitation & fair/poor health		1.009	0.979
		(0.251)	(0.246)
Any mental health barrier		1.506*	1.517*
		(0.348)	(0.363)
Caregiven child has learning/mental/ physical health problem		1.467	1.528
		(0.424)	(0.448)
Any substance dependence or hard drug use		0.779	0.718
		(0.358)	(0.334)
Severe abuse in past year		1.414	1.533
		(0.405)	(0.449)
Lagged unemployment rate in survey county		1.042	1.067
		(0.085)	(0.091)
After EBT rollout		0.464	0.459
		(0.287)	(0.284)
Assets used to determine eligibility		2.563	2.721
		(1.633)	(1.748)

Table 5.4 (continued)

	(1)	(2)	(3)
Assets used × owns a car		0.419	0.387
		(0.271)	(0.253)
Knows still eligible for food stamps			0.753
if working			(0.172)
N spells	344	336	330
N returns	112	109	106

NOTE: The models also include dummy variables for each calendar year. Exact partial likelihood method used for ties. * = $p < 0.10$; ** = $p < 0.05$; *** = $p < 0.01$. Standard errors in parentheses.
SOURCE: Authors' Calculations from the Women's Employment Survey.

when the county unemployment rate is higher and when women experience job loss, they are more likely to return to the Food Stamp Program. We also find that women with recent experiences with severe abuse are more likely than others to return to the food stamp rolls.

These findings tell us about the relative likelihood of staying on or returning to food stamps, not about the participation rate of eligible families. Increased outreach efforts might be warranted, given the confusion respondents express about food stamp rules and given their employment instability. Women who understand that they are allowed to combine food stamp receipt with low-wage work are significantly more likely to continue to receive food stamps. On the other hand, women who own vehicles are less likely to return to food stamps, perhaps indicating misunderstanding about car ownership rules. An outreach program that provided information about eligibility might increase participation rates.

Although the typical respondent in our Michigan sample worked in almost 70 percent of the months over the six-and-one-half-year panel, more than half experienced at least one spell of "unstable employment," defined as having been fired, laid off, or otherwise not having worked for more than four weeks (Johnson 2006). Food stamp receipt helps cushion earnings losses, but many who lost jobs did not return to the program. While some women find new jobs relatively quickly, many experience long spells of nonemployment without receiving food assistance.[10]

A study of local agency practices indicates that it may not be the particular type of outreach activity that matters but the number of activities in which an office engages (Bartlett, Burstein, and Hamilton 2004). Outreach is usually low-cost and includes activities such as preparing informational pamphlets and posters for distribution in community centers and other public places, operating a toll-free information hotline, and coordinating outreach activities with the local Medicaid and State Child Health Insurance Program (SCHIP) offices. Such activities better provide information about eligibility to eligible nonparticipants.

Although economic conditions in the nation have improved since the 2001 recession, many low-income families have not yet benefited from the recovery: poverty rates remain above 2000 levels, and the number of individuals who are food-insecure increased by six million between 1999 and 2004 (Rosenbaum 2006). The Food Stamp Program provides economic support for millions of working poor families, and our results suggest that more should be done to encourage eligible nonparticipants to apply for the benefits to which they are entitled.

Notes

This chapter comes from a paper presented at the conference "Income Volatility and Implications for Food Assistance Programs II," sponsored by the National Poverty Center, Gerald R. Ford School of Public Policy, University of Michigan, and by the Economic Research Service, U.S. Department of Agriculture, in November 2006. Pamela Loprest, Dean Jolliffe, Jeffrey Smith, and James Ziliak provided helpful comments on a previous draft. Any opinions expressed are solely those of the authors.

1. In the WES data, described below, a woman receiving TANF in April 1997 had received aid for at least 60 days since the sample was drawn from the February 1997 caseload.

2. Amounts were computed using the "marriage calculator" available from the Administration for Children and Families, U.S. Department of Health and Human Services. We assume that the woman has no assets, no vehicle, receives no child support, and has been on TANF for at least six months. The calculator is available at http://marriagecalculator.acf.hhs.gov/marriage/calculator.php (accessed April 28, 2008).

3. Michigan has since adopted a 48-month time limit that went into effect in late 2007.

4. The agency's name has since been changed to the Michigan Department of Human Services.

5. Respondents were asked if they were married or cohabiting and, if so, for how many months. Single women were asked to specify the month in which a previous marriage or cohabiting relationship ended.
6. These estimates use the cumulative incidence approach, so the probabilities add to one.
7. We use the exact partial likelihood method to handle ties (exits occurring in the same month) because our exits are measured in discrete time intervals.
8. To estimate these models, we augment our data using the methodology outlined in Lunn and McNeil (1995).
9. The WES survey asks a respondent if she owns a vehicle or has consistent, reliable access to one. We label all positive responses as vehicle ownership, even though some women do not own a vehicle. There is measurement error for these women, since their use of someone else's car would not affect their food stamp eligibility.
10. A limitation of our study is that our sample is drawn from a particular county in a single state. Both TANF and food stamp policies vary by state, and our findings may not be generalizable to states with different policy regimes. However, it seems reasonable to assume that lack of knowledge of program rules is a common problem that might be addressed by outreach efforts.

References

Bartlett, Susan, Nancy Burstein, and William Hamilton. 2004. *Food Stamp Program Access Study: Final Report.* Bethesda, MD: Abt Associates.

Blank, Rebecca M., and Patricia Ruggles. 1996. "When Do Women Use Aid to Families with Dependent Children and Food Stamps? The Dynamics of Eligibility versus Participation." *Journal of Human Resources* 31(1): 57–89.

Blank, Rebecca M., and Lucie Schmidt. 2001. "Work, Wages, and Welfare." In *The New World of Welfare*, Rebecca M. Blank and Ron Haskins, eds. Washington, DC: Brookings Institution Press, pp. 70–96.

Cadena, Brian, and Andreas Pape. 2006. "The Extent and Consequences of Attrition in the Women's Employment Study." Working paper. Ann Arbor, MI: University of Michigan. http://www.fordschool.umich.edu/research/poverty/pdf/WES_Attrition-06.pdf (accessed June 6, 2008).

Castner, Laura A., and Allen L. Schirm. 2005. *Reaching Those in Need: State Food Stamp Participation Rates in 2003.* Princeton, NJ: Mathematica Policy Research.

Cherlin, Andrew J., Karen Bogen, James M. Quane, and Linda Burton. 2002. "Operating within the Rules: Welfare Recipients' Experiences with Sanctions and Case Closings." *Social Service Review* 76(3): 387–405.

Cox, D.R. 1972. "Regression Models and Life-Tables." *Journal of the Royal Statistical Society, Series B* (Methodological) 34(2): 187–220.

Danielson, Caroline, and Jacob Alex Klerman. 2006. "Why Did the Food Stamp Caseload Decline (and Rise)? Effects of Policies on the Economy." Discussion Paper No. 1316-06. Madison, WI: Institute for Research on Poverty.

Edelman, Peter. 1997. "The Worst Thing Bill Clinton Has Done." *The Atlantic* 279(3): 43–58.

Food Research Action Center (FRAC). 2000. *State Government Responses to the Food Assistance Gap, 2000*. Third Annual Report by FRAC and America's Second Harvest. Washington, DC: FRAC.

Grogger, Jeffrey, and Charles Michalopoulos. 2003. "Welfare Dynamics under Time Limits." *Journal of Political Economy* 111(3): 530–554.

Heflin, Colleen M. 2004. "Who Exits the Food Stamp Program after Welfare Reform?" Discussion Paper No. 1279-04. Madison, WI: Institute for Research on Poverty.

Johnson, Rucker C. 2006. "Wage and Job Dynamics after Welfare Reform: The Importance of Job Skills." *Research in Labor Economics* 26(1): 231–298.

Kabbani, Nader S., and Parke E. Wilde. 2003. "Short Recertification Periods in the U.S. Food Stamp Program: Causes and Consequences." *Focus* 22(2): 64–66.

Kalil, Ariel, Kristin S. Seefeldt, and Hui-Chen Wang. 2002. "Sanctions and Material Hardship under TANF." *Social Service Review* 76(4): 642–662.

Lunn, Mary, and Don McNeil. 1995. "Applying Cox Regression to Competing Risks." *Biometrics* 51(2): 524–532.

McKernan, Signe-Mary, and Caroline Ratcliffe. 2003. *Employment Factors Influencing Food Stamp Program Participation: Final Report*. E-FAN No. 03-012. Washington, DC: U.S. Department of Agriculture, Economic Research Service.

Pavetti, LaDonna, and Dan Bloom. 2001. "State Sanctions and Time Limits." In *The New World of Welfare*, Rebecca M. Blank and Ron Haskins, eds. Washington, DC: Brookings Institution Press, pp. 245–264.

Ratcliffe, Caroline, Signe-Mary McKernan, and Kenneth Finegold. 2007. *The Effect of State Food Stamp and TANF Policies on Food Stamp Program Participation*. Washington, DC: Urban Institute.

Ribar, David C., Marilyn Edelhoch, and Qiduan Liu. 2008. "Watching the Clocks: The Role of Food Stamp Recertification and TANF Time Limits in Caseload Dynamics." *Journal of Human Resources* 43(1): 208–239.

Rosenbaum, Dorothy. 2006. "The Food Stamp Program is Growing to Meet Need." Washington, DC: Center on Budget and Policy Priorities. http://www.cbpp.org/6-6-06fa.pdf (accessed January 8, 2008).

Seefeldt, Kristin S., Sheldon Danziger, and Sandra K. Danziger. 2003. "Michigan's Welfare System." In *Michigan at the Millennium: A Benchmark and Analysis of its Fiscal and Economic Structure*, Charles L. Ballard, Paul N.

Courant, Douglas C. Drake, Ronald C. Fisher, and Elisabeth R. Gerber, eds. East Lansing, MI: Michigan State University Press, pp. 351–370.

Seefeldt, Kristin S., and Sean M. Orzol. 2005. "Watching the Clock Tick: Factors Associated with TANF Accumulation." *Social Work Research* 29(4): 215–229.

Turner, Lesley J., Sheldon Danziger, and Kristin S. Seefeldt. 2006. "Failing the Transition from Welfare to Work: Women Chronically Disconnected from Employment and Cash Welfare." *Social Science Quarterly* 87(2): 227–249.

U.S. Department of Agriculture (USDA). 2003. *Food Stamp Program State Options Report, Third Edition*. Washington, DC: USDA, Food and Nutrition Service. http://www.fns.usda.gov/fsp/rules/Memo/Support/State_Options/ 3-State_Options.pdf (accessed May 21, 2008).

———. 2004. *Food Stamp Program: State Options Report. Fourth Edition*. Washington, DC: USDA, Food and Nutrition Service. http://www.fns.usda .gov/fsp/rules/Memo/Support/State_Options/4-State_Options.pdf (accessed May 21, 2008).

U.S. Department of Health and Human Services (HHS). 2005. *Indicators of Welfare Dependence: Annual Report to Congress, 2004*. Washington, DC: HHS. http://aspe.hhs.gov/hsp/indicators04/index.htm (accessed January 8, 2008).

Zedlewski, Sheila R. 2004. "Recent Trends in Food Stamp Participation: Have New Policies Made a Difference?" Assessing the New Federalism, Series B, No. B-58. Washington, DC: Urban Institute.

Zedlewski, Sheila R., and Amelia Gruber. 2001. "Former Welfare Families and the Food Stamp Program: The Exodus Continues." Assessing the New Federalism, Series B, No. B-33. Washington, DC: Urban Institute.

Zedlewski, Sheila R., Pamela A. Holcomb, and Amy-Ellen Duke. 1998. *Cash Assistance in Transition: The Story of 13 States*. Assessing the New Federalism, Occasional Paper No. 16. Washington, DC: Urban Institute.

Part 3

Income Volatility and Implications for Serving Children and the Elderly

6

Income Volatility and Its Implications for School Lunch

Constance Newman
U.S. Department of Agriculture

Income volatility—month-to-month changes in a household's income—creates policy challenges for the administration of federal food assistance programs and potential hardship for families. As families shift in and out of eligibility, program designers must define eligibility rules that effectively target this changing population. And if volatility occurs involuntarily, a family might think of it as a short-term problem and forgo benefits for which they are eligible.

In this chapter, I examine the dynamic effects of monthly income volatility to better understand how it affects low-income populations. I also examine the implications of income volatility for household eligibility in the National School Lunch Program (NSLP). The analysis contributes to our understanding of the potential impacts of volatility on other USDA food assistance programs and on the changing economic conditions of low-income households.

First, I focus on the characteristics of income volatility for households with children. I compare the distributions of income volatility across six income groups using the coefficient of variation, a scale-independent measure of volatility. Then I examine the frequency of income changes occurring around the income-to-poverty ratio threshold of 185 percent, the figure used in the NSLP and other food assistance programs. Following that, I examine descriptive statistics and estimates from hazard models to understand which trigger events are most likely to explain eligibility changes.

Second, I examine the implications of income volatility for targeting efficiency in the NSLP. As this paper shows, an understanding of the interaction between income volatility and eligibility policy sheds light on recent concerns about NSLP integrity. A series of studies done in the late 1990s raised concerns about the accuracy of the NSLP application and eligibility certification procedures. Estimates of overcertification rates—the share of students receiving benefits for which they were not entitled—ranged from 12 to 33 percent.

The U.S. Congress recently amended the National School Lunch Act (signed into law in 1946) through the Child Nutrition and Women, Infants, and Children (WIC) Reauthorization Act of 2004. One of the most important changes to eligibility was to extend the eligibility period from one month to the entire school year. A student is eligible for the whole school year if eligible by monthly household income at the time of application. Before that, the rules stipulated that households report any changes in income and household composition to school authorities. Households seldom reported such changes, and the administrative burden would have been significant if they had. Under the old rules, schools had to verify the eligibility of a sample of students before December 15. This was moved up to November 15 in the new rules.

This chapter estimates how income volatility contributed to over-certification as defined under the pre–2004 act regulations. The extent to which income volatility contributed to total overcertification is unknown, but it was always suspected as a source of error. In this chapter, I trace how changes in income by month affect eligibility changes of initially eligible households. This process allows me to estimate the likely effects of income volatility on verification results in December. I also estimate how the use of one month of income to determine eligibility (in August) compares with the use of one year of income, which better matches the eligibility period under the new law. This allows us to understand the importance of another eligibility policy, the ability of households to apply throughout the year.

The analysis suggests that households experience substantial income fluctuations, especially those households that are eligible for free or reduced-price NSLP meals. The fluctuations come largely from changes in household labor market participation, and they may explain a large amount of overcertification error. The chapter does not estimate the size of other types of errors that could also be important, such as errors made by households or administrators. But the evidence on income volatility contributes an important piece to the puzzle of what caused overcertification error rates in the past. And the analysis of how income volatility affects NSLP eligibility can be extended to other USDA food assistance programs.

DATA AND ELIGIBILITY CRITERIA

SIPP: Description and Issue of Seam Bias

I use the 1996 panel of the Survey of Income and Program Participation (SIPP). Besides the benefits of its longitudinal design, SIPP has the advantage of supplying monthly rather than annual income. This provides the opportunity to analyze income dynamics over a shorter time frame than has been common. And for the problem of overcertification in the NSLP, annual data lack the needed detail for identifying eligibility changes within a year. The 1996 panel is a four-year panel that started in December 1995 and ended in February 2000.

SIPP has two important disadvantages: 1) attrition and 2) seam bias. I use the Census Bureau household weights for each month in order to match the initial sample design and control for attrition. The other problem, seam bias, occurs in surveys that ask for information from differentiated periods in the past. Earnings and total income data are susceptible to seam bias error (U.S. Census Bureau 1998).[1] However, I know of no research that examines the extent of seam bias for earnings or income data.[2] A common technique to avoid seam bias is to aggregate the monthly data by quarters. This technique is unavailable for this paper because I want to understand the differences that occur in very short time intervals in order to understand NSLP eligibility changes between September and December.

In the 1996 SIPP panel, I find seam bias in the income data. Table 6.1 shows the median percentage change in income in absolute terms by reference month, where the first month of the reference period is the month following the seam (Month 1). The magnitude of the percentage income change in Month 1 is much greater than the income changes in the other months: in Month 1, for each of the three school years examined, the percentage income change is 17–19 percent; for the other three reference months, the percentage income change is 2–6 percent.

Table 6.1 Medians of the Absolute Percentage Income Change by Reference Month: Unadjusted Data, Adjusted Data 1, and Adjusted Data 2 (%)

	Panel A: Unadjusted data			
	Reference month			
School year	Month 1	Month 2	Month 3	Month 4
1996–97	19	3	4	6
1997–98	18	3	4	5
1998–99	17	2	3	4

	Panel B: Adjusted data			
	Reference month			
School year	Month 1	Month 2	Month 3	Month 4
	Adjustment 1 (even distribution)			
1996–97	13	3	4	12
1997–98	12	3	4	11
1998–99	11	2	3	10
	Adjustment 2 (decreasing distribution)			
1996–97	7	9	9	9
1997–98	7	9	8	8
1998–99	7	9	8	8

SOURCE: SIPP 1996 Panel.

Seam bias creates a type of artificial volatility. Reported income may jump from one month to the next, either because of some combination of an actual income change—which I would want to identify to as great a degree as possible—or from misreporting at the seam. Using the raw, unadjusted data on reported income would result in overestimating the true extent of volatility. In order to differentiate between true income volatility and volatility from misreporting, I need to smooth the data in some way. I perform two kinds of adjustments to the data, each of which depends on different assumptions about the cognitive causes of the seam problem.[3]

Based on two fundamental explanations for seam bias error, memory failure, and inference strategy, I tested two ways of adjusting the data to smooth the differences across the seams.[4] In the first adjustment, I assumed that the income change that was misreported at the seam would have been evenly distributed over the first three months in the interview period if accurately reported and that the most recent month was accurately recalled. This inference strategy is one commonly used by interviewees and is referred to as a "constant wave response" (Rips, Conrad, and Fricker 2003). In the second adjustment, I assumed a decreasing distribution around the seam with a small amount spilling back into the last month of the previous period and the rest being distributed in decreasing order from the first month of the current reference period through the next two months. The cognitive basis for this adjustment is simply that respondents cannot pinpoint the exact date of the change. It assumes that the respondent knows about when the change occurred and that the change probably occurred close to the date reported but actually occurred slightly before or sometime afterward.

The effect of the two data adjustments on the measurement of data changes at the seams is shown in Table 6.2. The first adjustment does not fully remove the apparent seam bias as measured by absolute percentage income differences at the seams. The second adjustment, which has a decreasing function around the seam, appears to remove the seam bias: the absolute percentage income change across periods is fairly equal at the seam and within the reference period. In the following analysis I use the second adjustment for the analysis, and in some parts of the analysis I contrast the results using adjusted data with those using unadjusted data to show the adjustment effect.

Eligibility and Sampling Criteria

All children in participating schools can purchase an NSLP lunch at full price, and some qualify for reduced-price or free lunches. A student is eligible for a free meal if his or her household income is at or below 130 percent of the federal poverty guideline, and a student is eligible for a reduced-price meal if household income is between 130 and 185 percent of the guideline. If a student's household receives assistance from the Food Stamp Program, from Temporary Assistance for Needy Families, or from the Food Distribution Program on Indian Reservations (or if the student is homeless, a migrant, or a runaway), the student is categorically eligible for free lunch benefits.

In this study, eligibility is determined strictly by NSLP income limits, ignoring categorical eligibility. I use a pure income definition of eligibility in order to directly relate eligibility to income volatility. The

Table 6.2 Coefficient of Variation of Income Data: Distribution by Average Monthly Income-to-Poverty Status

Panel A: Unadjusted data

	≤ 0.75	0.75–1.30	1.30–1.85	1.85–2.40	2.40–3.00	> 3.00
No. of observations	792	1290	1402	1452	1387	4807
75%	0.77	0.57	0.47	0.41	0.37	0.37
50% (median)	0.52	0.39	0.32	0.28	0.25	0.24
25%	0.32	0.26	0.22	0.20	0.18	0.17
Mean	0.61	0.44	0.38	0.33	0.31	0.31
Std. dev.	0.45	0.28	0.26	0.19	0.24	0.23
Interquartile range	0.45	0.31	0.25	0.21	0.19	0.20

Panel B: Adjusted data

	≤ 0.75	0.75–1.30	1.30–1.85	1.85–2.40	2.40–3.00	> 3.00
No. of observations	792	1290	1402	1452	1387	4807
75%	0.68	0.51	0.42	0.36	0.33	0.33
50% (median)	0.45	0.34	0.28	0.25	0.23	0.21
25%	0.27	0.22	0.19	0.17	0.16	0.15
Mean	0.53	0.39	0.34	0.29	0.28	0.27
Std. dev.	0.40	0.25	0.23	0.17	0.22	0.20
Interquartile range	0.41	0.29	0.23	0.19	0.17	0.18

NOTE: CV over one year of monthly income data by average income-to-poverty status. The average CV in each income-to-poverty status group is significantly different from the average CV of all the other groups combined, and each average CV is significantly different from the average CV in the following and preceding income-to-poverty groups. The differences are all significant at the 0.01 level.
SOURCE: SIPP 1996 Panel.

restriction has little effect: in the SIPP data, less than 1 percent of the households that were categorically eligible were ineligible by income.

In the analysis, I often combine eligibility for either a free lunch or a reduced-price lunch into one eligible category. One reason for combining is that it simplifies the discussion. Another is that the savings to the USDA of catching errors related to differences in free and reduced-price status are much smaller than the savings from finding errors related to eligibility for either benefit. In 2004–2005, the amount reimbursed to schools by the USDA was $1.84 for a reduced-price lunch and $2.24 for a free lunch; both are much larger than the $0.21 reimbursed for a paid lunch.

INCOME VOLATILITY ANALYSIS

A 2003 study of poverty dynamics highlights the importance of income volatility. In a census report using the 1996 SIPP panel, John Iceland (2003) finds that the average monthly poverty rates for each year in the panel were higher than the corresponding annual poverty rates (1996–1999). Other, older studies find that annual poverty rates are lower than monthly poverty rates (Coder et al. 1987; Doyle and Trippe 1991; Ruggles and Williams 1987a). Stevens (1999) finds that half of all individuals exiting poverty reenter poverty within four years. Using annual data from the Panel Study of Income Dynamics for the years 1967–1988, she concludes that the amount of time spent in poverty has been underestimated by previous work that counted only single spells of poverty. She writes, "More than half of all blacks and around one-third of whites falling into poverty will spend five or more of the next ten years in poverty."

Analyses of the dynamics of participation in the USDA's Food Stamp Program (FSP) have highlighted the importance of multiple spells of participation. To be eligible for food stamps, an individual must have a gross monthly income of 130 percent of the poverty level or below (and meet other income and asset tests). Burstein (1993), using SIPP data from the late 1980s, finds that 38 percent of people who exit the program reenter within a year. Gleason, Schochet, and Moffitt (1998), also using SIPP, similarly find high FSP reentry levels in the early 1990s. They write, "More than half of those who stop receiving food stamps reenter the program within two years. . . . Among all individuals who exit food stamps, one-fourth start receiving food stamps again within four months and 42 percent within one year."

Income Volatility by Income Group

To compare volatility across income groups, I use the coefficient of variation (CV), since it measures relative volatility. Each household is assigned to one of the six income groups according to the household's average monthly income relative to the monthly poverty line, averaged over the number of months the household was in the survey.[5] Using the 55-percentage-point difference between the NSLP eligibility cutoffs at

130 and 185 percent of poverty as the yardstick for the three central groupings, the groups are broken down as follows: 0–75 percent, 76–130 percent, 131–185 percent, 186–240 percent, 241–300 percent, and 301 percent and over.

Figure 6.1 shows the CVs in monthly income across six income groups (adjusted for seam bias).[6] The graph shows a continuous decline, from the poorest group to the richest, in the medians of the groups' CV distributions. Table 6.2 shows that the CVs at the twenty-fifth and seventy-fifth percentiles of the distributions decrease for each higher income group. Mean CVs range from 0.27 to 0.53 across income groups, and the differences across groups are statistically significant. Whether adjusted or unadjusted data is examined, the mean CV of the lowest income group is double the mean CV of the highest income group.

Eligibility Status Changes

In this section, I calculate the number of changes in monthly eligibility status within one year and within three years. The frequency of changes in eligibility provides a measure of the implications of income volatility for administrative burden when schools have to reexamine a

Figure 6.1   Monthly Income Variation among Groups with Lower Income-to-Poverty Ratios

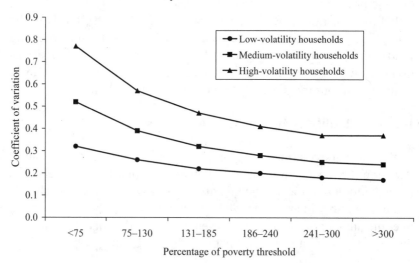

household's eligibility status for any change in income or household composition. Even though the rule was not generally enforced, it is an indicator of how the year-long eligibility rule reduces the schools' statutory responsibility and the amount of work that would have been required to fully enforce the previous law.

For the analysis in this section, I examine the frequency of income changes around the 185 percent poverty threshold. A change in status is defined as either exiting or entering eligibility; in order to get a simple, directionless measure, I do not distinguish between the directions of change. The reasons for change in one direction or the other may be different—and they have been shown to be[7]—but the frequency of eligibility change itself gives a distilled picture of the effects of volatility. I start the year in July because the monthly income for July is the first that may be used to determine eligibility if the household applies in August.

Figure 6.2 depicts the distribution of eligibility status changes across households with children during the 12-month period from July 1998 to June 1999. Of those, more than two-thirds (72 percent) never changed status. Of the households that changed status, it was just as common for them to change one time (9 percent of households) as it was for them to change two (9 percent) or three times or more (9 percent). Panel B of Figure 6.2 shows the status changes of the households that had at least one month of eligibility. This condition effectively narrows the sample to a low-income population. Among them, 37 percent had no change in status. Somewhat more (43 percent) had one or two status changes, while one-fifth (20 percent) had three or more status changes.

I also examine the number of eligibility changes within each of the income groups. As expected, most changes in eligibility status occur in the income groups closest to the eligibility limit. In the first income group, where average income was less than 75 percent of the poverty line, the average number of changes in status was 0.2. For the next income group, between 76 and 130 percent of poverty, the average number of status changes was 1.2. The two groups closest to the eligibility cutoff of 185 percent of poverty had the most changes. For the 131–185 percent group, the average number of status changes was 4.9, and for the 186–240 percent group, it was 5.0. The next two higher categories (241–300 percent and 301 percent and up) had an average number of changes of 2.2 and 0.6. The average number of 5.0 changes per year for

**Figure 6.2 Eligibility Changes in 1998–1999, a Representative
School Year**

Panel A: All households

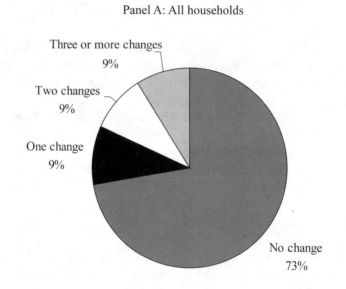

Panel B: Households eligible at least once, 1998–1999

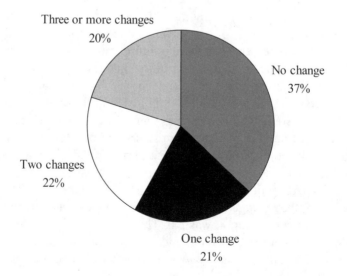

the income group immediately above and the one immediately below the 185 percent line reveals how important income volatility can be.

These results are consistent with the previously discussed findings of high rates of reentry into the FSP after exiting (Burstein 1993; Gleason, Schochet, and Moffitt 1998) and high rates of reentry into poverty after exiting (Stevens 1999). My results, like those cited, point to the importance of income volatility in understanding low-income population issues.

INCOME VOLATILITY TRIGGER EVENTS

While the previous section examined the magnitude of income volatility, this section investigates the sources of monthly income change that cause eligibility change. I use a hazard model to analyze the factors associated with entry into, and exit from, NSLP eligibility. This model is commonly used in studies of poverty dynamics (Bane and Ellwood 1986; McKernan and Ratcliffe 2002; Ruggles and Williams 1987b).

I use a discrete-time hazard model, which can be accurately estimated with a traditional logit specification (Allison 1984; Jenkins 1995). A discrete formulation of the probability is used to account for my data, which are in discrete monthly periods. Most studies of poverty and program participation dynamics use the discrete-time logit hazard model (Stevens 1999; McKernan and Ratcliffe 2002), which is written as

$$P(t) = \frac{1}{1 + e^{-z(t)}} \text{ , where } z(t) = c(t) + X\beta .$$

The model of eligibility, $z(t)$, is a function of $c(t)$, the baseline hazard function. $X\beta$ represents the matrix of explanatory factors and their respective parameters. The model is estimated by maximum likelihood, and I report the odds ratios. I use household weights and correct for standard errors using variables provided with SIPP to represent primary sampling units ("ghlfsam") and strata ("gvarstr").

I report results using eligibility determinations from both seam-adjusted income and unadjusted income. It is quite likely that seam bias exists in many of the independent variables, and rather than trying to correct for it where appropriate, I use unadjusted income, since that will show us what factors are at least contemporaneously associated (and jointly affected by survey respondents' memories of when events occurred). I also report results using the adjusted income to determine eligibility for the case of no seam bias on the right-hand side.

I look at the role of changes in circumstances—trigger events—as well as static characteristics such as household composition, labor force participation, state unemployment rates, and others. The full list is shown in Table 6.3, along with the variables' summary statistics. The trigger events are depicted by dummy variables, which equal one when a characteristic has changed. Among the trigger variables included are increases in total household hours worked and changes in the number of jobs held by different members of the household: the reference person, that person's spouse or partner, and other adults (as a composite). The number of jobs held is a coarser measure of employment than hours worked, and it is used here to identify job changes by household member type. The change-in-hours trigger provides an aggregate view of household work changes, and the change in the number of jobs held by a household member provides a more detailed view of the relative importance of jobs held by different members. Because employment changes can occur in so many ways in a household, I wanted to include as many aspects as possible. The results should not be interpreted as causal effects, because some of the independent variables may be endogenous.

I use changes in five different household wages as trigger dummy variables: wages for primary and secondary jobs of the household reference person, wages for primary and secondary jobs of the spouse, and a summed pay rate for all other adults in the house in all of their jobs. Wages are measured in one of two ways. The first is a wage reported as the regular hourly pay rate, which is separately provided for the primary and secondary jobs. The second, which is used only if the first is not available, is the sum of monthly gross earnings from the job divided by the product of the usual hours worked per week at this job and the number of weeks with a job in the month.

For most trigger variables, I allow the effects of a change in a given characteristic to be captured by the trigger dummy variables over one month. It is common in the literature to allow for delayed effects, but I wanted to test the effects of short-term events as much as possible. I made an exception for changes in marital status, public assistance receipt, disability status, presence or not of a subfamily in the household, and changes in the number of children. I thought that the effects of these variables, especially those that occur very infrequently, would be too hard to capture in one month. For marital status changes, the dummy variable for a change is equal to 1 if the change occurred one or two months prior to the current observation or if it occurred one month after the current observation. For the other types of changes, the dummy variable is equal to 1 if the event occurred in the last one or two months.

The data used for the analysis are from all years and months in the 1996 panel. Before any data are excluded, the sample has 436,479 household-month observations and 20,016 unique households. I exclude left-censored spells, the spells cut off at the beginning, but I keep right-censored spells, spells cut off at the end. The exclusion of left-censored spells reduces the sample size considerably and means I examine only households that underwent at least one change in eligibility.

The sample is divided into two parts: households that are in spells of ineligibility (the entry sample) and households that are in spells of eligibility (the exit sample). The exit sample is smaller because fewer households have incomes below 131 percent of the poverty line than have incomes of 131 percent or above. And the samples differ in size depending on the income measure used to define eligibility. Excluding left-censored spells of eligibility from the exit sample leaves 65,084 household-month observations in the adjusted income sample and 71,066 household-month observations in the unadjusted income sample. And excluding left-censored spells of ineligibility from the entry sample leaves 82,419 household-month observations in the adjusted income sample and 87,445 household-month observations in the unadjusted income sample. Results from the models of NSLP eligibility exit and NSLP entry are shown in Tables 6.4 and 6.5.

Exit Results

In the unadjusted income sample (last two columns, Table 6.4), the change most associated with exit from eligibility was that of a household changing from female-headed to married. This variable was not significant in the adjusted income sample. In a previous version of this analysis (Newman 2006) in which unadjusted income was not used, the result that getting married did not lead to exit raised many ques-

Table 6.3 Summary Statistics for Exit and Entry Model Variables

	Exit		Entry	
	Mean	Std. dev.	Mean	Std. dev.
Characteristics (weighted and SE-corrected)				
Dependent variable: end/beginning of eligibility spell	0.18	0.00	0.12	0.00
Log of time	1.38	0.02	1.70	0.01
State unemployment rate	4.85	0.03	4.71	0.03
No. of working adults per household member	0.28	0.00	0.42	0.00
No. of school-aged children	1.78	0.02	1.75	0.02
No. of jobs held by household reference person	0.73	0.01	0.88	0.01
No. of jobs held by spouse of reference person	0.38	0.01	0.60	0.01
No. of jobs held by other adults	0.29	0.01	0.54	0.01
Tenure of household reference	0.24	0.07	0.19	0.07
Tenure of spouse or partner	0.68	0.06	0.67	0.04
Tenure of other adults	0.19	0.02	0.13	0.01
Education of reference person	2.71	0.02	3.02	0.02
Education of spouse	1.70	0.03	2.28	0.03
Black/non-Hispanic reference person	0.19	0.01	0.12	0.01
Hispanic reference person	0.18	0.01	0.12	0.01
Native American reference person	0.02	0.01	0.01	0.00
Asian reference person	0.03	0.00	0.03	0.00
Disabled reference person	0.11	0.00	0.07	0.00
Disabled spouse or partner	0.06	0.00	0.05	0.00
Disabled other adults	0.05	0.00	0.05	0.00
Subfamily shares household[a]	0.08	0.00	0.07	0.00

Household receives public assistance	0.16	0.01	0.05	0.00
Single female–headed household	0.32	0.01	0.20	0.01
Single male–headed household	0.08	0.01	0.07	0.00
Group home household	0.00	0.00	0.00	0.00
Triggers				
Public assistance gained/lost	0.02	0.00	0.01	0.00
Reference person left disability rolls/became disabled	0.03	0.00	0.02	0.00
Female head of household to married change/married to female head of household change	0.00	0.00	0.00	0.00
Child left/entered household	0.01	0.00	0.02	0.00
Subfamily added to household[a]	0.00	0.00	0.00	0.00
Household total hours worked increased/reduced	0.27	0.00	0.33	0.00
Reference person gained one job or more	0.02	0.00	0.01	0.00
Spouse/partner gained one job or more	0.01	0.00	0.01	0.00
Other adults gained one job or more	0.02	0.00	0.02	0.00
Reference person's wage from primary job increased/decreased	0.10	0.00	0.15	0.00
Reference person's wage secondary job increased/decreased	0.02	0.00	0.03	0.00
Spouse/partner's wage primary job increased/decreased	0.08	0.00	0.10	0.00
Spouse/partner's wage secondary job increased/decreased	0.01	0.00	0.02	0.00
Other adults' wages increased/decreased	0.06	0.00	0.07	0.00
Increased/decreased % of working adults in household	0.04	0.00	0.03	0.00
N	71,066		87,445	

NOTE: SE = standard error of the odds ratio. The sample used here is the one in which unadjusted income was used to determine eligibility entry and exit.

[a] A subfamily is a nuclear family that is either related or not to the household reference person but does not include that person.

SOURCE: SIPP 1996 Panel.

Table 6.4 Logit Estimates of the Determinants of NSLP Eligibility Exit

	Adjusted income		Unadjusted income	
	Odds ratio	SE	Odds ratio	SE
Characteristics (weighted and SE-corrected)				
Log of time	0.66***	0.01	0.67***	0.01
State unemployment rate	0.99	0.01	0.99	0.01
No. of working adults per household member	2.20***	0.22	1.77***	0.18
No. of school-aged children	0.92***	0.02	0.91***	0.01
No. of jobs held by household reference person	1.20***	0.03	1.28***	0.03
No. of jobs held by spouse of reference person	1.23***	0.04	1.33***	0.03
No. of jobs held by other adults	1.27***	0.03	1.32***	0.03
Tenure of household reference	1.00***	0.00	1.00***	0.00
Tenure of spouse or partner	1.00	0.00	1.00***	0.00
Tenure of other adults	1.00	0.00	1.00	0.00
Education of reference person	1.09***	0.01	1.09***	0.02
Education of spouse	1.06***	0.01	1.05**	0.02
Black/non-Hispanic reference person	0.82***	0.03	0.80***	0.03
Hispanic reference person	0.81***	0.04	0.82***	0.04
Native American reference person	0.86	0.07	0.86	0.08
Asian reference person	0.73***	0.07	0.69***	0.06
Disabled reference person	0.92	0.04	0.91	0.04
Disabled spouse or partner	0.91	0.06	0.93	0.05
Disabled other adults	1.00	0.04	1.03	0.04
Subfamily shares household[a]	1.07	0.06	1.09	0.06

	OR	SE	OR	SE
Household receives public assistance	0.61***	0.03	0.59***	0.03
Single female–headed household	1.00	0.05	0.96	0.05
Single male–headed household	1.13	0.07	1.10	0.06
Group home household	1.18	0.40	1.19	0.33
Triggers				
Public assistance gained	0.98	0.11	0.93	0.09
Reference person left disability	1.00	0.06	0.72***	0.05
Female head of household to married change	1.44	0.34	2.06***	0.41
Child left household	0.82	0.09	0.82	0.08
Subfamily added to household[a]	0.93	0.16	0.83	0.13
Household total hours worked increased	1.37***	0.04	1.37***	0.04
Reference person gained one job or more	1.12	0.11	0.84	0.08
Spouse/partner gained one job or more	1.03	0.10	0.83	0.08
Other adults gained one job or more	1.00	0.08	0.82**	0.06
Reference person's wage from primary job increased	1.04	0.04	0.88***	0.03
Reference person's wage from second job increased	0.91	0.08	0.75***	0.06
Spouse's wage from primary job increased	1.14*	0.06	0.88*	0.04
Spouse's wage from secondary job increased	0.92	0.10	0.78	0.08
Other adults' wages increased	1.12	0.06	0.84***	0.04
Increased % of working adults in household	1.23***	0.07	1.04	0.06
N	65,084		71,066	

NOTE: SE = standard error of the odds ratio. * significant at the 0.10 level; ** significant at the 0.05 level; *** significant at the 0.01 level.

[a] A subfamily is a nuclear family that is either related or not to the household reference person but does not include that person.

SOURCE: SIPP 1996 Panel.

Table 6.5 Logit Estimates of the Determinants of NSLP Eligibility Entry

	Adjusted income		Unadjusted income	
	Odds ratio	SE	Odds ratio	SE
Characteristics (weighted and SE-corrected)				
Log of time	0.45***	0.01	0.40***	0.01
State unemployment rate	0.98	0.01	0.99	0.01
No. of working adults per household member	0.27***	0.03	0.42***	0.04
No. of school-aged children	1.01	0.02	1.04	0.02
No. of jobs held by household reference person	0.91***	0.02	0.95	0.02
No. of jobs held by spouse of reference person	0.94	0.03	0.93	0.03
No. of jobs held by other adults	0.79***	0.02	0.80***	0.01
Tenure of household reference	1.00	0.00	1.00***	0.00
Tenure of spouse or partner	1.00	0.00	1.00*	0.00
Tenure of other adults	1.00	0.00	1.00	0.00
Education of reference person	0.87***	0.01	0.88***	0.01
Education of spouse	0.89***	0.01	0.90***	0.01
Black/non-Hispanic reference person	1.18***	0.06	1.17***	0.05
Hispanic reference person	1.18***	0.05	1.17***	0.05
Native American reference person	1.33	0.22	1.41	0.22
Asian reference person	0.95	0.09	0.96	0.08
Disabled reference person	1.00	0.05	1.09	0.05
Disabled spouse or partner	0.94	0.06	1.01	0.06
Disabled other adults	0.89	0.05	0.96	0.05
Subfamily shares household[a]	0.98	0.06	1.00	0.05

	Odds ratio	SE	Odds ratio	SE
Household receives public assistance	1.12	0.06	1.13	0.05
Single female–headed household	0.95	0.05	0.92	0.04
Single male–headed household	0.85	0.05	0.85*	0.05
Group home household	0.79	0.26	0.86	0.26
Triggers				
Public assistance lost	1.05	0.12	0.94	0.09
Reference person became disabled	1.03	0.11	0.64***	0.06
Married to female head of household change	3.09***	0.55	5.50***	1.03
Child added to household	1.09	0.09	1.05	0.08
Subfamily left household[a]	0.55*	0.12	0.66	0.13
Household total hours worked reduced	1.54***	0.03	1.56***	0.03
Reference person lost one job or more	0.92	0.09	0.51***	0.06
Spouse/partner lost one job or more	0.78	0.11	0.49***	0.08
Other adults lost one job or more	0.74**	0.08	0.78	0.08
Reference person's wage from primary job decreased	1.21***	0.05	0.87***	0.03
Reference person's wage from second job decreased	1.11	0.08	0.86	0.06
Spouse's wage from primary job decreased	1.11	0.05	0.86***	0.04
Spouse's wage from secondary job decreased	1.45***	0.13	1.16	0.11
Other adults' wages decreased	1.27***	0.07	0.84***	0.05
Decreased % of working adults in household	1.48***	0.11	1.12	0.09
N	82,419		87,445	

NOTE: SE = standard error of the odds ratio. * significant at the 0.10 level; ** significant at the 0.05 level; *** significant at the 0.01 level.

[a]A subfamily is a nuclear family that is either related or not to the household reference person but does not include that person.

SOURCE: SIPP 1996 Panel.

tions. A change in the opposite direction (i.e., a household becoming female-headed) was a significant determinant of entry into eligibility, so it seemed somewhat odd that the results were asymmetric. Possible explanations were suggested, but this new result makes more sense, and the fact that getting married is a significant correlate with exiting eligibility when using the unadjusted income probably means that the timing of events is more in sync. Getting the joint timing right is especially important for events such as changing household marital status since such events are quite infrequent in the data.

In both the adjusted and unadjusted samples, the share of working adults in the household had a positive and significant effect on the odds of exit. Another significant static variable was the logarithm of time, indicating that the likelihood of exit decreased over time. Also, more school-aged children per household led to lower odds of exit. More jobs for the reference person, spouse or partner, or other adults led to higher odds of exit. The working tenure of the reference person and the spouse had significant but almost negligible effects on exit. A higher education level of the reference person and the spouse led to greater odds of exit. Households with a minority reference person had lower odds of exit than those with a white reference person. And anyone in the household receiving public assistance had lower odds of exit.

Three trigger events were significant determinants of exit in the adjusted income sample: 1) increases in total household hours worked, 2) increases in the share of working adults in the household, and (less significantly) 3) increases in the spouse's primary wage. In the unadjusted income sample, the only difference in those three adjusted sample results from the adjusted sample was that an increase in the share of working adults was not significant. More variables were significant in the unadjusted sample than in the adjusted sample, such as the change in marital status being significant, as mentioned above. And if a household reference person left disability, or was no longer disabled, he or she was significantly less likely to leave eligibility. One would expect the opposite result, but it is possible that the effects of a disability on income status are fairly persistent over time. Perhaps, for example, it is hard for a newly able person to enter the workforce after some time out. Other significant triggers were found in the unadjusted sample, and these too had the opposite effect of the one expected, including an increase in the reference person's wages, from either primary or secondary jobs; an increase in the number of jobs held by other adults in the household; an increase in other adults' wages; and an increase in the spouse's primary wages. That these factors made the odds of exit lower than 1 suggests that changes in wages and the number of jobs held by other adults are unimportant compared to other factors such as the total amount of time household members spent working.

Entry Results

The results from the hazard models of entry into NSLP eligibility are consistent with the results from the exit models (Table 6.5). As in the exit models, a change in marital status was the variable most strongly associated with entry in both the adjusted and unadjusted samples: in this case, the marital-status change is a household change from married to female-headed. In both the adjusted and unadjusted samples, the one significant household characteristic that was positively associated with entry was the race of the reference person being black or Hispanic. The significant factors that were negatively associated with entry were the log of time, the share of working adults in the household, the number of jobs held by the reference person and other adults, the education level of the reference person and spouse, and the household being single male–headed. All of these effects were significant in the expected directions.

Other trigger events that significantly and positively affected the odds of entry into eligibility were a reduction in total household hours worked; a reduction in the wages of the reference person, the spouse, and other adults; and, in the adjusted sample, a reduction in the share of working adults in the household. Two negative, significant triggers in the adjusted sample were the departure of a subfamily and an increase in the number of jobs held by other adults in the household. Negative, significant triggers in the unadjusted sample included the loss of a job by either the reference person or the spouse and the reference person becoming disabled. For all of these negative triggers, it must be remembered that they are less likely to lead to entry, meaning that these variables are less important than the positive ones. The most positive triggers in both samples were the change in household marital status to female-headed and the reduction in total household hours worked. A decrease in the share of working adults in the household was strongly associated with entry in the adjusted sample, as it was for the result in the exit model.

Overall, it would stand to reason that the unadjusted income sample is more likely to capture the important correlates, given that many of the independent variables are also likely to be affected by seam bias. According to results from the unadjusted income exit and entry models, the factors most associated with eligibility changes are changes in marital status and in total household hours worked. While changes in marital status occur infrequently in the data, when they do occur they appear to make a large difference in household income levels in both directions. Changes in hours worked occur much more frequently and are shown to be the most important change among the labor force participation variables in influencing volatility. The other trigger event significant in the adjusted sample is a change in the share of working household members, but the static share of working household members is significant in both samples. Wage changes and changes in the number of jobs per member appear to be unrelated to entry or exit. The results for labor market variables point to the relative importance of changes in total labor market participation at the household level as opposed to changes in labor market participation by a particular household member.

NSLP ELIGIBILITY AND INCOME VOLATILITY

In this section, I examine the effects of income volatility on eligibility under the pre-2004 rules for eligibility in the NSLP. Since 1981, schools have been required to verify the eligibility status of NSLP beneficiaries. Before 2004, schools did so by asking for proof of current income from a sample of recipients by December 15 of each year (changed to November 15 in 2004). The percentage of students found in the verification process to have received benefits that they were not entitled to, based on their December incomes, was referred to as the rate of overcertification error.

Studies in the 1990s raised concerns that the rate of overcertification error was somewhere between 15 and 27 percent (St. Pierre et al. 1990; USDA 1997, 1999). One study found, however, that the overcertification rate was only around 2 percent (Neuberger and Greenstein 2003). The USDA's Food and Nutrition Service launched more in-depth studies in the early 2000s to better understand the problem. In one of these, Gleason et al. (2003) found an estimated range of error of 12–33 percent: 12 percent under the assumption that nonresponding households were eligible, and 33 percent if nonresponding households were not eligible.

In several studies, income volatility was predicted to be an important determinant of NSLP eligibility dynamics. A 1992 study of household NSLP eligibility found that changes resulting from income and household composition changes were about 3 percent per month (St. Pierre and Puma 1992). A more recent study by Burghardt, Silva, and Hulsey (2004) assessed the verification results from a sample of 21 large metropolitan schools. They estimated that as much as 30–40 percent of the difference in household eligibility among respondents at the time of verification could be explained by changes in household income or household composition.

Income Changes Likely To Be Detected at Verification

Next, I examine the possible effects of volatility on verification findings. The purpose is to identify the extent to which income volatility may have accounted for verification error rates under the regulations in effect until 2004. Specifically, I count how many of the households eligible in August were still eligible for the same benefits in subsequent months. I look separately at three school years, 1996–1997, 1997–1998, and 1998–1999. In this section, I look at eligibility for free and reduced-price lunches, both together and separately. I combine them for reasons previously discussed, and I separate them in order to understand how much of the change in status was due to changes across these categories. I show the results from both the unadjusted data and the seam-bias-adjusted data, but I discuss only the adjusted results.

These results do not take into account possible household choices about whether to apply for the program or not, given the household's income situation, so the results represent solely the effect of income volatility if all income-eligible (at the time of application) households participate. Additionally, I assume that all eligible households were correctly certified at the start of the year. Thus, the analysis examines the extent to which income volatility for eligible households alone may account for overcertification.

Households can become eligible again in this counting framework—that is, households that become ineligible in one month are not excluded from the sample. Given the number of changes in eligibility we saw earlier, some households are known to be cycling in and out of eligibility status over the course of a year.[8]

Table 6.6 shows estimates from each different school year of the share of initially eligible households that are ineligible in each subsequent month of the school year. December is highlighted to show the share of initially eligible households that had become ineligible by the month of verification.

When I use adjusted income data, we see that, as expected, the share of households that became ineligible is lower month-by-month than in the unadjusted data.[9] The adjusted percentages for September for the three consecutive school years are 13.7, 11.8, and 7.2 percent. The data for December for the three school years are 19.5, 18.4, and 16.8 percent.

What about the error related to households eligible for free lunches becoming eligible for only reduced-price lunches by December? This change in eligibility is considered an overcertification error because it entails an unwarranted payment of benefits. Results from the adjusted income series show that, in the 1996–1997 school year, 9.4 percent of households that were eligible for free lunches in August were eligible for only reduced-price lunches by December (Table 6.7). For the next two years, the share was 8.2 and 7.9 percent.

Combining the two types of errors, which would lead to a benefit reduction or termination in December verifications under the old law, I estimate the overcertification error for the three school years at 28.9, 26.6, and 24.7 percent, or an average of 26.7 percent. These estimates are notable when compared with the estimates of errors found in the December verifications discussed above. My estimate of ineligibility stemming from an income volatility of 27 percent constitutes a large percentage of the high-end estimate of total error of 33 percent. Since I do not estimate the effects of participation that income volatility might also affect, this estimate may be upwardly biased.

I examine how changes in a household's month-to-month eligibility status differ from its original eligibility status—reduced-price or free

Table 6.6 Percentage Ineligible in Months Following August

Ineligible by the following month	August-eligible 1996–97		August-eligible 1997–98		August-eligible 1998–99	
	No adjustment	Seam-adjusted	No adjustment	Seam-adjusted	No adjustment	Seam-adjusted
September	15.6	13.7	13.9	11.8	8.7	7.2
October	14.4	12.9	14.3	13.1	13.1	11.1
November	19.0	17.6	22.2	21.1	18.6	17.0
December[a]	**21.1**	**19.5**	**19.2**	**18.4**	**17.9**	**16.8**
January	20.7	20.3	20.9	19.8	19.1	19.0
February	22.8	22.1	24.5	23.8	20.3	20.0
March	23.2	23.0	21.9	21.6	19.5	18.8
April	21.9	22.2	22.2	22.0	20.9	20.6
May	22.4	23.1	23.9	23.5	24.3	23.8
June	26.3	25.9	25.7	25.3	22.7	22.5
July	22.7	23.3	23.2	23.2	23.8	23.6

[a]December is set off in bold because this is the month when incomes were typically verified (before the 2004 change in the law).
SOURCE: SIPP 1996 Panel

Table 6.7 Changes in Free to Reduced-Price Eligibility by Month

	Seam-adjusted data		
	August-eligible 1996–97	August-eligible 1997–98	August-eligible 1998–99
Ineligible by the following month	% of free eligible that went to RP-eligible	% of free eligible that went to RP-eligible	% of free eligible that went to RP-eligible
September	7.2	6.9	4.5
October	6.8	6.0	7.1
November	8.9	9.1	8.2
December[a]	**9.4**	**8.2**	**7.9**
January	9.2	8.3	9.2
February	10.9	9.4	10.1
March	10.3	7.7	9.3
April	10.1	8.7	10.5
May	10.1	9.2	11.0
June	11.3	9.6	9.9
July	10.8	9.1	10.6

[a]December is set off in bold because this is the month when incomes were typically verified (before the 2004 change in the law).
SOURCE: SIPP 1996 Panel

lunch—using the adjusted data. Most of the households that became ineligible in the months immediately after August had been eligible for the reduced-price lunch. For example, in the 1996–1997 school year, 80.3 percent of households that were ineligible in September were households that had been in the reduced-price-meal category in August. In the other years, 79.3 and 70.0 percent of households that were ineligible in September had been eligible for the reduced-price lunch the month before. The preponderance of reduced-price households among the households that crossed the 185 percent income threshold is logical because these households were closest to the threshold.

Annual versus Monthly Eligibility Determination

Schools use monthly income most often to determine household eligibility at the time of application. This was the case under the old rules and still is under the new rules. Households apply for program benefits based on one month of income under the tacit assumption that monthly income is a good predictor of annual income. One would imagine that its power as a predictor would decline the more variable it was over the year. To explore the power of one month of income as a predictor in the context of NSLP eligibility, I compare estimates of eligibility using August income alone against estimates of eligibility based on annual income reported in the following months of the school year (using adjusted data). I do not think that August has any particular seasonal properties; any single month's income would provide similar results.

Table 6.8 allows us to view the complete overlap of the two categories of eligibility, determined by month and by year. Looking at the first section of the table, which shows the cross-tabulations for August 1996 and the school year 1996–1997, I see that the share of households eligible from the annual calculation is 33.8 percent. In contrast, the share of households eligible from the August (monthly) calculation is 29.9 percent, about 4 percentage points lower. Similarly, for the other two years, the August calculation is lower by about 3 percentage points in 1997–1998 and by almost 5 percentage points in 1998–1999.

In 1996–1997, of the households that were annually eligible, the monthly determination of eligibility counted 68.9 percent of them as eligible, whereas for the households annually ineligible, the monthly determination was closer—it counted 90.1 percent of them as ineligible. There are many more households above the eligibility limit, and thus, for them, one month of income is more likely to be representative of annual earnings. Italicized numbers in Table 6.8 show the results of analyzing the monthly cross-tabulations. In 1996, 78 percent of households that were eligible in August were also annually eligible; in that same year, 85 percent of households that were ineligible in August were also annually ineligible. The single-month determination appears to be better at capturing annually ineligible than annually eligible households. The same pattern was repeated in the other two years.

A household's income from a single month can be very different from its annual average income because of volatility. To the extent that households are not aware of their ability to apply for NSLP benefits throughout the year, using monthly income to determine eligibility could lead to a lower certification rate than that which would come from using annual income, which more accurately matches the certification period of a year. This outcome suggests that it is important for schools

**Table 6.8 Monthly (August) vs. Annual Eligibility Determinations:
Two Categories of Eligibility over Three School Years**

		Annual 1996–97		
		Ineligible	Eligible	Totals
August 1996	Ineligible	*85.0*	*15.0*	*100.0*
		90.1	31.1	70.1
	Eligible	*22.0*	*78.0*	*100.0*
		9.9	68.9	29.9
	Totals	*66.2*	*33.8*	*100.0*
		100.0	*100.0*	*100.0*
		Annual 1997–98		
		Ineligible	Eligible	Totals
August 1997	Ineligible	*86.6*	*13.4*	*100.0*
		90.5	29.4	70.7
	Eligible	*21.9*	*78.1*	*100.0*
		9.5	70.6	29.3
	Totals	*67.6*	*32.4*	*100.0*
		100.0	*100.0*	*100.0*
		Annual 1998–99		
		Ineligible	Eligible	Totals
August 1998	Ineligible	*86.2*	*13.8*	*100.0*
		92.4	32.3	73.5
	Eligible	*19.6*	*80.4*	*100.0*
		7.6	67.7	26.5
	Totals	*68.6*	*31.4*	*100.0*
		100.0	*100.0*	*100.0*

NOTE: Annual income uses data from months July to June of each respective school
year. Italicized numbers show the results of analyzing the monthly cross-tabulations.
SOURCE: SIPP 1996 Panel

to emphasize to families that they can apply for benefits at any time of the year.

CONCLUSION

In this chapter, I find that income volatility among households with children can cause frequent shifts in school lunch program eligibility. Using the coefficient of variation of monthly income, I find that lower-income households unequivocally have more volatile incomes than higher-income households do. I also find that, among households with children that were eligible for the school lunch program in at least one month of a year, almost two-thirds (63 percent) had one or more transitions into or out of eligibility, and that one-fifth (20 percent) had three or more transitions. Households with children whose average monthly income fell between 130 percent and 240 percent of poverty crossed the eligible line five times per year on average.

In hazard models of eligibility exit and entry, the most important factors were changes in household marital status (married or female-headed), changes in the total household hours worked in a month, and changes in the share of working adults in the household. I obtained the standard results with respect to static household-level determinants that one would expect in a model of poverty dynamics. For example, greater education levels led to higher chances of exit from eligibility, and households with black or Hispanic reference people were less likely to exit than those with white reference people. Corresponding results were obtained for the entry model.

In terms of the effects of income volatility on participation in the National School Lunch Program, I found that up to one-fifth of households that were eligible in August for either a reduced-price or a free lunch in the NSLP became ineligible in the following month of September. Moreover, the share of August eligibles that were ineligible increased through December to 27 percent on average. In the literature on certification errors, estimates of overcertification differ widely, with the extremes ranging from 12 to 33 percent. My estimate of overcertification of 27 in December from income volatility alone is higher than most estimated overcertification rates. However, an important qualifier to these results is that I had to assume that all households participate if eligible and that all certifications are made correctly. I conclude that income volatility has the potential to explain a large portion of NSLP overcertification error but that the exact amount is unknown.

I found that a certification process that uses a single month's income produces systematically fewer eligible households than a certification process that uses annual income. A single month's determination is more likely to err in the direction of ineligibility because of volatility.

Since the Child Nutrition and WIC Reauthorization Act of 2004 extended NSLP eligibility through the school year, income volatility will no longer affect NSLP eligibility. However, it remains an important issue to other USDA food assistance programs. The evidence here shows that income volatility is relatively higher for low-income households and that it is strongly linked to monthly changes in the characteristics of a household's labor force participation and marital status. For USDA food assistance programs, the volatility associated with low-income working households will become an increasing challenge to program administration.

Notes

This chapter is a revised and shortened version of a report published by the U.S. Department of Agriculture's Economic Research Service (Newman 2006).

1. Seam bias occurs when the differences in reported values for a given variable are much greater between time periods in which there is a break in survey administration than between time periods reported within a survey administration. For example, in SIPP, each time a survey respondent is visited to report his or her information, the respondent is asked to report about the past four months, one month at a time. The differences in variable values within the four months tend to be much smaller than the difference between the last month reported and the next month reported when the survey respondent is visited for the second round of questioning. This is referred to as seam bias, since it is a bias that occurs at the "seams" of reported information.
2. Research on the extent of seam bias has focused on how it affects estimates of program participation transition data (Doyle, Martin, and Moore 2000; see U.S. Census Bureau [1998] for a review).
3. I also tested other ways of adjusting and organizing the data that are not discussed here, such as using only the most recent month of data (the fourth reference month) and using three-month intervals that skip the seam instead of four-month

intervals. Both methods provided similar evidence of income volatility, as I show later.

4. See Kalton and Miller (1991), Marquis and Moore (1989), and Rips, Conrad, and Fricker (2003) for analysis of the cognitive roots of seam bias.

5. I include all households that were in the survey for 12 months or more in order to maximize observations (11,135). The median number of months in the survey for those in the survey 12 months or more was 31 months, and 39 percent of the households were in for the maximum of 36 months. The results are similar, if not more pronounced, when using the smaller sample sizes of households in the survey for 24 months or more (7,195 households) or in the survey for 36 months (4,333 households).

6. The same diagram using unadjusted data shows qualitatively the same result of lower CVs at higher income-to-poverty levels. But the unadjusted data show higher CVs for all groups than do the adjusted data, as expected.

7. See the next section, "Income Volatility Trigger Events," and McKernan and Ratcliffe (2002).

8. In other words, these are not life tables of the percentage of households with children who become ineligible by a certain month and are treated as no longer at risk for reentry or reexit in following months. Instead, these tables are a tally of ineligibility in any month, inclusive of those who may have reexited and reentered. This analysis is designed to estimate what percentage of households with children can be expected to be ineligible if a verification sample of these households is conducted in various months.

9. The data reverses in the 1996–1997 school year for some months after April in that the share from the adjusted data exceeds the share from the unadjusted data. I am not entirely sure why these adjustments would yield higher estimates in some cases. The differences, however, are not large enough that the 95-percent confidence intervals of each estimate do not also contain the other estimates.

References

Allison, Paul D. 1984. *Event History Analysis: Regression for Longitudinal Event Data*. A Sage University Paper. Series on Quantitative Applications in the Social Sciences, No. 46. Newbury Park, CA: Sage Publications.

Bane, Mary Jo, and David T. Ellwood. 1986. "Slipping Into and Out of Poverty: The Dynamics of Spells." *Journal of Human Resources* 21(1): 1–23.

Burghardt, John, Tim Silva, and Lara Hulsey. 2004. *Case Study of National School Lunch Program Verification Outcomes in Large Metropolitan School Districts*. Special Nutrition Programs Report No. CN-04-AV3. Washington, DC: U.S. Department of Agriculture (USDA), Food and Nutrition Service, Office of Analysis, Nutrition, and Evaluation.

Burstein, Nancy R. 1993. *Dynamics of the Food Stamp Program as Reported in the Survey of Income and Program Participation.* Washington, DC: USDA, Food and Nutrition Service, Office of Analysis, Nutrition, and Evaluation.

Coder, John F., Dan Burkhead, Angela Feldman-Harkins, and Jack McNeil. 1987. *Preliminary Data from the SIPP 1983-84 Longitudinal Research File.* SIPP Working Paper No. 8702. Washington, DC: U.S. Census Bureau.

Doyle, Patricia, Betsy Martin, and Jeff Moore. 2000. *The Survey of Income and Program Participation (SIPP) Methods Panel: Improving Income Measurement.* SIPP Working Paper No. 234. Washington, DC: U.S. Census Bureau.

Doyle, Patricia, and Carole Trippe. 1991. *Improving the Income Allocation Procedures in MATH.* Princeton, NJ: Mathematica Policy Research.

Gleason, Philip, Peter Schochet, and Robert Moffitt. 1998. *The Dynamics of Food Stamp Program Participation in the Early 1990s.* Washington, DC: U.S. Department of Agriculture (USDA), Food and Nutrition Service, Office of Analysis and Evaluation.

Gleason, Philip, Tania Tasse, Kenneth Jackson, and Patricia Nemeth. 2003. *Direct Certification in the National School Lunch Program—Impacts on Program Access and Integrity.* Final Report. E-FAN-03-009. Washington, DC: U.S. Department of Agriculture (USDA), Economic Research Service, Food Assistance and Nutrition Research Program.

Iceland, John. 2003. *Dynamics of Economic Well-Being: Poverty 1996–1999.* Current Population Report No. P70-91. Washington, DC: U.S. Census Bureau.

Jenkins, Stephen P. 1995. "Easy Estimation Methods for Discrete-Time Duration Models." *Oxford Bulletin of Economics and Statistics* 57(1): 129–138.

Kalton, Graham, and Michael E. Miller. 1991. "The Seam Effect with Social Security Income in the Survey of Income and Program Participation." *Journal of Official Statistics* 7(2): 235–245.

Marquis, Kent H., and Jeffrey C. Moore. 1989. "Using Administrative Record Data to Evaluate the Quality of Survey Estimates." *Survey Methodology* 15: 129–143.

McKernan, Signe-Mary, and Caroline Ratcliffe. 2002. *Transition Events in the Dynamics of Poverty.* Washington, DC: U.S. Department of Health and Human Services, Office of the Assistant Secretary for Planning and Evaluation.

Neuberger, Zoë, and Robert Greenstein. 2003. *New Analysis Shows "Overcertification" for Free or Reduced-Price School Meals Has Been Overstated.* Washington, DC: Center on Budget and Policy Priorities. http://www.cbpp.org/7-15-03wic.pdf (accessed January 25, 2008).

Newman, Constance. 2006. *The Income Volatility See-Saw: Implications for*

School Lunch. Economic Research Report No. 23. Washington, DC: U.S. Department of Agriculture (USDA), Economic Research Service.

Rips, Lance J., Frederick G. Conrad, and Scott S. Fricker. 2003. "Straightening the Seam Effect in Panel Surveys." *Public Opinion Quarterly* 67(4): 522–554.

Ruggles, Patricia, and Roberton Williams. 1987a. "Determinants of Changes in Income Status and Welfare Program Participation." Paper presented at the Annual Meeting of the American Statistical Association, held in San Francisco, August 17–20, 1987.

———. 1987b. *Transitions In and Out of Poverty: New Data from the Survey of Income and Program Participation*. SIPP Working Paper No. 8716. Washington, DC: U.S. Census Bureau.

Stevens, Ann Huff. 1999. "Climbing Out of Poverty, Falling Back In: Measuring the Persistence of Poverty over Multiple Spells." *Journal of Human Resources* 34(3): 557–588.

St. Pierre, Robert G., and Michael J. Puma. 1992. "Controlling Federal Expenditures in the National School Lunch Program: The Relationship between Changes in Household Eligibility and Federal Policy." *Journal of Policy Analysis and Management* 11(1):42–57.

St. Pierre, Robert G., Michael J. Puma, Michael Battaglia, and Jean Layzer. 1990. *Study of Income Verification in the National School Lunch Program National Survey*. Final Report. Washington, DC: U.S. Department of Agriculture (USDA), Food and Nutrition Service.

U.S. Census Bureau. 1998. *SIPP Quality Profile 1998*. 3rd ed. Survey of Income and Program Participation (SIPP) Working Paper No. 230. Washington, DC: U.S. Census Bureau.

U.S. Department of Agriculture (USDA). 1997. *National School Lunch Program Verification of Applications in Illinois*. Food and Nutrition Service Audit Report No. 27010-0011-Ch. Washington, DC: U.S. Department of Agriculture (USDA), Office of Inspector General.

———. 1999. *Current Population Survey Analysis of NSLP Participation and Income*. Nutrition Assistance Program Report Series. Washington, DC: U.S. Department of Agriculture (USDA), Food and Nutrition Service, Office of Analysis, Nutrition, and Evaluation.

7

The Age Gradient in Food Stamp Program Participation: Does Income Volatility Matter?

Craig Gundersen
University of Illinois

James P. Ziliak
University of Kentucky

With the passage of welfare reform in 1996, the Food Stamp Program became the sole program in the safety net that resembles an entitlement. Subject to basic income and asset tests, individuals are eligible to receive food stamps throughout their lifetimes, irrespective of family structure (as in Temporary Assistance for Needy Families), disability status (as in Supplemental Security Income), and employment status (except for able-bodied adults with no dependents). Total expenditures on the program, including administrative costs, exceeded $32 billion in fiscal year 2006, making it comparable in size to the Earned Income Tax Credit and Supplemental Security Income programs. Still, nonparticipation among eligibles is rampant, and rates of participation, unadjusted for other factors, decline with age. Indeed, Cunnyngham (2003) reports that in 2001 the participation rate among elderly persons eligible for food stamps was 28 percent, versus an average participation rate of about 62 percent for the full population. This lower participation rate holds despite the fact that the elderly do not have to meet the gross income test and they have higher asset limits than the nonelderly.

Numerous studies have been conducted on the determinants of participation in the Food Stamp Program, focusing on a variety of factors such as the business cycle and welfare reform (Wallace and Blank 1999; Ziliak, Gundersen, and Figlio 2003), recertification length (Kabbani and Wilde 2003), nutritive need for food stamps (Haider, Jacknowitz, and Schoeni 2003), and rates of food insecurity (Gundersen and Oliveira 2001). However, none of the research to date has focused on participation across the life course or on the role of income volatility. Knowledge of how participation varies across the life course is important to policymakers given the pending retirement of the first years of the post–World War II baby boom generation. This demographic bulge may lead to higher rates of participation at older ages than in the past because this is the first generation to grow up with the Food Stamp Program, which began in its modern form as part of the Great Society programs of the mid-1960s and became a national program in 1974. That is, historically participation has declined with age, but this could be a cohort phenomenon that may not carry forward in the future as younger generations have more exposure to the program and utilize it at higher rates. Many authors have documented a rise in earnings and income volatility over the past two decades (Blundell and Pistaferri 2003; Gottschalk and Moffitt 1994; Gundersen and Ziliak 2003; Haider 2001). Identifying the role of income volatility both on average and across the life course of food stamp participation is important to program design because participation is income-conditioned and strict reporting requirements apply to those participants who work and whose income varies. If potential recipients view the Food Stamp Program as an assistance program to be used in the face of negative income fluctuations but not when incomes are permanently low, changes in income volatility may be a factor. Because income volatility likely varies over the life cycle, we might expect the effect of volatility on the decision to use food stamps to vary across the age gradient.

In this chapter we narrow the gap in the literature by estimating the effects of age, birth cohort, and income volatility on Food Stamp Program participation. We use data from the 1980 to 2003 waves of the Panel Study of Income Dynamics (PSID), along with standard measures of income volatility from Gottschalk and Moffitt (1994) and a correlated random effects estimator for the linear probability model (Hausman and Taylor 1981). The correlated random effects estimator is advantageous in this context because it permits identification of both time-varying and time-invariant regressors, the latter of which include birth cohort and some of our measures of income volatility. For the sake of robustness we also estimate a correlated random effects estimator without birth cohorts and a standard fixed-effects linear probability model, which still permits identification of both the age gradient and the effect of volatility along the gradient.

We find that participation in food stamps is U-shaped across the life course, contrary to the conventional wisdom of simple summary statistics, which show participation declining monotonically across the age gradient. Consistent with the idea of greater familiarity with the Food Stamp Program encouraging participation, we find that younger birth cohorts have higher rates of food stamp participation than earlier birth cohorts. We also find that, in general, food stamp participation is higher across the age gradient among those with higher levels of income volatility.

PATTERNS OF FOOD STAMP PARTICIPATION AND INCOME VOLATILITY OVER THE LIFE COURSE

We begin our analysis with a description of our data and then present basic patterns of food stamp participation and income volatility over the life course.

Data

The data we use come from the Panel Study of Income Dynamics (PSID) for interview years 1980–2003 (calendar years 1979–2002). The survey has followed a core set of households since 1968, plus it has followed newly formed households as members of the original core have split off into new families. We begin in 1979 because this is when the Food Stamp Program ended the so-called purchase requirement, where recipients needed to pay for a set amount of discounted food stamps and the price was directly related to a household's income. The PSID is advantageous because it contains detailed information on income and household composition, which permits us to construct long time series of income for various age groups and family structures.

The sample we use is an unbalanced panel treating missing observations as random events. By eliminating only a missing person-year of data, the time series for each household can be of different lengths within 1980–2003. To be included in the full sample, the household head must 1) be in the sample at least three consecutive years, 2) not have year-to-year increases in real income[1] exceeding 300 percent or declines exceeding 75 percent, and 3) have annual family income of more than $1,000 in inflation-adjusted terms. We define date-of-birth cohorts in 10-year intervals in the PSID in order to maintain adequate within-cohort sample sizes. There are 72,311 person-years in the full sample. This sample is useful to gauge population-level statistics of food stamp participation and income volatility.

One disadvantage to the full sample is that many of the persons in this sample are unlikely ever to be eligible for food stamps. As a consequence, our estimates of the effects of income volatility and birth cohort on food stamp participation could be understated and less informative for policy. For example, if income volatility is very high but income levels are always above the food stamp eligibility cutoff, the volatility will not influence the participation decision. In response, we create a series of samples that contain households more likely to enter the Food Stamp Program. One is an *income-eligible sample*, where we only include households that in any given year have incomes below 130 percent of the poverty line, which is the gross income cutoff for food stamps. (The criteria for food stamp eligibility are defined in the next section.) There are 11,535 persons in this sample. Another is an *ever income-eligible sample*, where we broaden the income-eligible sample to contain households whose annual incomes dipped below 130 percent of the poverty line at least once during the sample period. There are 30,305 persons in this ever income-eligible sample. The income samples permit us to make statements on the effect of volatility on participation conditional on income eligibility.

Given our interest in the effect of income volatility, one may be concerned that choosing a sample based on income would impart an endogeneity bias into our estimated coefficients. This endogeneity bias could arise because eligibility for food stamps is income-conditioned and thus we are selecting a sample based on a variable that is correlated with the dependent variable. As an alternative we select a subsample of family heads with less than a high school diploma (a *low education sample*). The advantage of using education is that it is exogenous to the food stamp eligibility formula but at the same time is a common proxy in economics for permanent income; that is, this sample is likely to select individuals with low permanent incomes and thus a high ex ante probability of food stamp participation relative to family heads with higher levels of formal schooling (Bhattarai, Duffy, and Raymond 2005; Gundersen and Oliveira 2001). There are 17,560 person-years in this sample.

One potential drawback to the PSID is the smaller number of elderly persons in comparison to other surveys. In particular, it is smaller than the Survey of Income and Program Participation (SIPP) and the Health and Retirement Survey (HRS). Despite this smaller sample size, the PSID is the only data set with sufficient number of years to 1) adequately measure income volatility and 2) incorporate the effects of birth cohorts over an extended time period.

Food Stamp Participation

The Food Stamp Program, with a few exceptions, is available to all persons who meet income and asset tests. To receive food stamps, households must meet three financial criteria: 1) a gross income test, 2) a net income test, and 3) an asset test. A household's gross income before taxes in the previous month cannot exceed 130 percent of the poverty line, and net monthly income cannot exceed the poverty line.[2] Finally, income-eligible households with assets of less than $2,000 qualify for the program. The value of a vehicle above $4,650 is considered an asset unless it is used for work or for the transportation of disabled persons. Households receiving Temporary Assistance for Needy Families (TANF) and households where all members receive Supplemental Security Income (SSI) are categorically eligible for food stamps and do not have to meet these three tests. There are two distinctions for older persons. First, persons over the age of 60 do not have to meet the gross income test. (But they do have to meet the net income test.) Second, the asset limit for persons over the age of 60 is $3,000 rather than $2,000.

A large fraction of households eligible for food stamps do not participate. In 2005, for example, official estimates indicate that 35 percent of eligible households do not participate (Wolkwitz 2007). A common argument made for the existence of eligible nonparticipation is that there may be a stigma associated with receiving food stamps. Stigma encompasses a wide variety of sources, from a person's own distaste for receiving food stamps, to the fear of disapproval from others when redeeming food stamps, to the possible negative reaction of caseworkers

(Daponte, Sanders, and Taylor 1999; Moffitt 1983). Another reason often suggested is that transaction costs can diminish the attractiveness of participation.[3] A household faces these costs on a repeated basis when it must recertify its eligibility. Additionally, weighed against these costs, the benefit level may be too small to induce participation; food stamp benefits can be as low as $10 a month for a family. In light of the low participation rates of the elderly, these factors may be especially relevant for them.

In our first set of figures we display food stamp participation rates by year for five separate age categories: 1) under 30, 2) between 31 and 40, 3) between 41 and 50, 4) between 51 and 60, and 5) 61 and older. These age categories are defined for the head of household. Figure 7.1, Panel A, is for the full sample and Figure 7.1, Panel B, is for the low education sample. In each panel, the food stamp participation rate is calculated as the number of food stamp participants divided by the number of households in the sample. The rates are not weighted and thus the levels are likely upper-bound estimates, given the oversampling of the poor in the Survey of Economic Opportunity (SEO) subsample of the PSID. For both samples the participation rate of households headed by someone under the age of 30 exceeds that of all the other age categories (except the last two years in the low education sample) and, in some years, the under-30 versus over-30 gap can be quite large. Given the larger number of small children among households headed by someone under the age of 30 and the positive relationship between the presence of children and food stamp participation (Bartfeld 2003; Bollinger and David 1997; Hagstrom 1996), this is not entirely unexpected. Part of this age gap also likely arises from categorical eligibility for food stamps among families receiving AFDC/TANF; the latter program tends to be dominated by young families. Panels A and B of Figure 7.2 show our two income-based samples—income-eligible and ever income-eligible. The results for the latter look similar to the results for the low education sample in Figure 7.1. For the income-eligible sample in Panel A there are two primary differences with the other figures. First, the higher participation rates for households headed by someone under the age of 30 do not always hold. Second, the participation rates for households headed by someone over the age of 60 are substantially lower than for other groups.

In addition, the trends in Figures 7.1 and 7.2 shed some light on the demographic composition of the caseload underlying the much-studied rise in Food Stamp Program participation in the early 1990s followed by the subsequent decline in the late 1990s (Ziliak, Gundersen, and Figlio 2003). The increase in the late 1980s and early 1990s appears to have been initially driven by a surge in participation among families whose head was under age 30, followed by an increase in participation for families headed by someone in the 31–40 age group. However, participation among families with heads in the under 30 group started to decline around 1993 even though the peak in aggregate participation was not reached until 1995. Figures 7.1 and 7.2 suggest that the continued upward push came from those families whose heads were between the ages of 31 and 50. Participation then fell for all groups through 2001.

In Figures 7.3 and 7.4 we consider the influence of birth cohort on food stamp participation for the same samples as above. We separate the sample into six birth cohorts depending on whether the family head was born prior to 1919, between 1919 and 1928, between 1929 and 1938, between 1939 and 1948, between 1949 and 1958, or after 1958. In Panels A and B of Figure 7.3, when we do not condition on income, the lines reveal a cohort effect for those heads born after 1958. In Panel A, a head born in the most recent cohort is on average at least 50 percent more likely to participate in food stamps than heads from earlier cohorts, and this cohort gap more than doubles when the most recent cohort is compared to the 1939-to-1948 cohort. Among the low education sample (Panel B) the cohort effect between those born after 1958 and those born between 1949 and 1958 is narrower than in the full sample, but the differences are still rather stark. Once we condition on income, in Figures 7.4, Panels A and B, the higher food stamp participation rates among later cohorts no longer hold to the extent that they do in Figure 7.3. Instead, a pronouncedly lower participation rate holds for the earliest birth cohort (before 1918), especially in the income-eligible sample.

The post-1995 decline in food stamp participation is generally most pronounced among the post-1958 cohort and the pre-1919 cohort. The former is likely due to the strong macroeconomy and welfare reform–related reductions in AFDC/TANF participation (given the categorical eligibility of AFDC/TANF recipients for food stamps). However, the

178

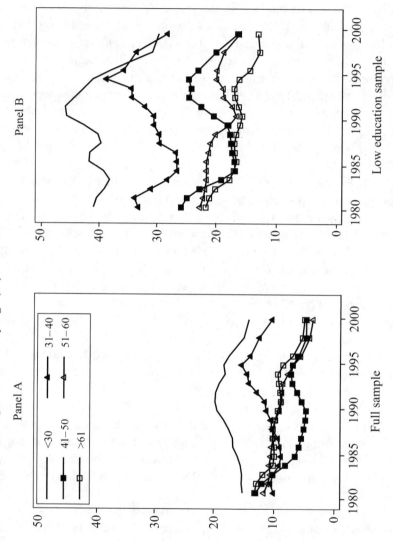

Figure 7.1 Food Stamp Participation Rates by Age (%)

Panel A   Panel B

Full sample   Low education sample

SOURCE: Authors' construction using data from 1980–2003 Panel Study of Income Dynamics.

Figure 7.2 Food Stamp Participation Rates by Age, Eligible Samples (%)

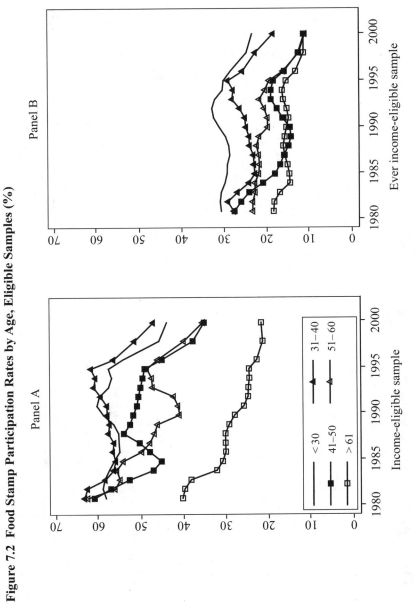

SOURCE: Authors' construction using data from 1980–2003 Panel Study of Income Dynamics.

180

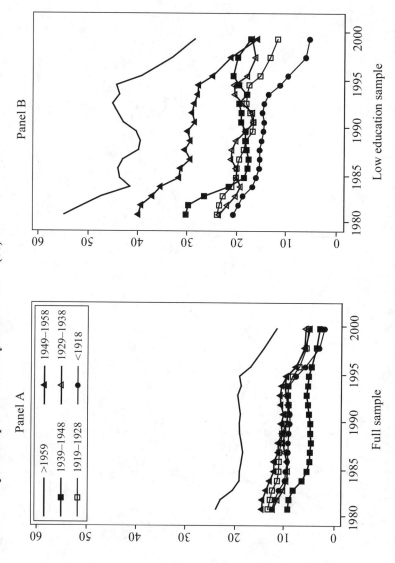

Figure 7.3 Food Stamp Participation Rates by Birth Cohort (%)

Panel A

Panel B

Full sample

Low education sample

SOURCE: Authors' construction using data from 1980–2003 Panel Study of Income Dynamics.

Figure 7.4 Food Stamp Participation Rates by Birth Cohort, Eligible Samples (%)

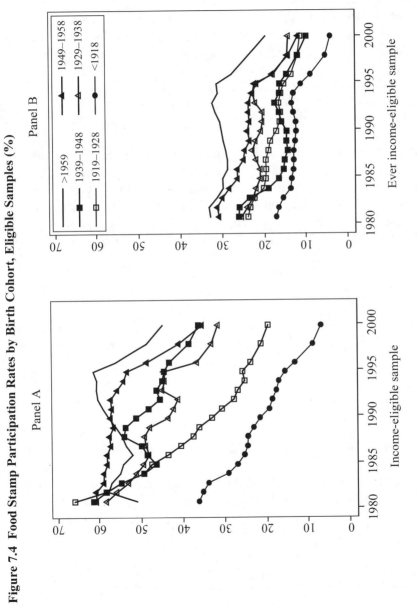

SOURCE: Authors' construction using data from 1980–2003 Panel Study of Income Dynamics.

decline among the pre-1919 cohort is quite surprising given that this demographic group is likely retired and thus was largely immune from the labor market effects of the expanding macroeconomy as well as welfare reform–related changes in the Food Stamp Program. At the same time, the late 1990s was also a time of nearly unprecedented growth in asset values, and thus the liquid asset test of $3,000 may have been binding for an increasing proportion of older Americans. These figures reveal possibly important cohort effects affecting both the level and trend in Food Stamp Program participation.

Income Volatility

We next examine basic trends in income volatility over the past two decades. For our analysis we adopt standard measures of income volatility as utilized in Dynarski and Gruber (1997), Gottschalk and Moffitt (1994), and Gundersen and Ziliak (2003), among others, by decomposing income into permanent and transitory components. Let y_{it} be the natural log of income for person i, $i = 1, \ldots, N$, in time period t, $t = 1, \ldots, T$, so that

$$(7.1) \quad y_{it} = \mu_i + \varepsilon_{it} ,$$

where μ_i is the permanent component and ε_{it} is the transitory component. The corresponding person-specific and time-invariant measure of transitory income volatility is given by

$$(7.2) \quad \sigma_{\varepsilon_i}^2 = \frac{1}{(T_i - 1)} \sum_{t=1}^{T_i} (y_{it} - \bar{y}_i)^2 ,$$

where $\bar{y}_i = \frac{1}{T_i} \sum_{t=1}^{T_i} y_{it}$ is the person-specific time mean and T_i reflects

the fact that the panel is unbalanced so that individuals are present in the sample for different lengths of time. The measure of permanent volatility is given by

$$(7.3) \quad \sigma_{\mu}^2 = \frac{1}{N-1} \sum_{i=1}^{N} (\bar{y}_i - \bar{y})^2 - \frac{\sigma_{\varepsilon}^2}{\overline{T}} ,$$

where $\bar{y}$ is the overall sample mean, σ_{ε}^2 is the average across i of the transitory income variances in Equation (7.2), and $\bar{T}$ is the average across the number of time periods T_i. The transitory variance in Equation (7.2) reflects within-group time series variation in income, whereas the permanent variance in Equation (7.3) reflects between-group variation. Following the methodology used in Gottschalk and Moffitt (1994), for each of our four samples we purge income of life-cycle age effects by replacing y in Equations (7.2) and (7.3) with the residuals from a regression of income on a quartic in age. Purging volatility of age effects also prevents the confounding of direct age effects on food stamp participation with the indirect effects of age through income volatility.[4]

We consider two variants of Equations (7.2) and (7.3), one based on all sample periods pooled together and one where we take higher-frequency measures of instability from 1980–1984, 1985–1989, 1990–1994, and 1995–2002. One way to view the low-frequency versus high-frequency estimates of transitory variances in Equation (7.2) is that the low-frequency estimates (which could be based on upwards of 20 years of data) are akin to person-specific permanent variances and the high-frequency estimates are more reflective of traditional transitory variances. Gottschalk and Moffitt (1994) split their sample into nine-year intervals to portray changes in earnings instability between the 1970s and 1980s. Although we are less interested in exploring broad, decadal trends in income volatility in the detail of Gottschalk and Moffitt, we do highlight some important trends and interactions of income volatility with food stamp participation.

In Table 7.1 we depict transitory and permanent low-frequency income volatility for each of our four samples. By columns, we consider these measures for all households within any given sample, followed by the same age breakdowns as in Figures 7.1 and 7.2. The volatility measures broken down by age use the residuals from a pooled regression across all ages—i.e., the regression coefficients are not allowed to vary by age; thus, the estimates in Table 7.1 reflect changes in sample composition and not changes in age-earnings profiles per se. There are a number of observations that should be noted about Table 7.1. First, permanent income volatility is substantially higher than transitory volatility regardless of sample. Second, transitory income volatility among the income-eligible, ever income-eligible, and low education samples exceeds that for the full sample across the age spectrum (with one exception). This is to be expected, given the greater labor market churning

Table 7.1   Transitory and Permanent Low Frequency Income Volatility by Age Groups

	All	Under 30	31–40	41–50	51–60	Over 61
			Full sample			
Transitory	0.15	0.16	0.15	0.14	0.15	0.15
Permanent	0.60					
			Low education sample			
Transitory	0.19	0.22	0.22	0.19	0.18	0.15
Permanent	0.51					
			Income-eligible sample			
Transitory	0.27	0.29	0.28	0.44	0.41	0.13
Permanent	0.54					
			Ever income-eligible sample			
Transitory	0.32	0.32	0.31	0.35	0.45	0.24
Permanent	0.62					

SOURCE: Data are from the 1980–2003 Panel Study of Income Dynamics (PSID).

among poorly educated and low-income adults in the United States. Third, in general, income volatility is lowest for the over-61 group across all four samples.

Table 7.2 replicates the results in Table 7.1 for the high-frequency income volatility measures. A comparison of Tables 7.1 and 7.2 demonstrates that the estimated high-frequency volatility across all age groups is substantially smaller than the level of volatility measured at low frequency (again, with only one exception). This is consistent with our conjecture that estimates from Equation (7.2) based on all sample years are more akin to a person-specific permanent volatility measure. (Note that the levels of volatility, even at five-year intervals, exceed those in Gottschalk and Moffitt [1994]. This occurs because they use earnings as opposed to income and they restrict their sample to white male heads of household while we admit nonwhites and female-headed families.) We also note that for most age groups income volatility spikes in the mid-1990s, though it did so a bit earlier among the currently income-eligible population, which may have helped spur the growth in caseloads in the early 1990s.

We conclude our descriptive section by examining a simple bivariate relationship between income volatility and Food Stamp Program participation. Specifically, in Table 7.3 we split the sample by quartiles

Table 7.2 Transitory and Permanent High-Frequency Income Volatility by Age Groups

	All	Under 30	31–40	41–50	51–60	Over 61
			Full sample			
			1985			
Transitory	0.08	0.10	0.07	0.07	0.08	0.08
Permanent	0.57					
			1990			
Transitory	0.07	0.09	0.07	0.05	0.08	0.06
Permanent	0.67					
			1995			
Transitory	0.09	0.13	0.08	0.07	0.09	0.10
Permanent	0.71					
			2000			
Transitory	0.08	0.10	0.08	0.08	0.08	0.08
Permanent	0.63					
			Low education sample			
			1985			
Transitory	0.09	0.12	0.08	0.10	0.10	0.08
Permanent	0.64					
			1990			
Transitory	0.09	0.13	0.10	0.07	0.10	0.07
Permanent	0.62					
			1995			
Transitory	0.11	0.14	0.14	0.10	0.11	0.10
Permanent	0.59					
			2000			
Transitory	0.10	0.12	0.11	0.11	0.12	0.07
Permanent	0.62					
			Income-eligible sample			
			1985			
Transitory	0.12	0.25	0.08	0.10	0.08	0.04
Permanent	0.66					
			1990			
Transitory	0.17	0.20	0.30	0.09	0.25	0.03
Permanent	1.00					
			1995			
Transitory	0.14	0.10	0.24	0.09	0.11	0.12
Permanent	0.80					

(continued)

Table 7.2 (continued)

	All	Under 30	31–40	41–50	51–60	Over 61
		Income-eligible sample				
		2000				
Transitory	0.07	0.08	0.08	0.09	0.08	0.04
Permanent	0.29					
		Ever income-eligible sample				
		1985				
Transitory	0.17	0.23	0.13	0.28	0.21	0.09
Permanent	0.65					
		1990				
Transitory	0.20	0.25	0.19	0.12	0.42	0.12
Permanent	0.93					
		1995				
Transitory	0.21	0.22	0.24	0.12	0.32	0.21
Permanent	0.92					
		2000				
Transitory	0.11	0.12	0.01	0.11	0.12	0.09
Permanent	0.65					

SOURCE: Data are from the 1980–2003 Panel Study of Income Dynamics (PSID).

Table 7.3 Food Stamp Participation by Quartiles of Transitory Income Volatility

	First quartile	Second quartile	Third quartile	Fourth quartile
	Low-frequency income volatility			
Full sample	0.04	0.06	0.12	0.21
Low education sample	0.15	0.19	0.25	0.36
Income-eligible sample	0.27	0.43	0.58	0.58
Ever income-eligible sample	0.18	0.19	0.23	0.28
	High-frequency income volatility			
All income sample	0.06	0.07	0.10	0.18
Low education sample	0.20	0.18	0.24	0.32
Income-eligible sample	0.30	0.44	0.53	0.55
Ever income-eligible sample	0.19	0.17	0.22	0.28

SOURCE: Data are from the 1980–2003 Panel Study of Income Dynamics (PSID).

of transitory income volatility (at high and low frequencies) and then for each quartile we depict the level of food stamp participation for each of our samples. The results indicate that food stamp participation is increasing in income volatility. The difference is especially clear when comparing the fourth and first quartiles across each of the samples. This suggests that, in addition to age and cohort, income volatility may be an important determinant of food stamp use.

The Age Gradient in Food Stamp Program Participation

Estimation methods

The standard static model of welfare participation in economics is to postulate that participation occurs if and only if the net utility gain is positive—that is, if the utility of participating less the cost of participating and less the utility of not participating is positive. Defining

$$V(y_{it}^1; FSP_{it} = 1)$$

as the indirect utility obtained from income y_{it}^1 while on food stamps ($FSP_{it} = 1$), and

$$V(y_{it}^0; FSP_{it} = 0)$$

as the corresponding indirect utility when not participating in food stamps, then the individual participates if

$$V(y_{it}^1; FSP_{it} = 1) - V(y_{it}^0; FSP_{it} = 0) > 0.$$

Note that for simplicity we assume the indirect utility function as defined incorporates any direct utility costs of program participation such as the stigma and transaction costs described above. If direct preferences are additive over time, then under two-stage budgeting (whereby the individual equates the discounted marginal utility of wealth across periods and then maximizes current period preferences over consumption, leisure, and welfare participation), the static model of welfare participation is "life cycle–consistent" (Blundell and Macurdy 1999). This implies that all lifetime preference parameters are identified except for the time discount rate and the intertemporal substitution elasticity. As the latter parameters are typically not focal parameters of interest in welfare applications, the static model is fairly general.

To estimate the roles of age and income volatility in the food stamp decision we adopt a reduced-form, index-function version of food stamp participation. Let

(7.4) $FSP_{it} = 1$ if $FSP_{it}^* = Z_{it}\pi + X_i\gamma + u_{it} > 0$;

$FSP_{it} = 0$ otherwise ,

where FSP_{it}^* is the latent propensity to participate in food stamps, Z_{it} is a $(1 \times L)$ vector of time-varying variables determining participation, X_i is a $(1 \times L)$ vector of time-invariant variables, and π and γ are vectors of unknown parameters to estimate, and u_{it} is a compound-error term equal to $u_{it} = \alpha_i + \eta_{it}$. The elements of Z_{it} include the age gradient as represented by the same series of indicators as in Figures 7.1 and 7.2— interactions between transitory income volatility and the age gradient, marital status, homeownership status, and family size. Elements of X_i include the race of the head, whether the head is a high school graduate, date-of-birth cohorts as defined in Figures 7.3 and 7.4, and transitory income volatility as defined in Equation (7.2). Permanent volatility will be absorbed in the constant term. When we use income volatility defined over five-year time horizons, this measure will be included in Z_{it}.

Because the model is in reduced form we assume that

$E[\eta_{is} \mid Z_{it}, X_i] = 0 \forall s, t,$

which is the typical strict exogeneity assumption between covariates and the time-varying idiosyncratic error term. However, α_i, which represents latent time-invariant preferences for Food Stamp Program participation, is in general not uncorrelated with the regressors, i.e.,

$E[\alpha_i \mid Z_{it}, X_i] \neq 0.$

This correlated random effect can arise for a number of reasons, including preferences for welfare participation that vary across education levels or birth cohorts.

Estimation of nonlinear discrete choice models in the presence of correlated unobserved heterogeneity is complicated because simple transformations such as first differencing do not eliminate the time-invariant unobserved heterogeneity, α_i, the exception being the conditional logit estimator of Chamberlain (1980). Most estimators such as the panel probit estimator require a large number of time periods for consistent estimation of both $\hat{\pi}$ and $\hat{\alpha}_i$. A transparent alternative is a panel version of the linear probability model. A concern with this estimator is that predictions may lie outside the unit interval. However, this concern is not germane to this chapter insofar as the focus is on the effects of age and income volatility on food stamp participation and not on the predicted probability of participation per se.

Admitting unrestricted correlation between unobserved heterogeneity and the covariates would lead one to apply OLS to the transformed model

$$(7.5) \quad \widetilde{FSP}_{it} = \widetilde{Z}_{it}\pi + \widetilde{\eta}_{it} \, ,$$

where

$$\widetilde{FSP}_{it} = FSP_{it} - \overline{FSP}_i \, , \qquad \widetilde{Z}_{it} = Z_{it} - \overline{Z}_i \, , \qquad \widetilde{\eta}_{it} = \eta_{it} - \overline{\eta}_i$$

are the deviations from time means, with the person-specific time means defined as

$$\overline{FSP}_i = \frac{1}{T_i}\sum_{t=1}^{T_i} FSP_{it}, \overline{Z}_i = \frac{1}{T_i}\sum_{t=1}^{T_i} Z_{it} \, .$$

Estimation of Equation (7.5) yields the so-called within or fixed-effects estimator. Although providing consistent estimates of π, the cost of this approach is that it is no longer possible to identify the coefficients on the time-invariant variables X_i. This implies that it is still possible to identify the interaction between time-invariant low-frequency income volatility and the age gradient, but not the level effects of low-frequency volatility, education, or cohort on food stamp participation. (Level effects of high-frequency volatility from the five-year estimates are identified given sufficient time series variation.)

To identify the effect of time-invariant factors, we use the correlated random effects estimator of Hausman and Taylor (1981). The idea here is to exploit the fact that some of the regressors are correlated with the unobserved heterogeneity and some are not.[5] Any time-varying variables that are uncorrelated with the latent heterogeneity α_i can be used as instrumental variables for time-invariant variables that are correlated. Provided that the number of uncorrelated time-varying variables is at least as large as the number of correlated time-invariant variables, the coefficients on the latter are identified.

More specifically, let

$$Z_{it} = [Z_{it}^1, Z_{it}^2] \, ,$$

where Z_{it}^1 is a $(1 \times K_1)$ vector of time-varying variables uncorrelated with

$$\alpha_i, E[\alpha_i \mid Z_{it}^1] = 0,$$

and Z_{it}^2 is a $(1 \times K_2)$ vector of time-varying variables correlated with

$$\alpha_i, E[\alpha_i \mid Z_{it}^2] \neq 0.$$

Likewise, let

$$X_i = [X_i^1, X_i^2]$$

be the corresponding $(1 \times L_1)$ and $(1 \times L_2)$ vectors of time-invariant regressors, with

$$E[\alpha_i \mid X_i^1] = 0 \text{ and } E[\alpha_i \mid X_i^2] \neq 0 \, .$$

Ignoring for the moment the fact that our panel is unbalanced, we rewrite the estimating equation of interest in matrix form as

(7.6) $FSP = Z\pi + X\gamma + \alpha + \eta,$

where FSP is $(NT \times 1)$, Z is $(NT \times [K_1 + K_2])$, and X is $(NT \times [L_1 + L_2])$.

Then let

$$\text{cov}(\alpha + \eta) = \sigma_\eta^2 \Omega, \qquad \Omega^{-1} = Q_a + \theta^2 P_a, \qquad \Omega^{-1/2} = Q_a + \theta P_a,$$

$$Q_a = I_{NT} - P_a, \ P_a = I_N \otimes T^{-1} e_T e_T', \qquad \text{and } \theta = \left[\frac{\sigma_\eta^2}{\sigma_\eta^2 + T\sigma_\alpha^2} \right]^{1/2},$$

where Q_a is the within (deviation from time mean) transformation, P_a is the time-mean operator, I_N and I_{NT} are $(N \times N)$ and $(NT \times NT)$ identity matrices, and e_T is a $(T \times 1)$ vector of ones. Letting $D = [Z, X]$ be the matrix of regressors and $\Gamma = [\pi, \gamma]$ be the vector of parameters, then in order to make the error covariance matrix in Equation (7.6) homoskedastic it is necessary to premultiply both sides of the equation by $\Omega^{1/2}$, as follows:

(7.7) $\Omega^{-1/2} FSP = \Omega^{-1/2} D\Gamma + \Omega^{-1/2} (\alpha + \eta).$

Hausman and Taylor (1981) then suggest the following instrumental variables estimator for Equation (7.7):

(7.8) $\hat{\Gamma} = [D'\Omega^{-1/2} P_w \Omega^{-1/2} D]^{-1} D'\Omega^{-1/2} P_w \Omega^{-1/2} FSP,$

where $P_w = W(W'W)^{-1} W'$ is the projection matrix of instruments W. For instruments they suggest

$$W = [Q_a Z_1, Q_a Z_2, P_a X_1, P_a Z_1];$$

that is, the deviation from time means $Q_a Z_1, Q_a Z_2$ are instruments for Z_1 and Z_2, while the time mean of Z_1, $P_a Z_1$, serves as an instrumental variable for the correlated time-invariant regressor X_2. The time mean of X_1 is an instrument for itself. So long as the order condition $K_1 > L_2$ is met then all model parameters are identified. As our base case we categorize the regressors as follows:

$$Z_{it}^1 = [Age_{it}^j, \hat{\sigma}_{\varepsilon_i}^2 * Age_{it}^j, year_t],$$

$$Z_{it}^2 = [married_{it}, owner_{it}, family_{it}],$$

$$X_i^1 = [\hat{\sigma}_{\varepsilon_i}^2, race_i],$$

and

$$X_i^2 = [education_i, cohort_i] \; ,$$

where Age_{it}^j represents the various indicators for the age gradient ($j = \leq 30, > 30$ and $\leq 40, > 40$ and $\leq 50, > 50$ and $\leq 60, > 60$). We assume that preferences for marriage, home ownership, family size, and education are correlated with latent preferences to participate in food stamps, and that different birth cohorts through varied socialization mechanisms have different (and possibly correlated) preferences for food stamp use. We have no strong priors to assume that race is correlated with latent preferences to participate conditional on the other covariates and therefore assume it is uncorrelated. Likewise, we assume that income volatility is uncorrelated with unobserved heterogeneity. Note that this does not imply that the *level* of income is uncorrelated with α_1, but the variance is assumed to be uncorrelated. This is a standard assumption that is justified provided that volatility is driven by demand-side market forces or other factors unrelated to time-invariant latent heterogeneity.

To make the estimator operational we first need to replace θ with a consistent estimate. It is recommended that initial consistent estimates be obtained by the within-fixed-effects estimator (FE) and that the variance terms be constructed as

$$\hat{\sigma}_\eta^2 = \frac{1}{NT - N - K} \sum_i \sum_t (\widetilde{FSP}_{it} - \tilde{D}_{it} \hat{\Gamma}_{FE})^2$$

and

$$\hat{\sigma}_\alpha^2 = \frac{1}{N} \sum_i (\overline{FSP}_i - \bar{D}_i \hat{\Gamma}_{FE})^2 - T^{-1} \hat{\sigma}_\eta^2 \; ,$$

whereas, before,

$$\widetilde{FSP}_{it} = FSP_{it} - \overline{FSP}_i$$

and

$$\tilde{D}_{it} = D_{it} - \bar{D}_i$$

were the deviations from time mean. Under the correlated random effects structure this estimator is asymptotically more efficient than the within estimator. However, in the event that the assumed lack of correlation between Z_{it}^1 and α_1 is violated, then the Hausman and Taylor estimator is inconsistent. For robustness, then, we compare our results to those estimated from the within estimator. We also compare our results with a Hausman and Taylor estimator, which does not include birth cohorts. It is well known that separate identification of age, year, and cohort effects is complicated without strong functional form assumptions (Heckman and Robb 1985), though in our case the presence of an unbalanced panel aids in identification because new cohorts enter the panel later in the sample period. That said, we are interested in understanding how sensitive the estimated age gradient is to the inclusion of cohort effects.

Results

Our results from the Hausman and Taylor estimator with endogenous cohort effects are presented in Table 7.4 for our four samples. Here we look at the low-frequency measures of income volatility; below we consider the high-frequency measures. Recall that in the low-frequency model transitory volatility is time-invariant and thus is an element of X_i^1, whereas in the high-frequency model transitory volatility varies over time for each individual and thus is an element of Z_i^1. The respective transitory income volatility measures are de-meaned prior to interacting with the age gradient, implying that the direct effect of volatility yields the mean effect and the interactions reflect deviations from the mean. In both cases permanent volatility is absorbed into either the constant term or year dummies and thus is not identified.

The results in Table 7.4 indicate that there is a U-shaped pattern to food stamp participation across the age gradient for the full, low education, and ever income-eligible samples. Across all three of the samples, the bottom of the U is for those between the ages of 41 and 50. The peak for all three samples is for households headed by someone over the age of 60. These results suggest that, controlling for other factors, Food Stamp Program participation is not monotonically declining across the age gradient. The results for the income-eligible sample are not U-shaped, nor are they decreasing across the age gradient. Instead they are flat across the age gradient.

The direct effect of transitory income volatility on food stamp participation at the mean level of volatility depends on the sample. For the

Table 7.4 The Effect of Age and Income Volatility on Food Stamp Participation: Hausman–Taylor with Endogenous Cohort Effects, Low Frequency Income Volatility

	Full sample	Low education sample	Income-eligible sample	Ever income-eligible sample
Age between 31 and 40	-0.02	-0.04	0.00	-0.02
	(0.00)	(0.01)	(0.02)	(0.01)
Age between 41 and 50	-0.02	-0.07	-0.01	-0.04
	(0.01)	(0.02)	(0.02)	(0.01)
Age between 51 and 60	0.02	0.00	0.07	0.03
	(0.01)	(0.02)	(0.04)	(0.02)
Age greater than 60	0.04	0.01	0.05	0.04
	(0.01)	(0.03)	(0.05)	(0.02)
Income volatility	0.23	0.07	-0.06	-0.02
	(0.03)	(0.07)	(0.02)	(0.01)
Age between 31 and 40 × income volatility	0.03	0.08	0.03	0.01
	(0.01)	(0.04)	(0.01)	(0.01)
Age between 41 and 50 × income volatility	0.00	0.18	0.05	0.03
	(0.02)	(0.05)	(0.02)	(0.01)
Age between 51 and 60 × income volatility	0.05	0.42	0.04	0.02
	(0.03)	(0.07)	(0.02)	(0.01)
Age greater than 60 × income volatility	-0.21	0.14	0.07	0.03
	(0.03)	(0.08)	(0.02)	(0.01)
Homeowner	-0.03	-0.03	-0.06	-0.05
	(0.00)	(0.01)	(0.02)	(0.01)

Married	−0.02	−0.02	−0.01	−0.03
	(0.00)	(0.01)	(0.02)	(0.01)
High school graduate	−0.08		−1.12	−0.02
	(0.08)		(0.13)	(0.17)
White	−0.14	−0.17	0.00	−0.18
	(0.02)	(0.03)	(0.04)	(0.04)
Family size	0.02	0.03	0.04	0.04
	(0.00)	(0.00)	(0.00)	(0.00)
Born between 1949 and 1958	−0.07	−0.14	0.03	−0.09
	(0.02)	(0.07)	(0.08)	(0.04)
Born between 1939 and 1948	−0.10	−0.16	−0.24	−0.07
	(0.02)	(0.08)	(0.10)	(0.07)
Born between 1929 and 1938	−0.07	−0.20	−0.59	−0.16
	(0.07)	(0.12)	(0.18)	(0.15)
Born between 1919 and 1928	−0.19	−0.29	−0.48	−0.11
	(0.08)	(0.14)	(0.22)	(0.17)
Born before 1918	−0.03	−0.13	−0.83	−0.16
	(0.10)	(0.13)	(0.21)	(0.19)

NOTE: Standard errors are in parentheses. There are 72,150 person-years in the full sample, 17,463 in the low education sample, 11,535 in the income-eligible sample, and 30,305 in the ever income-eligible sample. Each model controls for a vector of year dummies. Blank = not applicable.

SOURCE: Data are from the 1980–2003 Panel Study of Income Dynamics (PSID).

full sample, persons with high levels of volatility over long time horizons—i.e., permanently high volatility—are more likely to participate in the Food Stamp Program. In the low education sample this effect is also positive but it is statistically insignificant. That food stamp use is higher among those with high volatility over low frequencies is in accord with Blundell and Pistaferri (2003), who find that food stamps are very effective in smoothing consumption in the face of permanent income shocks. In contrast, for the income-eligible and the ever income-eligible samples the effect of income volatility is negative and significant. Across the different samples, as the probability of being eligible for food stamps increases, there is a corresponding decline in the effect of income volatility. One possible explanation for these differences for the samples that may not always be eligible for food stamps (i.e., for all the samples except the income-eligible sample) is that higher volatilities among those at greater risk of food stamp participation include spells above the food stamp eligibility cutoff, which highlights the possible endogeneity of this sample selection.

We now consider the effects of income volatility across different ages. To do so, we depict the total effect of age and interactions of age with income volatility (along with the respective 95 percent confidence interval) for a representative individual at each age range, with income volatility one standard deviation below or one standard deviation above the mean level of volatility. Panels A–D of Figure 7.5 refer to the four samples at low-frequency volatility. For the full sample, the effect of income volatility is relatively constant across the age spectrum with the exception of those over age 61 with lower income volatility—they have higher probabilities of food stamp participation in comparison to those younger than 30. For the low education sample, lower income volatility is associated with lower probabilities of food stamp participation for those aged 31–50 in comparison to those younger than 30, and higher income volatility is associated with higher probabilities of food stamp participation for those aged 51–60. More consistent patterns emerge for the income-eligible samples: there, household heads aged 51 and older with higher income volatilities are more likely to participate in the Food Stamp Program. One caution in interpreting these results is that the distributions of both low- and high-frequency income volatility are skewed and widely dispersed so that one standard deviation above the mean is in the far right tail of the distribution.

197

Figure 7.5 Effects of Low Frequency Income Volatility on Food Stamp Program Participation

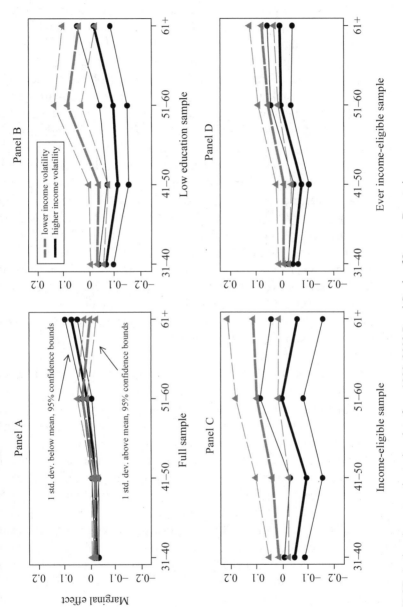

SOURCE: Authors' construction using data from 1980–2003 Panel Study of Income Dynamics.

Figure 7.5, Panels A and B, also provides insights into the role of income volatility at any given age. Comparisons of income volatilities one standard deviation above the mean and below the mean indicate that in general households with higher income volatility are more likely to receive food stamps.

While the effect of age on food stamp participation is U-shaped, the effect of birth cohort is generally declining with respect to earlier birth cohorts. In comparison to the base group (those born after 1959), for each of the samples every birth cohort either has statistically the same probability of food stamp participation or a lower probability. In terms of other variables in the regression model they generally align as expected; namely, food stamp participation is lower among those with a high school diploma or more, among white families, among homeowners, among married couples, and among those with small families.

We now turn to the results (Table 7.5) where we use a high-frequency measure of income volatility. Like the results for the low-frequency measures, the effect of age is still, except for the income-eligible sample, U-shaped, but this is primarily due to dips in participation rates in the ages between 31 and 50 rather than increases in the post-50 age group. The effect of high-frequency income volatility is statistically insignificant with the exception of the low education sample, where it is negative and significant. As seen in the flat lines in Figure 7.6, Panels A–D, the effect of income volatility at all age levels is insignificant. At any given age, the differences between higher and lower levels of income volatility are much more narrow than is the case with low-frequency income volatilities. Earlier birth cohorts, as in Table 7.4, are in general as likely or less likely to receive food stamps in comparison to more recent birth cohorts, for all samples.

As mentioned previously, separate identification of age, period, and cohort effects is generally achieved by imposing functional form restrictions on the respective parameters. One such restriction is to zero out the cohort effects and examine how the age coefficients change with the omission of controls for birth cohort. In Table 7.6 we present the results from the Hausman-Taylor estimator without cohort effects under low-frequency income volatility. One primary difference in the results in Table 7.4 is that, for the low education and income-eligible samples, across all age groups participation in food stamps is lower than for the under 30 group. In other words the U-shaped pattern for the former sample and the flat age profile for the latter sample no longer hold.

An alternative restriction that can be imposed to eliminate birth cohorts is to assume that all covariates are correlated with the unobserved propensity to participate in food stamps, though at the cost of no longer identifying other time-invariant variables such as our measure of low-frequency income volatility. In Table 7.7 we impose this assumption for the low-frequency income volatility measures and present results from fixed-effects linear probability models. Here, the results regarding the relationship between the age profile and food stamp participation are more similar to those found in Table 7.4.

In Tables 7.8 and 7.9 we repeat the exercises from Tables 7.6 and 7.7, only now for the high-frequency income volatility measure. One key difference from the results for Table 7.5 is that income volatility has a positive and significant effect on food stamp participation in the low education sample in Tables 7.8 and 7.9 while it has a negative and significant effect in Table 7.5.

CONCLUSION

We used data from the Panel Study of Income Dynamics over the past two decades to estimate the effect of age, income volatility, and interactions of age and volatility on the probability of participating in the Food Stamp Program. We employed the correlated random effects estimator of Hausman and Taylor (1981), which permits identification of parameters on both time-varying and time-invariant regressors. We found that participation in food stamps is U-shaped across the life course and that younger birth cohorts have higher rates of food stamp participation than earlier birth cohorts. We also find that, in general, food stamp participation is higher across the age gradient among those with higher levels of income volatility.

Our results have four main implications for policymakers and Food Stamp Program administrators. First, contrary to common expectations, we found that, after controlling for relevant factors, older persons actually have higher rates of participation than younger persons, especially in comparison to those between the ages of 31 and 50. While outreach

Table 7.5 The Effect of Age and Income Volatility on Food Stamp Participation: Hausman-Taylor with Endogenous Cohort Effects, High Frequency Income Volatility

	Full sample	Low education sample	Income-eligible sample	Ever income-eligible sample
Age between 31 and 40	-0.02	-0.05	0.00	-0.03
	(0.00)	(0.01)	(0.02)	(0.01)
Age between 41 and 50	-0.02	-0.08	-0.01	-0.05
	(0.01)	(0.02)	(0.03)	(0.01)
Age between 51 and 60	0.01	-0.02	0.05	0.01
	(0.01)	(0.02)	(0.04)	(0.02)
Age greater than 60	0.02	-0.01	0.02	0.02
	(0.01)	(0.03)	(0.05)	(0.02)
Income volatility	-0.02	-0.18	-0.02	0.00
	(0.02)	(0.05)	(0.02)	(0.01)
Age between 31 and 40 × income volatility	0.09	0.32	-0.01	0.00
	(0.02)	(0.06)	(0.02)	(0.01)
Age between 41 and 50 × income volatility	0.09	0.30	0.21	0.01
	(0.02)	(0.07)	(0.09)	(0.01)
Age between 51 and 60 × income volatility	0.15	0.44	0.01	0.00
	(0.03)	(0.07)	(0.02)	(0.01)
Age greater than 60 × income volatility	-0.01	0.16	0.01	0.00
	(0.02)	(0.06)	(0.02)	(0.01)
Homeowner	-0.03	-0.03	-0.06	-0.05
	(0.00)	(0.01)	(0.02)	(0.01)

Married	-0.02	-0.03	0.00	-0.03
	(0.00)	(0.01)	(0.03)	(0.01)
High school graduate	-0.48		-1.20	-0.11
	(0.13)		(0.14)	(0.12)
White	-0.06	-0.19	0.04	-0.17
	(0.04)	(0.03)	(0.04)	(0.03)
Family size	0.02	0.03	0.04	0.04
	(0.00)	(0.00)	(0.00)	(0.00)
Born between 1949 and 1958	-0.02	-0.04	0.17	-0.02
	(0.04)	(0.08)	(0.08)	(0.04)
Born between 1939 and 1948	-0.09	-0.21	-0.29	-0.13
	(0.05)	(0.08)	(0.11)	(0.05)
Born between 1929 and 1938	-0.14	-0.04	-0.50	0.04
	(0.13)	(0.12)	(0.20)	(0.10)
Born between 1919 and 1928	-0.23	-0.36	-0.40	-0.34
	(0.15)	(0.13)	(0.22)	(0.12)
Born before 1918	-0.20	0.01	-0.80	0.03
	(0.18)	(0.12)	(0.21)	(0.12)

NOTE: Standard errors are in parentheses. There are 72,150 person-years in the full sample, 17,463 in the low education sample, 11,535 in the income-eligible sample, and 30,305 in the ever income-eligible sample. Each model controls for a vector of year dummies. Blank = not applicable.

SOURCE: Data are from the 1980–2003 Panel Study of Income Dynamics (PSID).

202

Figure 7.6 Effects of High Frequency Income Volatility on Food Stamp Program Participation

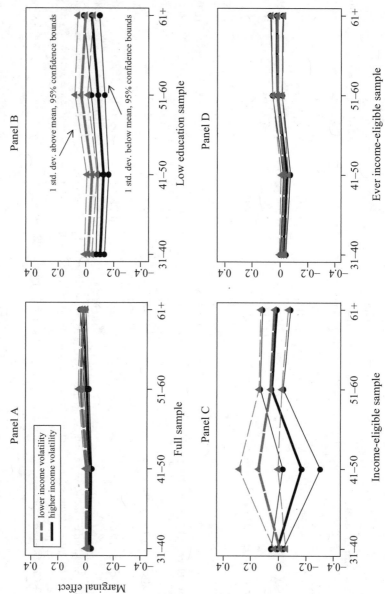

SOURCE: Authors' construction using data from 1980–2003 Panel Study of Income Dynamics.

to the elderly may remain an important policy intervention for other reasons, our results demonstrate that concerns about low participation rates among the elderly may be overstated. Second, if any age group should be targeted for outreach, it is probably those between the ages of 31 and 50, perhaps by improving the application and recertification procedures to better accommodate the working-age population. Third, our results show that later birth cohorts have higher rates of participation than earlier birth cohorts. As a consequence, in the absence of other factors, in the future there may be a permanent increase in the number of food stamp recipients. Fourth, our results show some evidence that lower income volatility is associated with lower probabilities of receiving food stamps. One possible reason for this result is that potential recipients with low but steady incomes may perceive food stamps as a program to be used only in response to negative income shocks. In response, outreach to those known to have more constant income patterns may be worthwhile.

We conclude with a few suggestions for future research directions. Although we have taken reports of food stamp participation as accurate in this chapter, previous work has established that food stamp receipt is underreported in surveys (Bollinger and David 1997, 2001, 2005; Marquis and Moore 1990). This underreporting can have consequences for the understanding of the relationship between food stamps and various outcomes of interest (Gundersen and Kreider 2008). Moreover, even though income in the PSID is among the best measured in social surveys, there is some evidence of income misreporting, and if this is correlated with food stamp participation then our results may be biased. Future research should explore the dual roles of income and food stamp misreporting on both the determinants of participation and other correlated outcomes. Finally, we have not explored the possible role of risk aversion with respect to the food stamp participation decision. In the 1996 wave of the PSID several questions were asked regarding risk aversion, and these variables could potentially be utilized to better understand how food stamp recipients respond to income volatility. These and related issues portend a vibrant research agenda on food assistance for many years to come.

Table 7.6 The Effect of Age and Income Volatility on Food Stamp Participation: Hausman-Taylor without Birth Cohort Effects, Low Frequency Income Volatility

	Full sample	Low education sample	Income-eligible sample	Ever income-eligible sample
Age between 31 and 40	−0.03	−0.07	−0.03	−0.03
	(0.00)	(0.01)	(0.01)	(0.01)
Age between 41 and 50	−0.03	−0.11	−0.08	−0.06
	(0.01)	(0.01)	(0.02)	(0.01)
Age between 51 and 60	0.00	−0.07	−0.07	0.00
	(0.01)	(0.02)	(0.03)	(0.01)
Age greater than 60	0.01	−0.08	−0.15	0.01
	(0.01)	(0.02)	(0.04)	(0.02)
Income volatility	0.26	0.08	−0.03	−0.01
	(0.03)	(0.06)	(0.02)	(0.01)
Age between 31 and 40 × income volatility	0.03	0.09	0.03	0.01
	(0.01)	(0.04)	(0.01)	(0.01)
Age between 41 and 50 × income volatility	0.00	0.18	0.03	0.02
	(0.02)	(0.05)	(0.02)	(0.01)
Age between 51 and 60 × income volatility	0.05	0.40	0.02	0.02
	(0.03)	(0.07)	(0.02)	(0.01)
Age greater than 60 × income volatility	−0.22	0.11	0.05	0.02
	(0.03)	(0.08)	(0.02)	(0.01)
Homeowner	−0.03	−0.04	−0.07	−0.05
	(0.00)	(0.01)	(0.01)	(0.01)

Married	-0.03	-0.02	-0.02	-0.04
	(0.00)	(0.01)	(0.02)	(0.01)
High school graduate	0.01		-0.28	0.13
	(0.03)		(0.08)	(0.05)
White	-0.17	-0.17	-0.16	-0.21
	(0.01)	(0.02)	(0.03)	(0.02)
Family size	0.02	0.03	0.04	0.04
	(0.00)	(0.00)	(0.00)	(0.00)

NOTE: Standard errors are in parentheses. There are 72,150 person-years in the full sample, 17,463 in the low education sample, 11,535 in the income-eligible sample, and 30,305 in the ever income-eligible sample. Each model controls for a vector of year dummies. Blank = not applicable.
SOURCE: Data are from the 1980–2003 Panel Study of Income Dynamics (PSID).

Table 7.7 The Effect of Age and Income Volatility on Food Stamp Participation: Fixed Effects Estimator, Low Frequency Income Volatility

	Full sample	Low education sample	Income-eligible sample	Ever income-eligible sample
Age between 31 and 40	-0.02	-0.04	0.00	-0.02
	(0.00)	(0.01)	(0.02)	(0.01)
Age between 41 and 50	-0.02	-0.07	-0.01	-0.04
	(0.01)	(0.02)	(0.03)	(0.01)
Age between 51 and 60	0.02	0.00	0.07	0.03
	(0.01)	(0.02)	(0.04)	(0.02)
Age greater than 60	0.04	0.01	0.05	0.04
	(0.01)	(0.03)	(0.05)	(0.02)
Age between 31 and 40 × income volatility	0.03	0.09	0.03	0.02
	(0.03)	(0.06)	(0.01)	(0.00)
Age between 41 and 50 × income volatility	0.00	0.20	0.02	0.03
	(0.03)	(0.09)	(0.02)	(0.01)
Age between 51 and 60 × income volatility	0.05	0.47	0.01	0.02
	(0.05)	(0.11)	(0.02)	(0.01)
Age greater than 60 × income volatility	-0.22	0.21	0.04	0.03
	(0.06)	(0.13)	(0.03)	(0.01)
Homeowner	-0.03	-0.03	-0.06	-0.05
	(0.00)	(0.01)	(0.02)	(0.01)
Married	-0.02	-0.02	0.00	-0.03
	(0.00)	(0.01)	(0.03)	(0.01)

| Family size | 0.02 | 0.03 | 0.04 | 0.04 |
| | (0.00) | (0.00) | (0.01) | (0.00) |

NOTE: Standard errors are in parentheses. There are 72,150 person-years in the full sample, 17,463 in the low education sample, 11,535 in the income-eligible sample, and 30,305 in the ever income-eligible sample. Each model controls for a vector of year dummies.
SOURCE: Data are from the 1980–2003 Panel Study of Income Dynamics (PSID).

Table 7.8 The Effect of Age and Income Volatility on Food Stamp Participation: Hausman-Taylor without Birth Cohort Effects, High Frequency Income Volatility

	Full sample	Low education sample	Income-eligible sample	Ever income-eligible sample
Age between 31 and 40	-0.03	-0.07	-0.03	-0.03
	(0.00)	(0.01)	(0.01)	(0.01)
Age between 41 and 50	-0.04	-0.12	-0.09	-0.06
	(0.01)	(0.01)	(0.02)	(0.01)
Age between 51 and 60	-0.02	-0.08	-0.08	-0.01
	(0.01)	(0.02)	(0.03)	(0.02)
Age greater than 60	-0.02	-0.08	-0.17	-0.01
	(0.01)	(0.02)	(0.04)	(0.02)
Income volatility	0.00	0.33	-0.01	0.00
	(0.02)	(0.06)	(0.02)	(0.01)
Age between 31 and 40 × income volatility	0.09	0.30	0.20	0.01
	(0.02)	(0.07)	(0.08)	(0.01)
Age between 41 and 50 × income volatility	0.09	0.44	-0.01	0.00
	(0.02)	(0.07)	(0.02)	(0.01)
Age between 51 and 60 × income volatility	0.14	0.15	0.00	0.00
	(0.03)	(0.06)	(0.02)	(0.01)
Age greater than 60 × income volatility	-0.03	-0.18	-0.01	0.00
	(0.02)	(0.05)	(0.02)	(0.01)
Homeowner	-0.03	-0.03	-0.08	-0.05
	(0.00)	(0.01)	(0.02)	(0.01)

Married	−0.02	−0.03	−0.01	−0.03
	(0.00)	(0.01)	(0.02)	(0.01)
High school graduate	−0.14		−0.33	0.05
	(0.03)		(0.08)	(0.05)
White	−0.14	−0.18	−0.15	−0.20
	(0.01)	(0.02)	(0.03)	(0.02)
Family size	0.02	0.03	0.04	0.04
	(0.00)	(0.00)	(0.00)	(0.00)

NOTE: Standard errors are in parentheses. There are 72,150 person-years in the full sample, 17,463 in the low education sample, 11,535 in the income-eligible sample, and 30,305 in the ever income-eligible sample. Each model controls for a vector of year dummies. Blank = not applicable.

SOURCE: Data are from the 1980–2003 Panel Study of Income Dynamics (PSID).

Table 7.9 The Effect of Age and Income Volatility on Food Stamp Participation: Fixed Effects Estimator, High Frequency Income Volatility

	Full sample	Low education sample	Income-eligible sample	Ever income-eligible sample
Age between 31 and 40	0.02	0.05	0.01	0.03
	(0.02)	(0.05)	(0.01)	(0.03)
Age between 41 and 50	0.02	0.08	0.01	0.05
	(0.01)	(0.02)	(0.02)	(0.01)
Age between 51 and 60	0.01	0.02	0.06	0.01
	(0.01)	(0.02)	(0.03)	(0.01)
Age greater than 60	0.02	0.01	0.03	0.02
	(0.01)	(0.01)	(0.04)	(0.02)
Income volatility	0.02	0.31	0.00	0.00
	(0.03)	(0.08)	(0.02)	(0.00)
Age between 31 and 40 × income volatility	0.09	0.30	0.19	0.01
	(0.03)	(0.10)	(0.12)	(0.01)
Age between 41 and 50 × income volatility	0.10	0.44	0.00	0.00
	(0.04)	(0.09)	(0.00)	(0.00)
Age between 51 and 60 × income volatility	0.15	0.17	0.01	0.00
	(0.04)	(0.08)	(0.02)	(0.00)
Age greater than 60 × income volatility	0.00	0.19	0.02	0.01
	(0.03)	(0.07)	(0.02)	(0.00)
Homeowner	0.02	0.03	0.07	0.05
	(0.00)	(0.01)	(0.02)	(0.01)

Married	(0.02)	(0.02)	0.01	(0.03)
	(0.00)	(0.01)	(0.03)	(0.01)
Family size	0.02	0.03	0.03	0.04
	(0.00)	(0.00)	(0.01)	(0.00)

NOTE: Standard errors are in parentheses. There are 72,150 person-years in the full sample, 17,463 in the low education sample, 11,535 in the income-eligible sample, and 30,305 in the ever income-eligible sample. Each model controls for a vector of year dummies.
Blank = not applicable.
SOURCE: Data are from the 1980–2003 Panel Study of Income Dynamics (PSID).

Notes

This chapter comes from a paper originally prepared for presentation at the National Poverty Center/Economic Research Service conference on "Income Volatility and Implications for Food Assistance Research II." The authors thank conference participants—in particular, Dean Jolliffe and Jeff Smith—and participants in a seminar held at Iowa State University's Department of Economics for excellent comments. The authors also thank Brandie Ward for excellent research assistance. The views expressed herein are solely those of the authors and do not necessarily reflect the views of of ERS, NPC, or any other sponsoring agency.

1. Income is the sum of labor earnings plus income from rent, interest, and dividends. Transfers include social insurance (Social Security, SSI, Aid to Families with Dependent Children [AFDC], and veterans' benefits) and private transfers (child support, alimony, and gifts from relatives).
2. Net income is calculated by subtracting a standard deduction from a household's gross income. In addition to this standard deduction, households with labor earnings deduct 20 percent of those earnings from their gross income. Deductions are also taken for child care and care for disabled dependents, medical expenses, and excessive shelter expenses.
3. Examples of such costs include travel time to a food stamp office and time spent in the office, the burden of transporting children to the office or paying for child care services, and the direct costs of paying for transportation.
4. Another approach is to not purge income of these life-cycle age effects. To test the robustness of our results, we also considered this alternative approach. While the coefficients on our income volatility measures and their interactions with age did change under this alternative approach, the combined effects were very similar to the combined effects in the preferred model. Results are available from the authors upon request.
5. For example, Hausman and Taylor (1981) assume that age in an earnings regression is not correlated with the latent heterogeneity but that education is correlated.

References

Bartfeld, Judi. 2003. "Single Mothers, Emergency Food Assistance, and Food Stamps in the Welfare Reform Era." *Journal of Consumer Affairs* 37(2): 283–304.

Bhattarai, Gandhi Raj, Patricia A. Duffy, and Jennie Raymond. 2005. "Use of Food Pantries and Food Stamps in Low-Income Households in the United States." *Journal of Consumer Affairs* 39(2): 276–298.

Blundell, Richard, and Thomas Macurdy. 1999. "Labor Supply: A Review of Alternative Approaches." In *Handbook of Labor Economics,* Orley C.

Ashenfelter and David Card, eds. Vol. 3A. Amsterdam: Elsevier, pp. 1559–1695.

Blundell, Richard, and Luigi Pistaferri. 2003. "Income Volatility and Household Consumption: The Impact of Food Assistance Programs." *Journal of Human Resources* 38(Supplement): 1032–1050.

Bollinger, Christopher R., and Martin H. David. 1997. "Modeling Discrete Choice with Response Error: Food Stamp Participation." *Journal of the American Statistical Association* 92(439): 827–835.

———. 2001. "Estimation with Response Error and Nonresponse: Food-Stamp Participation in the SIPP." *Journal of Business and Economic Statistics* 19(2): 129–141.

———. 2005. "I Didn't Tell, and I Won't Tell: Dynamic Response Error in the SIPP." *Journal of Applied Econometrics* 20(4): 563–569.

Chamberlain, Gary. 1980. "Analysis of Covariance with Qualitative Data." *Review of Economics and Statistics* 47(1): 225–238.

Cunnyngham, Karen. 2003. *Trends in Food Stamp Program Participation Rates: 1999 to 2001.* Alexandria, VA: U.S. Department of Agriculture (USDA), Food and Nutrition Service.

Daponte, Beth Osborne, Seth Sanders, and Lowell Taylor. 1999. "Why Do Low-Income Households *Not* Use Food Stamps? Evidence from an Experiment." *Journal of Human Resources* 34(3): 612–628.

Dynarski, Susan, and Jonathan Gruber. 1997. "Can Families Smooth Variable Earnings?" *Brookings Papers on Economic Activity* 1(1997): 229–284.

Gottschalk, Peter, and Robert Moffitt. 1994. "The Growth of Earnings Instability in the U.S. Labor Market." *Brookings Papers on Economic Activity* 25(2): 217–254.

Gundersen, Craig, and Brent Kreider. 2008. "Food Stamps and Food Insecurity: What Can Be Learned in the Presence of Nonclassical Measurement Error?" *Journal of Human Resources* 43(2): 352–382.

Gundersen, Craig, and Victor Oliveira. 2001. "The Food Stamp Program and Food Insufficiency." *American Journal of Agricultural Economics* 83(4): 875–887.

Gundersen, Craig, and James P. Ziliak. 2003. "The Role of Food Stamps in Consumption Stabilization." *Journal of Human Resources* 38(Supplement): 1051–1079.

Hagstrom, Paul A. 1996. "The Food Stamp Participation and Labor Supply of Married Couples: An Empirical Analysis of Joint Decisions." *Journal of Human Resources* 31(2): 383–403.

Haider, Steven J. 2001. "Earnings Instability and Earnings Inequality of Males in the United States: 1967–1991." *Journal of Labor Economics* 19(4): 799–836.

Haider, Steven J., Alison Jacknowitz, and Robert F. Schoeni. 2003. "Food Stamps and the Elderly: Why Is Participation So Low?" *Journal of Human Resources* 38(Supplement): 1080–1111.

Hausman, Jerry A., and William E. Taylor. 1981. "Panel Data and Unobservable Individual Effects." *Econometrica* 49(6): 1377–1398.

Heckman, James, and Richard Robb. 1985. "Using Longitudinal Data to Estimate Age, Period, and Cohort Effects in Earnings Equations." In *Cohort Analysis in Social Research: Beyond the Identification Problem*, William M. Mason and Stephen E. Fienberg, eds. New York: Springer-Verlag, pp. 137–150.

Kabbani, Nader S., and Parke E. Wilde. 2003. "Short Recertification Periods in the U.S. Food Stamp Program." *Journal of Human Resources* 38(Supplement): 1112–1138.

Marquis, Kent H., and Jeffrey C. Moore. 1990. "Measurement Errors in SIPP Program Reports." In *Proceedings of the Bureau of the Census, Sixth Annual Research Conference*. Washington, DC: U.S. Census Bureau, pp. 721–745.

Moffitt, Robert. 1983. "An Economic Model of Welfare Stigma." *American Economic Review* 73(5): 1023–1035.

Wallace, Geoffrey, and Rebecca M. Blank. 1999. "What Goes Up Must Come Down? Explaining Recent Changes in Public Assistance Caseloads." In *Economic Conditions and Welfare Reform*, Sheldon H. Danziger, ed. Kalamazoo, MI: W.E. Upjohn Institute for Employment Research, pp. 49–89.

Wolkwitz, Kari. 2007. *Trends in Food Stamp Program Participation Rates: 1999 to 2005*. Alexandria, VA: U.S. Department of Agriculture (USDA), Food and Nutrition Service.

Ziliak, James P., Craig Gundersen, and David N. Figlio. 2003. "Food Stamp Caseloads over the Business Cycle." *Southern Economic Journal* 69(4): 903–919.

Part 4

Design of Food Assistance Programs

8
Design of Assistance Programs to Address Real Income Volatility

Robin Boadway
Queen's University

Katherine Cuff
McMaster University

Nicolas Marceau
Université du Québec à Montréal

Over the past two decades, changes in income volatility and its sources have received increasing attention (Blundell, Pistaferri, and Preston 2004; Gottschalk and Moffit 1994; Haider 2001). Increases in income volatility raise issues of public concern. What impact will greater volatility have on household consumption and welfare? More specifically, how does a change in volatility affect recipients of government assistance? Obviously the answer will depend in part on the source of the volatility. It could be due to exogenous shocks or household decisions. Furthermore, the design of assistance programs will help determine the impact of income volatility on assistance recipients. This raises the question of how assistance programs should be designed when potential recipients face income instability? Determining the principles involved in designing assistance programs for low-income persons when their income and needs are volatile is the focus of this chapter.[1]

Many of the issues that arise in designing assistance programs when income is stable also apply when it is volatile. Welfare and social insurance programs are typically targeted on the basis of some measures of need, such as income, assets, employment, and family circumstances. Standard approaches to program design stress both the normative issues involved in defining need and eligibility and the administrative issues involved in implementing the eligibility criteria and delivering and distributing cash or goods. Implementation must deal with asymmetric information problems, which preclude program administrators from achieving perfect targeting. This leads to both Type I and Type II errors, resulting in (for Type I) less than full coverage of the target population and (for Type II) leakage of funds from the program. Undercoverage may also occur because eligible persons are ill-informed about their entitlements or because of the stigmatization associated with receiving welfare. Information problems include hidden actions that make it difficult to screen out ineligible persons. Households may change their behavior to become eligible or may fail to take actions that are required for eligibility, such as engaging in a job search or reapplying for benefits. Moreover, informational asymmetries enjoyed by administrators may lead to agency problems and consequently imperfect targeting of assistance. For example, only administrators may be able to observe the characteristics of welfare applicants, and if they have different preferences than the government regarding which individuals should receive assistance then there could be undercoverage of the target population. Agency problems may also arise if the effort to classify welfare applicants is costly for administrators and unobservable by the government. Again in this case, administrators may incorrectly (from the point of view of the government) classify welfare applicants.

These standard problems of welfare program design are exacerbated when the need for assistance is volatile and low-income households are unable to insure fully against the volatility. The possibility of unexpected changes in circumstances makes the eligibility requirements for assistance—including the targeting of benefits, the frequency of certification, the reporting mechanisms, and the timeliness of support—very important. An ideal program would react quickly and accurately to persons unexpectedly moving from noneligibility to eligibility, while avoiding adverse incentive effects. It would also respond quickly to those whose circumstances change in the opposite direction, though presumably with less urgency.

SOURCES OF REAL INCOME VOLATILITY

Complexity in designing low-income support programs to address volatility arises mainly because volatility comes from a variety of sources. Some of these will be exogenous and beyond individual control. Others will be in part a consequence of individual actions.

Exogenous Sources of Volatility

The most obvious exogenous shock that employable low-income persons might face is a change in employment income. For example, an individual might be laid off or incur a workplace injury. Real income shocks can also occur from changes in the various prices facing low-income households. They might also be the result of a partially or completely uninsured adverse event. An individual may suffer from a change in health status, either temporary or permanent, that entails sudden medical expenses and often a loss of employment income. A supporting person may suffer a similar fate, which also may affect the individual. The individual may also face a loss of community support because of a shock to the local community, such as the closure of an industry or a natural disaster. Some of these shocks can be either anticipated or observed. For others, detecting the changed circumstances of affected persons may take time, and even then may be subject to some errors in observation. That constitutes a significant problem for program design.

Volatility Resulting from Individual Choice

Changes in real income might be the result of personal decisions affecting the low-income individual's employment status, living circumstances, consumption, or social capital. Changes in employment income might be in part a result of individual behavior. Workers might lose their jobs for cause, or they might voluntarily quit or reduce their hours of work. Their income can also change if they engage in nonmarket or underground activities, either to supplement or to substitute for formal work.

Real income changes can also occur if low-income individuals change their living circumstances. They may decide to cohabitate or to terminate cohabitation, or to change the size of their family. Their economic well-being can also change because of consumption choices. If they overspend by borrowing, the subsequent financing of the debt may leave insufficient resources for other needs and may even force them into personal bankruptcy. Similarly, they may commit themselves to housing costs that exceed their means and that are hard to escape in the short run because of contractual obligations. Their personal behavior may even result in eviction from existing housing.

Finally, they may suffer a loss in social capital because of personal decisions. If they choose to move to a different city or neighborhood, they lose their network of friends and other social support mechanisms, at least temporarily. There is also the loss of social capital for those who have been incarcerated after being convicted of committing a crime.

The government may prefer to address the consequences of adversity arising from voluntary choices differently from those arising exogenously. However, distinguishing the two may be difficult.

Labor Market Rigidities as a Source of Uncertainty

If low-income individuals could immediately find suitable work after either a voluntary or an involuntary leave from employment, then changes in employment income as a source of income volatility would greatly be reduced. Rigidities in the labor market, however, generally prevent this from happening, so even those looking for work may remain unemployed for an uncertain length of time.

Involuntary unemployment can arise from various sources. Firms may find it in their interest to offer an efficiency wage, which will generally be larger than the market-clearing wage. Structural unemployment can also arise when a portion of the labor market is unionized or when there is economic restructuring or outsourcing. Labor market rigidities induced by the government (such as a binding minimum wage and unemployment insurance) may also be a source of involuntary unemployment. There will also generally be some frictional unemployment because of business cycles and job searches.

The labor market may also entail indivisibilities that make it more difficult for some individuals to enter or remain attached to it. For various technological and coordination reasons, many jobs require a minimum number of work hours, and this may not suit low-income individuals with other demands on their time (Saez 2002). Low hourly wage jobs may not be attractive because they do not offer long enough hours to be worth taking. Time spent on household production may be more valuable than earning a low wage in the market. Indivisibilities as a source of unemployment may be viewed as involuntary or voluntary depending on the circumstances.

RESPONSES TO REAL INCOME VOLATILITY

Individual responses to volatility depend upon both market options and support programs available from government and nongovernment sources.

Individual Responses to Volatility

Suppose that low-income individuals are subject to an unexpected negative shock to their real income. Some of this may be offset by previously acquired market insurance or by government support programs. It is likely, though, that some residual consequences will remain. Thus, unemployment insurance does not fully replace lost income: individuals cannot insure against shocks in their cost of living, insurance against many forms of accident are available only with a deductible or coinsurance, and so on. Government support programs will also leave individuals to bear part of the shock. Because the government cannot perfectly observe either the actions of affected individuals or the source of the shock, it will not offer full insurance. By the same token, government support programs will not respond instantaneously. It will take time for the changed circumstances of potential recipients to be registered and verified. At the very least, individuals will need to respond temporarily to real income shocks. The following list summarizes six ways in which low-income persons might respond to such shocks.

1.   They might deplete their assets—including financial assets, housing and other consumer durables, and valuable objects. If

in debt, they may not be able to make interest payments and may even declare personal bankruptcy.

2.   The composition of consumption expenditures might change. They may spend a higher proportion of their incomes on basic necessities, such as food and shelter, while forgoing less necessary items, such as new clothing and entertainment.

3.   To obtain cash quickly, they might resort to high-cost sources of borrowing, such as credit cards, cash marts, loan sharks, pawn shops, and personal acquaintances.

4.   They may change the number of hours worked, seeking part-time work or changing jobs. Other family members, including children, might enter the workforce. They may obtain some earnings through self-employment or odd jobs. In extreme cases, they may participate in the underground economy or engage in illegal activities.

5.   They may take advantage of sources of outside support (nongovernmental). This can include members of their extended family or charities (food banks, secondhand clothing shops, public shelters, etc.).

6.   Finally, they may be forced to move from their neighborhood or city and reestablish themselves elsewhere, losing social networks that they have built up.

These actions obviously have potentially serious consequences, but some caveats should be mentioned. First, some low-income persons facing income shocks will have taken precautionary measures, especially if their circumstances were uncertain ex ante. Others will have social support networks to help them through.

Second, these individuals may be responsible to varying degrees for their plight. The temporary shocks they face may be a consequence of their own actions. They may have overextended themselves financially or undersaved, committed themselves to expensive housing, or taken actions that brought about their own loss of income.

Third, the consequences of adverse income shocks may depend upon the preferences and circumstances of households. Persons who are more risk-averse or living close to subsistence levels will feel more urgently the need to compensate for the effect the shock has had on their consumption. They will try to smooth their consumption, despite the costs. The consequence, as Chetty and Looney (2006) have pointed out, is that observations of relatively smooth consumption streams do not necessarily indicate that social insurance programs are of no value. On the contrary, if persons are highly risk-averse, social insurance will be valuable to them even if their consumption streams are relatively smooth in its absence. With social insurance, they will no longer have to rely on costly and inefficient mechanisms to insure themselves against income shocks. These caveats make the problem of government policy more complicated, both from the point of view of being able to obtain the relevant information on individuals and from the point of view of deciding on who deserves support.

Market and Policy Failures May Preclude Full Self-Protection

Informational problems affecting insurance markets make it difficult for the market to properly assist households in protecting themselves against income uncertainty. First, moral hazard—the difficulty of observing the actions of insurees—implies that competitive insurers would not break even if they offered actuarially fair insurance contracts. For that reason, insurers will require coinsurance from buyers who, by definition, will be left with incomplete insurance. Second, adverse selection—the difficulty of observing the risk characteristics of the insurees—will give an incentive to insurers to screen insurees by offering them a menu of contracts. In one standard case, insurees who are a good risk will be offered less than full insurance to prevent bad risks from purchasing the contract destined for those insurees that represent a good risk. In the most severe case of adverse selection, insurance contracts will simply not be offered (Rothschild and Stiglitz 1976).

Informational problems also affect credit markets. Because of moral hazard, lenders may be reluctant to finance some projects and may require cofinancing from the borrowers. Obviously, for households who need to borrow quickly because of an adverse income shock, and who can only offer, as a guarantee of repayment, that they will, say, find a new job, this may mean that they will simply be unable to borrow. As for adverse selection, creditors may be unable to distinguish loans by the quality of borrowers and the chances that the loan will be repaid. This can cause higher interest rates for all individuals who want to borrow (Stiglitz and Weiss 1981). It may also imply that individuals with some characteristics will simply be unable to borrow because they are deemed to be too risky on average (Mankiw 1986). For these reasons, some individuals will be shut out of the credit markets. Usually the most vulnerable are those most likely to be shut out.[2]

The design of low-income support programs can also inadvertently preclude self-insurance. Often a condition for qualifying for support programs is that an individual cannot own more than a given amount of assets (Currie 2006). Such a restriction is equivalent to forbidding precautionary savings above some level, and it obliges recipients to find more costly ways to respond to risk.[3] Stores in poor neighborhoods may exploit the timing of support payments by increasing prices to extract as much surplus as possible from welfare recipients (Tanguay, Hunt, and Marceau 2005). Welfare recipients may circumvent that by storing some items, but for perishable products that is infeasible. Finally, the possibility of government support may induce risky behavior in instances where the government cannot commit to not helping out those in need; thus the government faces the Samaritan's dilemma (Bruce and Waldman 1991). If individuals understand that governments cannot resist providing help to those in need, some might reason that there is no need to save since they will nevertheless be offered welfare assistance (Ziliak 2003).

Limited Ability to Self-Insure

Even when risks can be insured, low-income households may not have the financial resources to purchase insurance. The more comprehensive an insurance contract is, the more costly it should be to purchase. The relative demand for insurance is likely to be greater for low-income than for high-income persons. Ihori and McGuire (2006) show that if preferences exhibit decreasing absolute risk aversion, which is the usual assumption, insurance will be an inferior good. Low-income households will therefore be especially affected by the costliness of insurance. For some types of insurable events, such as theft, low-income persons may face higher premiums because of living in riskier areas, or they may not own enough valuables to make the purchase of insurance worthwhile. The form of available insurance contracts may also preclude its purchase by low-income individuals. For example, individuals without access to the formal credit market will only have cash to pay for insurance, a payment option that might not be acceptable.

Low-income individuals are also less likely to be covered by employer-sponsored insurance. This may be because they choose not to participate in an employer-sponsored insurance system, possibly because of cost or because their employer does not offer it. If skilled workers are relatively scarce in the market and workers value insurance, then firms may offer them relatively more attractive compensation packages than those offered to unskilled workers. By offering group insurance, employers can pool the risk of all of their workers and thereby face lower insurance cost per insured person than what the individual would pay on his or her own. Employer-sponsored insurance contracts may also be longer-term than those offered to individuals. Indeed, the short-term nature of individual health insurance contracts is often cited as a major source of market failure in health insurance (Cutler 2002). In addition, employer payments for health insurance often receive preferential tax treatment. Finally, such in-kind compensation could also help bind workers to firms. The potential profitability of offering in-kind compensation in lieu of wages is more likely to occur at firms employing high-wage workers, since firms employing minimum-wage workers are restricted from reducing wages. The end result is that skilled (high-income) workers may be better protected against adverse events.

Even if low-income persons have equal access to self-insurance, it might be more costly for low-income persons to self-insure than high-income ones. First, if the marginal utility of income is decreasing, then to set a given fraction of one's income aside for the eventuality of bad luck is more costly for low-income than for high-income individuals. Second, there are transaction costs in financial markets, a portion of which are fixed costs, so transacting is relatively more expensive for those who own fewer assets. Diversifying risk using financial markets is more costly for low-income individuals because they tend to own fewer assets. Third, and related to the above discussion, it may be that risk aversion is decreasing in income. Finally, assuming an individual's network is made up of similar individuals, low-income individuals will have more difficulty borrowing from family and friends than high-income ones, because the former have less discretionary income, and therefore savings, available to lend to others.

Supply-Side Responses to Circumvent Market Failures

Because low-income individuals tend to be less educated, and because of the complexity of some government insurance and assistance programs, some private companies provide services to help potentially eligible individuals access government programs. Generally these private companies will charge the individuals for their services and thereby reduce the net assistance received by those using them.

Many alternative sources of credit for low-income persons outside of the formal credit market have also developed. Some of these are legal, such as pawn shops or cash-in-advance stores, while others are illegal. At pawn shops, individuals may leave some collateral good at the store in exchange for credit. If the loan is repaid within a certain period, the individual regains possession of the collateral good. Otherwise, the collateral good remains the possession of the store, which may sell it to other customers. Cash-in-advance stores or cash marts offer individuals advances on their pay at some fixed cost or may cash checks immediately at a fee. Pawn shops and cash-in-advance stores constitute a costly source of finance for low-income persons because of the high default rates and the associated loss of collateral goods or high service fees. In some cases, innovative institutional mechanisms have evolved to help address the failure of standard credit markets. For example, cooperative savings arrangements that provide microcredit to participants might alleviate some of the liquidity constraints faced by low-income households. Illegal credit obtained from loan sharks, gambling schemes, and the fencing of stolen goods constitutes another costly source of credit for low-income individuals. But because these are often the sole sources of finance available for such persons, they continue to exist. In addition to being costly, they can put users at personal risk of going to jail or suffering bodily harm.

Low-income households facing an adverse income shock may not be able to afford products in the formal or regulated sector and may turn to the informal sector. They might live in dwellings not up to building codes, use unlicensed repair persons, or leave their children in unlicensed home day-cares. Consumption of these unregulated services may put the individuals and their families at risk for injury or other health problems. These households may also be tempted to work in the black market. This is risky since they might be detected by the authorities, resulting not only in termination of the employment relationship but also in the possibility of criminal punishment. Furthermore, employees in the black market have no insurance coverage, be it public or private, and no recourse against their employer in the event of a conflict.

Finally, private charities have developed to assist those in need who have no insurance or access to credit, and for whom government help is insufficient. Then there are some individuals who simply refuse government assistance. For all of these cases, charities offer a wide range of programs and services. Some, such as food banks, shelters, and community outreach programs, provide services specifically for individuals with immediate needs. Charities might also offer services to help individuals gain access to government resources as well as help provide medical services to uninsured individuals and legal services for low-income persons. While these charities provide useful assistance, those who use them have no guarantee they will obtain help in the future. Because of the discretion of private charities in the way they distribute aid and uncertainty about their ongoing budgets, low-income individuals using them face the risk of eventually being without help (Allard, forthcoming). This is a significant risk and may explain why public assistance is far more developed than private charities.

GOVERNMENT OBJECTIVES

The design of support programs depends on the government's objectives. From a normative perspective, there are many possible objectives for low-income support programs. Policy intervention could be motivated by equity, social insurance, equality of opportunity, or paternalism. Each of these might prescribe a different type of program.

Welfaristic Objectives

The standard analysis of redistribution supposes that governments judge policy outcomes according to how they affect the welfare of individuals in the economy. A major issue, then, is how to aggregate individual welfare levels into a social ordering. Conceptually, there are two approaches to addressing this issue. One is to suppose that redistribution to the poor is motivated by the altruism of the nonpoor (Hochman and Rodgers 1969). According to this view, redistribution can be efficiency-enhancing, but because of a free-riding problem associated with altruistic transfers to the poor, the government must step in on behalf of the nonpoor. This altruism approach essentially sidesteps normative issues of equity by putting all the weight on the preferences of the nonpoor.

An alternative approach is to suppose that there is a social welfare function that aggregates the utilities of all persons in the economy based on some ethical precepts. The problem is that it is not clear how such a social welfare function is agreed upon. A common approach is to suppose that persons will have social preferences that are distinct from their individual preferences based on self-interest (Arrow 1951). They might, for example, imagine themselves before they learn the characteristics that they will be endowed with—that is, behind the "veil of ignorance" (Rawls 1971). Even here, there is unlikely to be full agreement on the social welfare function, given that it embodies important value judgments about the measurement and aggregation of individual utilities. Nonetheless, the social welfare function approach is useful as a methodological device since it allows one to consider the consequences of various initial value judgments.

A useful way to proceed is to consider a social welfare function exhibiting constant aversion to inequality in individual real incomes. Formally, it may be written as

$$W(y_1, y_2, \ldots, y_n) = \sum_{i=1}^{n} \frac{y_i^{1-\rho}}{1-\rho} \; ,$$

where y_i is the real income of household i with $i = 1, \cdots, n$. The advantage of using this function is that it captures the weight put on equity in the economy in a single parameter, ρ.[4] Assuming that the aversion to inequality is nonnegative, ρ can take values between zero (the utilitarian case) and infinity (the maximin or Rawlsian case). The greater the aversion to inequality, the more redistribution will be called for in the sense that the more equal will be the final outcomes.

The single-parameter social welfare function approach seems reasonable when households vary according to only one characteristic, but difficult issues arise in more general settings. If households have different preferences, comparing welfare across households becomes conceptually problematic. There is no well-defined comparable measure of real income across households when individual preference orderings are heterogeneous. How then should welfare comparisons be made among persons with different preferences? One approach, following Roemer (1998) and Fleurbaey and Maniquet (forthcoming), is to argue that circumstances that are the consequence of personal choice should not affect redistribution; only differences in well-being that result from exogenous characteristics over which households have no influence should. Thus, if preferences are regarded as a matter of personal choice—and that is not entirely obvious—they are the responsibility of individuals and should not affect redistribution. Redistribution should only compensate persons for things over which they have no control, such as their innate ability. Applying these principles of compensation and responsibility in practice is not easy, although some attempts have been made (Roemer 1998). In a world with full information and lump-sum taxes, it is impossible to satisfy both principles simultaneously. Without full information, matters are even more problematic because it is difficult to tell whether low income is due to a preference for leisure or to low innate ability. This will be important for low-income support programs since there are many dimensions along which both preferences and characteristics may differ.

Difficulties also arise when persons have more than one characteristic. For one thing, multidimensional screening problems can occur if households differ by two or more characteristics, such as productivity and riskiness, and this makes program design difficult (Besley and Coate 1995). For another, policy prescriptions can become unclear when persons differ in ways other than productivity.[5]

Nonwelfaristic Objectives

The social welfare function approach ranks social outcomes solely according to how they affect individual utilities. Policymakers may also attach weight to objectives that do not reflect individual preferences (Sen 1970). Indeed, altruistic approaches may also take account of nonwelfare consequences of policies. There are several examples of this that are relevant for considering low-income support programs. One widespread objective is equality of opportunity. Equality of opportunity can be taken to mean many things, but broadly it refers to the idea of persons being put on an equal footing with respect to their options to participate in society. Thus, equality of opportunity can include resources devoted to improving the skills of low-income persons, or more generally the assets they require to prosper in the market (Sen 1999). It can also involve improving their physical or mental fitness. Equality of opportunity can be seen as a form of ex ante redistribution as opposed to equalizing ex post market outcomes through the tax transfer system.

Another nonwelfaristic objective is poverty alleviation, where the objective may be to remove as many people as possible from below some poverty line in consumption or income (Kanbur, Keen, and Tuomala 1995). Since poverty alleviation typically ignores the value of leisure to those in poverty, it is nonwelfaristic.

There may be other nonwelfaristic objectives taken into account by policymakers, such as social cohesion, crime reduction, various freedoms, nondiscrimination, the fostering of family and social values, and so on. In the literature on redistribution, fairness or absence of envy has been investigated as a property of redistribution programs (Nishimura 2003). As well, the sanctity of property rights has been emphasized by some, either as an objective or as a constraint on redistribution (Nozick 1974).

The government might also be concerned with the cost of a given assistance program, program take-up, the social stigma associated with the program, and how the program will affect the assistance that recipients receive from private sources. It may put more weight on Type I errors (incomplete coverage of the target population) than on Type II errors (leakages to the nondeserving). Targeting programs to a subset of the population may be less costly since assistance is only given to a group of individuals. On the other hand, obtaining the information needed to identify the target group might make the program more costly. Targeted programs might also generate greater stigma since only some individuals are receiving assistance (Atkinson 1995). Such design issues are discussed further below.

Paternalistic Objectives

Finally, governments may take a quasiwelfaristic approach in the sense of giving weight to the well-being of persons yet evaluating that well-being not according to the preferences revealed by individuals themselves but according to preferences chosen by the government.

These paternalistic preferences may be justified from an altruistic perspective as reflecting the weights that the nonpoor put on the consumption patterns of the poor. Thus, nonpoor taxpayers may put relatively high weight on the consumption of some products, such as food, shelter, and clothing, and relatively low weight on others, such as alcohol, cigarettes, and even leisure. While this paternalistic approach to redistribution may offend those who adopt a normative perspective, it is a consequence of the altruistic view of redistribution.

Paternalism may also emerge in an otherwise welfaristic framework if one adopts recent findings from the behavioral economics literature. That literature has stressed various ways in which individual behavior does not conform to the rational, well-informed, farsighted, self-interested view of standard economic theory (Bernheim and Rangel 2007; Rabin 1998). Of particular relevance for redistribution is the suggestion that persons may sometimes take decisions that are not in their own self-interest. This may reflect bounded rationality, whereby they do not understand fully the options available to them. For example, many people do not understand the various types of financial instruments or the risks associated with the choices they have to make. Some government policies seem to be influenced by these shortcomings in consumer knowledge and perceptions, such as rules governing the disclosure of product information, regulations on interest rates that can be charged on credit card debt, safety regulations, seat belt rules, and even mandatory savings in managed financial accounts.

As well, households may exhibit shortsightedness and impatience in various contexts. This has been modeled using the concept of time-inconsistent intertemporal preferences (Laibson 1997; Strotz 1956). The idea, based on experimental research, is that persons systematically discount the next period's consumption relative to consumption today at a higher rate than consumption between two periods in the future. As time goes on, this bias in favor of today's consumption persists so that, effectively, preferences change over time. This leads to a tendency to overconsume (undersave) in the sense that if households could choose at some time before t their consumption stream for periods t onwards, they would consume less at time t and more later on. This kind of impatience can have other consequences than simply undersaving. It might cause persons to discount future adverse consequences of current behavior, leading to problems of addiction, risky behavior, procrastination, obesity, lack of exercise, underexertion in education, and perhaps even criminal behavior. Given that people typically come to regret the shortsighted decisions that they have taken, there may be grounds for government policies to offset these tendencies by regulation, in-kind transfers, or taxation and subsidization. One might expect the incidence of impatience to be higher among low-income persons, if only because the actions themselves tend to reduce income-generating activities.

The argument for government intervention in the face of impatience in individual behavior is controversial. Some might object to government paternalism on principle and argue that people ought to bear the consequences of their own actions. Others might argue that the findings of behavioral economics have yet to be established with sufficient certainty. A further line of argument is that people should be able to recognize that their preferences lead to time-inconsistent behavior. These relatively more sophisticated persons should be able to take actions that precommit themselves to avoiding the full consequences that happen to those who are simply myopic. However, even these farsighted persons are not likely to overcome the problem completely.

GOVERNMENT CONSTRAINTS

One source of complexity in designing support programs to address real income volatility of low-income households is the enormous heterogeneity of potential recipients. In a first-best world (i.e., one in which the government has full information and access to any policy instrument), the government could perfectly insure low-income individuals against real income volatility. This first-best outcome is not attainable when individual characteristics and circumstances are not perfectly observable by the government.

Characteristics of Potential Recipients

We begin with a consideration of three key classes of characteristics that can vary widely among persons, can contribute to low-income status, and can involve private information: individual preferences, endowed personal characteristics, and attachment to the labor market.

Individual preferences

Dealing with differences in preferences poses challenging policy problems that only recently have come to the fore in the public economics literature, as discussed above. The following are some important sources of preference heterogeneity.

Preferences for leisure. Individuals may differ in their preferences for leisure or, more generally, in their willingness to provide work effort that will affect their real incomes. Apart from the difficulties that differences in preferences for leisure pose for welfare comparisons, the government will have difficulty in distinguishing recipients on the basis of their preferences for leisure. The consequence of such differences will be observationally equivalent to differences in the ability to earn income if the government cannot observe ability either (Cuff 2000; Boadway et al. 2002).

Preferences for goods. Individuals may also differ in their preferences for various goods. They may devote differing proportions of their income to cigarettes, alcohol, and gambling, as well as to expensive cars, large houses and other consumer durables. This will have consequences for the design of support programs to the extent that they involve in-kind transfers. It can also affect cash transfer programs—for example, if there are limits to asset ownership in the welfare system. And, it may also have implications for dealing with real income volatility, such as would be the case if some persons have incurred contractual obligations for consumer durable purchases. Another important issue is the preference for immediate over future consumption. Those who want to consume heavily when young, when their wages are low, tend to have low income in the future because they are less willing to forgo income in order to invest in schooling. On the contrary, those who are willing to accept a low consumption level when young—or who are simply more patient—will invest in schooling and earn a higher income when old. These choices affect both the number of income support recipients and the way that support should be financed.

Risk aversion. The extent to which a person has risk aversion is particularly important in an environment of real income volatility. It affects both the costs of risk associated with volatility as well as the incentives to take measures to deal with it (Chetty and Looney 2006). Moreover, differences in degrees of risk aversion will affect the extent to which an individual is willing to engage in risky activities and thus be exposed to real income volatility.

Propensity to commit crime. Criminal behavior can be both a source and a consequence of adverse personal outcomes, and persons might be tempted into criminal behavior with varying propensities, an assumption often found in the literature on law and economics (Becker 1968). While there are no doubt various underlying causes for persons to have different propensities to engage in criminal behavior, for our purposes we can take these propensities as exogenous and imperfectly observable to the government. Criminal behavior itself can take a wide number of forms, including tax evasion, working in the underground economy, fraud with respect to support programs, dealing in illegal substances, property crime, and crime against persons. The potential interdependence of criminal behavior and income volatility is an important consideration in designing support programs.

Propensity to exploit support programs. Persons might also differ in their willingness to change their behavior simply to take advantage of government support programs, even if such behavior is not, strictly speaking, illegal. The analogue would be with tax avoidance as a way of reducing one's tax burden or reducing work effort to qualify for training programs (Ashenfelter 1978). The design of most government programs relies to a degree on the willingness of persons to comply voluntarily with the programs' purposes and requirements. The possibility that households will exploit programs by not acting in good faith affects both the generosity of programs and the need to build in detection and enforcement mechanisms to preclude access by those for whom the programs are not intended.

Problems of self-control. As mentioned, recent work in behavioral economics has stressed that persons may systematically overdiscount future outcomes and behave in a myopic way, and that they subsequently may regret their choices (Bernheim and Rangel 2007; Rabin 1998). They may overspend in the aggregate and on particular goods, adopt an unhealthy lifestyle, and make choices that can lead to future addictions (e.g., to nicotine, alcohol, gambling, or drugs). The intensity of this type of self-control problem can vary across persons and will not be observable to the government, although some of the consequences will be.

Stigmatization. Support programs may depend on voluntary take-up by targeted recipients. To the extent that targeting engenders a feeling of stigma by recipients or causes other members of the population to stigmatize program recipients, the effectiveness of the program in reaching the target population may be limited (Atkinson 1995; Jacquet and Van der Linden 2006). Feelings of stigmatization likely vary in intensity among different persons.

Beliefs in the source of success. Finally, some recent literature theorizing about the source of differences in the generosity of social protection among countries, and especially between the United States and other countries in the Organisation for Economic Co-operation and Development (OECD), has suggested that persons may hold differing beliefs about the relative importance of hard work versus luck in generating personal success (Bénabou and Tirole 2006). Those who believe luck is more important than effort may put in less effort and the consequences will be self-enforcing. It is difficult to know the extent to which such beliefs are motivating factors. If policymakers themselves believe that effort is a more important determinant of success, they may offer less generous redistribution programs.

Personal characteristics

The standard literature on redistribution has long emphasized endowed characteristics as the main determinants of differences in well-being. It has focused especially on those characteristics that were correlated with earning power (Mirrlees 1971). However, the scope of relevant characteristics can be broader than that, especially for lower-income persons. The following summarizes some of the more important exogenous characteristics affecting individual welfare.

Skills. Household skills may be innate, as in the traditional approach, or may be acquired through experience, training, or human capital investment. Skill differences may result in different wage rates, but they may also reflect differences in employability (Parsons 1996). Skills can be very different in type. They can be general or specific skills. They can include communication skills, multitasking skills, intellectual skills, or physical skills. In the extreme, persons may be unemployable because of very low skills or because of a disability. Moreover, households may have acquired skills that are obsolete or inappropriate for the jobs that are available. These variations in personal skills have implications for the types of policy instruments used in support programs.

Needs. Individuals may differ in their ability to obtain utility from income and therefore will have different income needs to obtain the same level of well-being (Boadway and Pestieau 2006; Rowe and Woolley 1999). These differences can reflect their permanent physical condition or their current health status, leading to disability expenses on the one hand and medical expenses on the other. Differences in the need for income can also reflect their living circumstances, such as whether they live alone or cohabitate, or whether they have dependents to support. Some of these personal characteristics will be exogenous; others are a matter of choice. Many of them will be observable to the government, as will changes in them. Support programs will generally try to address the volatility in such needs. Of course, in some cases, the government may not be able to fully compensate individuals for whatever their expenditure needs are, even if the needs could be observed.

Risk of illness. Individuals may differ systematically in their risk of becoming ill. Not only will high-risk persons face a greater chance of suffering an adverse shock to their well-being, but they may find it more difficult to get insured, depending on whether insurance companies can observe their risk class (Boadway et al. 2006). Illness is one source of volatility in real incomes, and government intervention may involve either cash support or the provision of health care.

Assets. At any given time, households may vary in the assets that they acquired in the past or inherited, including financial assets, real property, and Social Security wealth. They may even be in a negative asset position, having acquired debt that has not been repaid. Moreover, their credit rating may have been adversely affected by past financial problems. The ownership of assets, including durable goods such as automobiles, typically plays a role in eligibility for income support programs. For example, to qualify for assistance under TANF the value of a household's countable assets, including savings and possibly some portion of the value of its automobile, must fall below a certain level. Such asset limits clearly restrict the asset holdings of recipient households and prevent them from saving. Along with these traditional forms of asset wealth, individuals may have access to varying degrees of social capital, including extended families or support networks of different sizes that may be drawn on in times of need (Putnam 2000).[6] Such social capital could also influence individuals' decisions about education, occupation, and other long-term decisions affecting their earning ability and ultimately their potential need for support programs. For example, a person is more likely to be on welfare if his or her parents were on welfare, thus creating a dependency cycle. Or, that person may drop out of school because that is what friends or role models are doing (Akerlof 1997).

Labor market attachment

Labor income is an important source of volatility for some low-income persons. Its relevance depends on the extent to which individuals are attached to the labor market, and that can vary from person to person in a number of dimensions.

Employables with some labor market attachment. Persons who are potentially employable—that is, who have some capability of working productively—can be in a variety of states of employment. Some may be employed full time, albeit in jobs with varying degrees of earnings and security. Others might be in part-time jobs, either by choice or by necessity. These jobs may also be more or less secure. Even these employed persons might be potential candidates for income support, depending on their personal circumstances. Some of them may not be working in the short term because of illness, injury, or family responsibilities such as parental leave or caring for an ill dependent. Employable persons might also be temporarily unemployed, having been laid off or being in the process of changing jobs. Their status may reflect the riskiness or seasonal nature of their jobs, or it may reflect an economy-wide shock. Other, less fortunate persons may be employable in principle, but nonetheless they are in long-term unemployment. Their skills may be too low for potential employers, given their location or the existence of rigidities like minimum wages. Or, they may be involuntarily unemployed because of efficiency wages or search inefficiencies. These are persons who are able to work but either cannot find jobs or are not actively seeking them because of discouragement or preference. Regardless of the employment status of these employables, they may also be engaged in nonmarket work or even black market work. Presumably, which of the above conditions employables are in will be affected by their innate characteristics, their education, and their health, as well as by their preference for leisure.

Unemployables. Some people may be deemed to be unemployable and therefore not able to hold a job. Unemployability may stem from disability or poor health or from a very low skill level. In fact, defining the status of unemployability is fraught with difficulty. The distinction between being employable and being unemployable is bound to be somewhat arbitrary. There may be a continuum of one or more of the above personal characteristics (e.g., health status, skills) along which there is some point at which persons are deemed to be unemployable. Not only is this cutoff arbitrary, but it will be not be perfectly observable to the government or to potential employers. Indeed, government agencies and private firms may have different ideas as to what this cutoff should be. Moreover, strictly speaking, almost all persons—including those who are mentally or physically disabled—could be employed doing some kind of work, even if fairly menial. However, their productivity may be such that the private sector would not hire them without the aid of a carrot or a stick.

Voluntarily out of the labor market. Finally, there are groups of people who choose not to enter the labor market. One such group is the retired, who have worked and now draw pension and capital incomes, and who may also draw support from family or charitable organizations. Even for these persons, withdrawal from the labor force may only be partial. Another group consists of persons who opt out of the labor market to be homemakers or to raise children. Finally, there are the young, who are in school or college.

The informational problems regarding the individual's attachment to the labor market, his or her income, and other personal characteristics in designing low-income support programs can in part be addressed by different screening, auditing, and tagging mechanisms. As well, self-selection mechanisms can sometimes be devised that make it unattractive for some undeserving persons to apply. The lack of information regarding individual preferences and the type of uncertainty facing households is much more difficult to address.

Characteristics of Program Administrators

Another type of informational problem facing the government stems from the fact that someone has to administer the program, and the government might not have complete information about who is doing so. There may be agency problems. For example, if the effort to obtain information is costly for the social workers and unobservable by the government, then welfare applicants could be incorrectly classified (tagged) unless social workers are highly diligent. The government might then have to ensure that social workers put forth an appropriate level of effort by paying them according to results (Boadway, Marceau, and Sato 1999). It might also be the case that program workers have different objectives from the program designers. Since program workers often make decisions about the eligibility of recipients, those who end up being served by the program may differ from the group the program designers intended to target. These problems are very difficult to overcome. In the end, they may affect the extent to which discretion for program delivery is left in the hands of program administrators and how finely program benefits are targeted.

ASPECTS OF PROGRAM DESIGN

There are a variety of problems in designing support programs to address real income volatility. We summarize them in this section.

Who Deserves Support?

The target population, a subset of which will be deemed to deserve support, includes those whose real incomes have fallen and who are not otherwise taken care of by unemployment insurance, workers' compensation, disability insurance, or ordinary pensions. Nor are they able to self-insure through savings against uncertain circumstances—unlike, say, the self-employed in seasonal industries for whom reductions in income are expected, or maybe even those in risky industries whose earnings effectively compensate for the risk. For people in this situation, a difficult issue arises concerning the next-best remedy: it may be the case that persons who ought to be covered by contributory social insurance programs are not covered because of the deficiency of existing programs. The ideal remedy would be to revise those programs rather than use low-income support programs as a device for insuring against adverse outcomes. However, if such remedies are not forthcoming, presumably low-income support programs are the second-best instruments.

Even if the government could observe the actions and the characteristics of all households whose real incomes have fallen, the policy problem would not be straightforward. An issue arises as to whether policy ought to distinguish between deserving and undeserving persons, along the lines of the principles of compensation versus responsibility. The principle of compensation states that in achieving some social objective, individuals should be compensated for inequalities in personal characteristics, but only for those characteristics for which they are not responsible. Thus, deserving persons might be those whose fate is a consequence of exogenous factors over which they have no influence. Nondeserving persons might be those whose actions have caused them to be in a needy state. The distinction between deserving and nondeserving persons is not clear, even in the absence of imperfect information. Behavioral economics emphasizes that individuals might have self-control problems that lead to overspending, addictions, etc., and that they may regret the ex post outcomes that their earlier choices have caused. Should these persons be regarded as being responsible for their adverse states, or should self-control problems be regarded as part of one's exogenously given preferences? (Public health care systems typically do not distinguish between those whose personal behavior has led to bad health outcomes and those who lead exemplary lives.) What about persons who acquire spending obligations because they have changed their household characteristics, such as by having a baby or separating from a partner? Perhaps a more clear-cut case concerns persons whose incomes fall because of their own premeditated choices: they quit their jobs or reduced their hours of work. Should they be held responsible for their actions or should they be entitled to support? The matter is complicated not just by the ethical dilemma but also because there may be consequences to other persons. For example, other persons may depend on the income of the person in question, in which case the others suffer if support is not forthcoming. Or those suffering reductions in real income may turn to crime, which is a realistic alternative in many cases and involves various social costs.

The heterogeneity of potential recipients reinforces the complexity of the problems confronted in designing support programs for real income volatility. Not only may persons differ in many dimensions, but also such differences can lie along a continuum, blurring the distinction between the needy and the nonneedy.

How to Elicit Information from Potential Recipients?

To complicate matters further, the government is likely to be imperfectly informed about the circumstances faced by given persons. The implication is that policies will typically need to have multiple components and will include different means of targeting to ensure that resources go to those most in need. Targeting can include instruments of self-selection that ensure unintended recipients do not receive assistance (Blackorby and Donaldson 1988). Targeting may also include proactive measures to elicit information, such as tagging or monitoring (Boadway and Cuff 1999; Parsons 1996).

Broadly speaking, eligibility for assistance may be based on self-selection or it may be determined by screening applicants for eligibility. In the case of self-selection mechanisms, recipients freely choose whether to take up the benefits of the program with limited constraints, such as income or asset restrictions. Targeting is effectively achieved by designing the terms of the program in such a way that it is attractive only for intended recipients. Thus, public housing, public day care, or food stamps may be valued relatively more by needy families than by the nonneedy. Self-selection mechanisms are likely to be relatively crude means of targeting, so to avoid Type I errors such mechanisms may have to be fairly generous and universal. Their advantage is that they require minimal discretionary monitoring by administrative agencies.

Screening mechanisms to determine eligibility can involve either ex post or ex ante monitoring. Ex post screening involves self-reporting of eligibility criteria by recipients and subsequent random auditing. An example of this would be transfers or refundable tax credits delivered through the tax system, the magnitude of which depends on income tax information provided by recipients. Governments would then conduct audits on the individuals by means such as taking stock of their assets, looking at bank records, making visits to the home, etc., to determine whether they had made accurate reports. Another example might be unemployment insurance benefits if they apply as soon as an individual becomes unemployed.

Ex ante screening, or tagging, involves determining eligibility on the basis of information made available at the time of application. Welfare and disability programs are typically of this sort. To determine the employability of individuals, the government must verify whether an individual is medically able to work. Medical conditions can often be determined through assessment by medical professionals, although such assessments may vary from professional to professional. Changes in the employability of an individual for medical reasons will also require some continued monitoring of the individual's condition, such as in the case of an injury or a curable disease, when the inability to work may only be temporary. Other individuals might find it difficult to obtain work because of very low skill levels. They may not be able to read or may lack basic communication skills that most employers require to make them employable. The government can use observable characteristics that are correlated with the ability to work—such as literacy, education, and employment history—to tag an individual as employable. Finally, individuals might not be able to work because they are caring for dependents, such as an elderly parent or a young child. Again, the government can use available, observable information to verify the individual's personal circumstances. Even if individuals are deemed employable, the government must try to determine whether the individual is voluntarily or involuntarily unemployed. To do this, the government will need to know not only the individual's employment opportunities but also why the individual became unemployed (e.g., was laid off, quit, was fired, etc.) and whether he or she is looking for work. Unemployed individuals could also differ in their assets, expenditure needs, skills, or health status, characteristics that may or may not be observable but would also affect their need for assistance. Again, the government could gather information on observable characteristics to try to determine the actual need of the individual, or it could design the assistance program to try to screen out the nonneedy from the needy.

Both ex post and ex ante screening may involve continual subsequent ex post monitoring to ensure that recipients abide by the terms of the support. Individuals would have to be reassessed on a regular basis if the circumstances preventing them from working were subject to change—for example, if dependent children are cared for by another individual or enter public school. Likewise, some form of monitoring for job search activities and quits will be required, and to be effective the monitoring should apply to the various phases of job search, from application to job acceptance (Boadway and Cuff 1999). This form of monitoring might be difficult to do since an individual could impede his or her job search in many ways that would be virtually impossible to detect. With imperfect monitoring, the ability to design transfers that treat the involuntarily unemployed more generously than the voluntarily unemployed will be impeded (Boadway, Cuff, and Marceau 2003).

There are advantages and disadvantages to each type of screening. Ex ante screening is more flexible and can readily respond to changes in circumstances, but it will be more costly than ex post screening, since every applicant must be screened. Both types of screening are bound to lead to errors of classification and will result in both Type I and Type II errors. Type II errors increase the cost of the program by using up resources on those who should not be eligible for full support. Type I errors, on the other hand, compromise the integrity of support programs because deserving individuals are not receiving the support to which they are entitled. The incidence of Type I and Type II errors may be affected by the type of screening. In the case of ex post screening, some Type II errors are detected ex post, by which time overpayments may be difficult to correct. With ex ante screening, the incidence of Type I errors may be affected by individuals' behavior. Deserving persons might simply not apply, whether because they are not fully informed about their eligibility, because it is costly to apply, or because they feel stigmatized by the process. As well, given the uncertainty of the eligibility cutoff, potential applicants might not apply because of uncertainty about whether they will be deemed eligible.

Universal or Targeted Support Programs?

Program design must take into account the fact that the govern-ment is not fully informed about the circumstances of households or the reasons for them. The program will be prone to having Type I and Type II errors, and, depending on the weight it puts on those errors, the generosity and design of the program will be affected. Type I errors are primarily a concern because they imply that some deserving persons are not obtaining support. The more averse to inequality the government is, the more it will try to avoid Type I errors. Type II errors represent leakages of funds to undeserving persons and are more of a concern for program costs. The government may have a limited budget to devote to support programs. The greater the Type II errors are, the less will be the level of assistance than can be afforded for the target population. The extent of Type I and Type II errors will depend both on the design of the program and on the extent of monitoring. Universal programs requiring less information regarding potential recipients will limit Type I errors to those who choose not to take up the program but will have large Type II errors, which are costly. An extreme form of universal program is the proposed basic income grant (Murray 2006; Wright 2006), in which all individuals, regardless of circumstance, receive a set amount of money. The rationale is to provide everyone with a basic income without stig-matization so that they can participate more fully in society. It is not designed to address problems of volatility, so presumably it would need to be supplemented by targeted support programs.

Type II errors can be reduced by targeting. Programs can be tar-geted along several different dimensions: they may be means-tested, asset-tested, targeted to a specific demographic group, to a specific pop-ulation such as pregnant women, or to a population in a specific region. The downside of a more targeted program is that Type I errors may be increased because of imperfect targeting. A targeted program might, however, have greater value when uncertainty of needs is an issue. It will be possible—indeed, necessary—for the government to improve its information by monitoring. But since monitoring is costly, both the form and the magnitude of monitoring will have to be traded off against the improvement of accuracy.

How Much Support to Provide?

A key issue is the extent to which reductions in real income should be replaced by government support. Even among the deserving target population, persons will face a variety of circumstances. They will have different real incomes, different numbers of dependents, and different expenditure needs. The question of how much support to award to each type of person will involve making comparisons of persons in heterogeneous circumstances. Even among persons who differ only in income, the extent to which those differences should be compensated involves a judgment about equity based on the decision maker's aversion to inequality. In a world of perfect information, one might argue that full social insurance would be optimal. Applying this in practice is not straightforward, particularly in the case of reductions in employment income. For one thing, the amount of ideal income replacement of a full insurance scheme will not generally be 100 percent; it will only be so if household preferences take a particular form (e.g., additively separable in consumption and leisure). Perhaps more important, full income insurance will almost never be incentive-compatible in a world of imperfect information. That is because, unless consumption and leisure are perfect substitutes, persons will typically be better off receiving support than working, since in the latter case they forgo leisure and the utility that it yields. The extent of income insurance will be limited because of the incentive that it gives for potential recipients to become eligible for support and to stay on support as long as possible: the generosity of the program cannot lead to an expected outcome from obtaining support that exceeds the expected outcome from being in the workforce. Monitoring then becomes important as a device for relaxing that incentive constraint. Ex ante monitoring can detect some persons whose income falls because they voluntarily reduce their income by quitting work or reducing their hours; it can also detect those who misreport their incomes. Ex post monitoring can detect some persons who prolong their stay on support programs by not searching for employment or accepting job offers. From this point of view, more intensive monitoring essentially allows insurance to be more complete by relaxing the incentive constraint (Boadway and Cuff 1999).

How Feasible Are Monetary Sanctions?

A further problem facing the government concerns the sanctions that can be imposed on persons who are found to have misrepresented their circumstances (e.g., their income or their living arrangements) or who fail to abide by the requirements of receiving support (e.g., by quitting or by not engaging in job searches). By imposing a very large penalty, full conformity with program objectives should result, even if monitoring is very limited (Becker 1968). However, in the context of low-income support programs, there will be a limit to which sanctions can be relied on to reduce exploitation by the nondeserving. Those who have been detected exploiting the system will typically have limited resources, so there will be a problem of limited liability (Polinsky and Shavell 1991). Even if they are able to pay, a monetary sanction would be onerous. (This has been a problem with refundable tax credit programs targeted at low-income persons, where recovering overpayments has been difficult.) An alternative to monetary sanctions is to restrict future eligibility, but that might also be problematic given that the persons involved already have low incomes. On top of this, there may be errors associated with monitoring. The implication is that there is a limit to the ability to rely on sanctions, which puts more pressure on monitoring to preclude Type II errors.

What Form Should Government Support Take?

The form that support should take is judgmental even with perfect information. The classic view, based on a welfaristic objective function, would be that cash transfers are desirable since they lead to the highest level of welfare of the recipients. However, the welfaristic approach is not necessarily the one that an optimizing government would choose. If the government's redistribution goals are motivated by the perceived altruism of taxpayers, and if that altruism is based on paternalistic preferences, efficient redistribution may involve in-kind transfers, depending on the form that paternalism takes. If taxpayers value the consumption of all goods and services of low-income recipients but not their leisure, cash transfers are desirable. However, if their altruistic preferences include only a narrower set of goods, then transfers or subsidies of those goods may be more efficient. Behavioral considerations might also justify support that is contingent on the consumption of particular goods, such as those that favor food and shelter over alcohol and tobacco. Finally, cash transfers might be insufficient if markets are missing or imperfect. If the market for medical insurance is incomplete, it may be more efficient for support based on medical needs to take the form of direct provision of medical care.

There are serious problems with operationalizing paternalism, whatever the argument for it. The altruistic preferences of taxpayers are likely to be heterogenous, implying that even if the preferences were known it would not be possible to obtain a consensus on the correct form of the transfer. Even if there were a consensus on the form of paternalistic preferences, as there might be in the case of behavioral-based paternalism, translating that consensus into a specific policy might be difficult. For example, if paternalism favored basic commodities, such as food, shelter, clothing, and other necessities, resale possibilities might make it difficult to constrain recipients from using the in-kind transfer in ways not intended. It may, however, be possible to use electronic payment mechanisms, such as those used for food stamps, to restrict retrading.

The choice of transfer instrument may also be affected by stigmatization, although this might be expected to work in favor of cash transfers (at least in the absence of administrative arguments). The use of in-kind transfers like food stamps typically requires that recipients identify themselves. To the extent that this induces feelings of stigmatization in recipients, it might be regarded as a disadvantage. Cash transfers, on the other hand, have no such stigma attached to their use. There may well be stigmatization associated with both cash and in-kind transfers through the process of application, recertification, and monitoring; however, the possibility of stigma might actually be an advantage in the sense that it may induce self-selection into the program by those who are needy.

It is also conceivable that incentive effects will differ between cash and in-kind transfers. Recipients can use cash transfers as they see fit, whereas in-kind transfers will generally not be a perfect substitute for earned income. Recipients may therefore have an incentive to supplement in-kind transfers with earnings that can be spent on other goods. As a result, work effort may be discouraged less under in-kind transfers than under cash transfers, and that may constitute an important argument enhancing the paternalistic case for in-kind transfers. Of course, the force of this argument depends on the nature of income conditions attached to the receipt of support.

Related to this is the role of in-kind transfers in deterring time-consistency or Samaritan's Dilemma consequences. Potential recipients of income support have an incentive to engage in actions that increase the chances that they will receive support in the future. The form of aid will affect a potential recipient's incentive to make these short-sighted decisions. If aid comes as cash, recipients can easily replace any lost income stemming from their poor decisions with the cash transfers. If, on the other hand, aid comes in the form of in-kind transfers of necessities, they may find these actions less attractive than taking more farsighted actions that leave them with higher incomes in the future, as the in-kind transfers cannot perfectly replace their lost income from their earlier decisions. Moreover, to preclude potential recipients from underproviding for their long-term needs, low-income persons could be provided training or other forms of forced investment rather than income support that they may squander.

The choice of policy instrument can also be influenced by the information problems faced by the government. The use of in-kind transfers rather than cash may be justified on informational grounds. By offering lower-quality goods rather than cash, the government might ensure that only those truly in need will receive assistance. Similar arguments might also be made in favor of using in-kind transfers over subsidies for the purchase of particular goods and services. There may be other economic arguments, however, in favor of implicit subsidies like housing or education vouchers. Other policy instruments might also act as screening tools to help separate the deserving from the nondeserving, such as workfare, employment assistance services, or training programs.

What Are the Incentive Effects of Support Programs?

Assistance programs may affect individuals' incentives to work, to save, to participate in the underground economy, to undertake training or education, to cohabitate, to have children, and to move to a different locale. Often programs are designed with such incentive effects in mind, although unintended effects might arise. As well, the fact that the government is imperfectly informed implies that it cannot observe fully the incentive effects that the program induces. This includes the incentives that persons have to make themselves eligible for the program by influencing their own real incomes, as well as the incentives that they have to change their situation once their real incomes have fallen. Again, monitoring by the government will mitigate this problem. But the design of the program will also be compromised to avoid adverse incentive effects.

The level and form of support might also be affected by the possibility that private support (e.g., charity) might be crowded out. It is efficient to exploit private support as much as possible since the efficiency cost of this support is less than the cost of public funds. That is, the cost per dollar of public funds can be significantly higher than one dollar because of the incremental deadweight loss associated with raising additional revenue through the tax system (Browning 1976). Income and other support transferred voluntarily do not incur a deadweight loss. This is one reason why it is efficient to subsidize voluntary donations made by households to charitable causes (Diamond 2006).

How Often Should Recipients Be Recertified?

As highlighted by Ribar and Edeloch in this volume, qualified households may fail to undertake the necessary paperwork to be recertified for program benefits. It is not entirely clear why even those who are eligible to take public benefits are not doing so. Perhaps it is difficult to understand what is needed to be recertified for the program, or perhaps recipients lack important information about recertification deadlines. The time involved to be reassessed on a continual basis might be substantial. Furthermore, the assistance program might not be an entitlement program, so even if the programs are designed well, only a fraction of eligible persons may receive benefits. As such, some individuals may choose not to bother applying. There could also be long waiting periods before benefits are actually received. A consequence of a slow certification period is that it is possible to imagine cases in which a household switches from qualifying to not qualifying as its real income fluctuates, and so is penalized by the slowness of the response of the programs to changing circumstances. There might also be an asymmetric response of the program: it may take more time to qualify than to be disqualified. Or, certification may take place at a fixed point in time, such as in the National School Lunch Program, where applications are administered at the beginning of the school year. It is possible the program may fail to offer help to those who find themselves in need during the school year. Assistance in the form of refundable and nonrefundable tax credits is also very slow to respond to changes in household circumstances: such credits are calculated only once a year based on the previous total annual income. Households might also have to reapply every so often to the program to continue to receive benefits.

How Responsive Is the Support Program?

Finally, how effective an assistance program will be in helping those facing real income volatility will in part be determined by how readily the program can respond to changes in an individual's circumstances. Those in the relevant target population will typically have limited resources to fall back on, so the need for timely provision of support is paramount. The responsiveness of support programs will depend on how quickly the program administrators can obtain and verify information regarding changes in an individual's circumstances. Along some dimensions the government may be able to respond more quickly than others. For example, verifying the termination of an individual's employment may be easier than verifying changes in family support. From the point of view of responsiveness to changes in need, it may be useful to consider mechanisms that do not require ex ante monitoring to determine eligibility. Temporary support might be granted on the basis of limited ex ante screening, with more permanent support being awarded only with further monitoring of an individual's circumstances. This might be prudent, given that some persons have very limited ability to self-insure against sudden misfortune and they also have limited access to outside social support networks.

An issue of program design is how to harmonize support for income variability with longer-term support for those in chronic need. Some arguments support the notion that the short-term response to income variability should differ from long-term support. One could argue that erring on the generous side makes sense in the context of variability of income for low-income persons. These persons are likely to find it difficult to self-insure, which means they cannot easily adjust to a decline in real income. They may have commitments that are difficult to undo in the short run, such as housing rental contracts. Type II errors may be more tolerable and Type I errors less tolerable in the short run than in the long run, given that it takes time to sort out persons according to their need. Incentive effects may be limited in the short run since it takes time to adjust one's earnings from employment or self-employment. These arguments suggest that support should be more generous and eligibility less restrictive for temporary than for long-run support. Administrative considerations complement these policy considerations. In the case of policies to respond to reductions in real income, the key consideration is timeliness—that is, determining eligibility as quickly as possible. That precludes delivering support through the income tax system, such as by refundable tax credits, since this is not responsive to sudden changes in circumstances. Other mechanisms with ex post monitoring might be feasible, such as allowing individuals to report their own eligibility, subject to ex post auditing for verification accompanied by appropriate penalties. The fear is that this would lead to excessive Type II errors, which could not be corrected by ex post monitoring because sanctions might be difficult to enforce.

It seems more reasonable to determine eligibility using an ex ante monitoring approach where persons apply and are subject to initial screening. The mechanisms already exist to do this. Given the special urgency that might be attached to the need for assistance in this case, as well as the time it takes to screen fully, one might argue for reasonably lenient screening initially, followed by more detailed screening subsequently for continuing eligibility. Lenient screening will minimize Type I errors initially, although it may well invite Type II errors. Perhaps the possibility of Type II errors can be reduced by using the past history of applicants as a source of information. For example, repeat users could be discouraged. Leniency for first-time applicants might also increase the take-up rate for persons who might be deterred from applying for fear of being turned down.

The timeliness issue might also have implications for the form of the transfer. Support that can be processed rapidly would be preferred. Cash certainly fits this criterion. Food transfers might as well, given that mechanisms are already in place for administering them, although presumably there is some time delay in setting up recipients with food-stamp electronic cards initially. Other types of in-kind transfers, such as rent subsidies, might be more costly to implement in a short time frame.

CONCLUSION

Our purpose in this chapter has been to explore the issues involved in designing and implementing income support programs to deal with real income volatility. Many of the same issues arise with these types of programs as arise with support programs designed to respond to needs of a more persistent nature. These issues include the identification of those deserving of support, the quantification of needs, the choice of cash versus subsidies versus in-kind transfers, the availability of other forms of support, the incentive effects created by programs that are either too generous or not generous enough, the type of targeting to employ, and the role of monitoring or auditing to ensure compliance. Resolving these issues is difficult because of the unavoidability of making value judgments and because of that fact that the government faces informational constraints. It is not surprising that low-income support programs rely on a multitude of instruments and approaches involving combinations of cash transfers, in-kind transfers (such as food), subsidies, work and training programs, and social services of various types.

Support programs to deal with the consequences of volatility face additional problems. Most important is the need for timeliness in identifying and assisting those whose real incomes have fallen unexpectedly. Low-income persons will typically have difficulty insuring against adverse shocks, and to the extent that they can insure it will be very costly and sometimes carry long-term consequences. Moreover, incentive effects may well be less severe in the short run than in the long. This suggests that the response to short-term volatility should be more generous than for more persistent need, and that the issue of Type II errors should be given less weight. At the same time, the need to distinguish between short-term need and long-term need implies reasonably short recertification periods as well as other measures, such as monitoring and auditing, that facilitate compliance.

Despite the long list of difficulties associated with designing support programs to deal with real income volatility, it is important to stress that the downside of not offering adequate support for low income volatility should not be underestimated. The options for those needing assistance are often more costly to society in the long run than providing the assistance when needed.

Notes

We are grateful for comments by the editors, Dean Jolliffe and Jim Ziliak; the discussant, Luigi Pistaferri; and participants in the conference "Income Volatility and Implications for Food Assistance Programs II," November 16–17, 2006, sponsored by the University of Michigan's National Poverty Center and by the USDA's Economic Research Service.

1. For the reader interested in details about actual low-income support programs, Currie (2006) provides an excellent overview of current U.S. assistance programs.

2. Information problems can also affect access to housing for low-income households. Adverse selection can arise when the probability of defaulting on one's rent is not observable. Landlords may find it profitable to lower the rent they charge to a level below the market-clearing rent, thereby reducing the average probability of default but generating excess housing demand and homelessness (Cuff and Marceau 2007).

3. Whether or not these asset limits actually constrain low-income individuals is unclear. Recent empirical papers have examined the effect of such limits on the assets of households with high probabilities of welfare receipt. Increases in asset limits appear to have had no impact on the liquid assets held by these households but some positive effect on vehicle assets (Hurst and Ziliak 2006; Sullivan 2006).

4. This social welfare function with constant relative aversion to inequality can be derived from underlying axioms about social preferences. Such a form is possible under the assumption that individual utility functions are comparable and measurable up to a ratio scale. That is, proportional changes in utility are comparable across individuals. See Boadway and Bruce (1984), Chapter 5. Another single-parameter social welfare function is one where the absolute aversion to inequality is constant. The social choice foundations for this are discussed in Bossert and Weymark (2004).

5. To use an example cited by Sen (1973), suppose two persons of equal productivity differ in the utility they obtain from a given amount of income. If society's aversion to inequality is high, one would want to redistribute from those who are more efficient utility-generators to those who are less, while if aversion to inequality is low, one might want to redistribute from those who are less efficient at generating utility to the more efficient ones. The analogue would be with education or health expenditures (Arrow 1971). Should educational resources be concentrated on those who are most able to use them? Or should those who have more difficulty learning be favored? Similarly, should health expenditures be allocated to persons with afflictions that are easier to treat, or to those with afflictions more difficult to treat?

6. The idea that social capital can help poor people insure their consumption against adverse shocks is controversial. In a recent paper, Gertler, Levine, and Moretti

(2006) find, using Indonesian data, that families hit by a health shock suffer a decline in consumption that is unrelated to the presence of a social network or a wealthy extended family. Thus, social capital seems to be of no help for those families. This is in contrast to the previous literature on the subject, surveyed in Gertler, Levine, and Moretti (2006), which finds that social capital can play the role of an insurance policy against adverse consumption shock.

References

Akerlof, George A. 1997. "Social Distance and Social Decisions." *Econometrica* 65(5): 1005–1028.

Allard, Scott W. Forthcoming. "Mismatches and Unmet Need: Access to Social Services in Urban and Rural America." In *Welfare Reform and Its Long-Term Consequences*, James P. Ziliak, ed. Cambridge: Cambridge University Press.

Arrow, Kenneth J. 1951. *Social Choice and Individual Values*. New Haven, CT: Yale University Press.

———.1971. "A Utilitarian Approach to the Concept of Equality in Public Expenditures." *Quarterly Journal of Economics* 85(3): 409–415.

Ashenfelter, Orley C. 1978. "Estimating the Effect of Training Programs on Earnings." *Review of Economics and Statistics* 60(1): 47–57.

Atkinson, Anthony B. 1995. "On Targeting Social Security: Theory and Western Experience with Family Benefits." In *Public Spending and the Poor: Theory and Evidence*, Dominique van de Walle and Kimberly Nead, eds. Baltimore, MD: Johns Hopkins University Press, pp. 25–68.

Becker, Gary S. 1968. "Crime and Punishment: An Economic Approach." *Journal of Political Economy* 76(2): 169–217.

Bénabou, Roland, and Jean Tirole. 2006. "Belief in a Just World and Redistributive Politics." *Quarterly Journal of Economics* 121(2): 699–746.

Bernheim, B. Douglas, and Antonio Rangel. 2007. "Behavioral Public Economics: Welfare and Policy Analysis with Nonstandard Decision-Makers." In *Behavioral Economics and Its Applications*, Peter Diamond and Hannu Vartiainen, eds. Princeton, NJ: Princeton University Press, pp. 7–77.

Besley, Timothy, and Stephen Coate. 1995. "The Design of Income Maintenance Programmes." *Review of Economic Studies* 62(2): 187–221.

Blackorby, Charles, and David Donaldson. 1988. "Cash Versus Kind, Self-Selection, and Efficient Transfers." *American Economic Review* 78(4): 691–700.

Blundell, Richard, Luigi Pistaferri, and Ian Preston. 2004. "Consumption Inequality and Partial Insurance." IFS Working Paper 04/28. London: Institute for Fiscal Studies.

Boadway, Robin W., and Neil Bruce. 1984. *Welfare Economics*. Oxford: Basil Blackwell.

Boadway, Robin W., and Katherine Cuff. 1999. "Monitoring Job Search as an Instrument for Targeting Transfers." *International Tax and Public Finance* 6(3): 317–337.

Boadway, Robin W., Katherine Cuff, and Nicolas Marceau. 2003. "Redistribution and Employment Policies with Endogenous Unemployment." *Journal of Public Economics* 87(11): 2407–2430.

Boadway, Robin W., Manuel Leite-Monteiro, Maurice Marchand, and Pierre Pestieau. 2006. "Social Insurance and Redistribution with Moral Hazard and Adverse Selection." *Scandinavian Journal of Economics* 108(2): 279–298.

Boadway, Robin W., Nicolas Marceau, and Motohiro Sato. 1999. "Agency and the Design of Welfare Systems." *Journal of Public Economics* 73(1): 1–30.

Boadway, Robin W., Maurice Marchand, Pierre Pestieau, and Maria del Mar Racionero. 2002. "Optimal Redistribution with Heterogeneous Preferences for Leisure." *Journal of Public Economic Theory* 4(4): 475–498.

Boadway, Robin W., and Pierre Pestieau. 2006. "Tagging and Redistributive Taxation." *Annales d'Économie et de Statistique* 2006(83–84): 123–147.

Bossert, Walter, and John A. Weymark. 2004. "Utility in Social Choice." In *Handbook of Utility Theory*. Vol. 2, *Extensions*, Salvador Barberà, Peter J. Hammond, and Christian Seidl, eds. Boston: Kluwer Academic Publishers, pp. 1099–1177.

Browning, Edgar K. 1976. "The Marginal Cost of Public Funds." *Journal of Political Economy* 84(2): 283–298.

Bruce, Neil, and Michael Waldman. 1991. "Transfers in Kind: Why They Can Be Efficient and Nonpaternalistic." *American Economic Review* 81(5): 1345–1351.

Chetty, Raj, and Adam Looney. 2006. "Consumption Smoothing and the Welfare Consequences of Social Insurance in Developing Economies." *Journal of Public Economics* 90(12): 2351–2356.

Cuff, Katherine 2000. "Optimality of Workfare with Heterogeneous Preferences." *Canadian Journal of Economics* 33(1): 149–174.

Cuff, Katherine, and Nicolas Marceau. 2007. "Tenancy Default, Excess Demand, and the Rental Market." Department of Economics Working Paper Series. Hamilton, Ontario: McMaster University.

Currie, Janet M. 2006. *The Invisible Safety Net: Protecting the Nation's Poor Children and Families*. Princeton, NJ: Princeton University Press.

Cutler, David M. 2002. "Health Care and the Public Sector." In *Handbook of Public Economics*. Vol. 4, *Handbooks in Economics*. Alan J. Auerbach and Martin Feldstein, eds. Amsterdam, the Netherlands: North-Holland, pp. 2143–2243.

Diamond, Peter. 2006. "Optimal Tax Treatment of Private Contributions for Public Goods with and without Warm Glow Preferences." *Journal of Public Economics* 90(4–5): 897–919.

Fleurbaey, Marc, and François Maniquet. Forthcoming. "Compensation and Responsibility." In *Handbook of Social Choice and Welfare.* Vol. 2, Kenneth J. Arrow, Amartya K. Sen, and Kotaro Suzumura, eds. Amsterdam, the Netherlands: North-Holland.

Gertler, Paul, David I. Levine, and Enrico Moretti. 2006. "Is Social Capital the Capital of the Poor? The Role of Family and Community in Helping Insure Living Standards against Health Shocks." *CESifo Economic Studies* 52(3): 455–499.

Gottschalk, Peter, and Robert Moffitt. 1994, "The Growth of Earnings Instability in the U.S. Labor Market." *Brookings Papers on Economic Activity* 25(2): 217–272.

Haider, Steven J. 2001. "Earnings Instability and Earnings Inequality of Males in the United States: 1967–1991." *Journal of Labor Economics* 19(4): 799–836.

Hochman, Harold M., and James D. Rodgers. 1969. "Pareto Optimal Redistribution." *American Economic Review* 59(4): 542–557.

Hurst, Erik, and James P. Ziliak. 2006. "Do Welfare Asset Limits Affect Household Saving? Evidence from Welfare Reform." *Journal of Human Resources* 41(1): 46–71.

Ihori, Toshihiro, and Martin McGuire. 2006. "Group Provision against Adversity, Security Spending, and Growth." Paper presented at the 62nd Congress of the International Institute of Public Finance, held in Paphos, Cyprus, August 28–31.

Jacquet, Laurence, and Bruno Van der Linden. 2006. "The Normative Analysis of Tagging Revisited: Dealing with Stigmatization." *FinanzArchiv: Public Finance Analysis* 62(2): 168–198.

Kanbur, Ravi, Michael Keen, and Matti Tuomala. 1995. "Labor Supply and Targeting in Poverty-Alleviation Programs." In *Public Spending and the Poor: Theory and Evidence*, Dominique van de Walle and Kimberly Nead, eds. Baltimore: Johns Hopkins University Press, pp. 91–113.

Laibson, David. 1997. "Golden Eggs and Hyperbolic Discounting." *Quarterly Journal of Economics* 112(2): 443–477.

Mankiw, N. Gregory. 1986. "The Allocation of Credit and Financial Collapse." *Quarterly Journal of Economics* 101(3): 455–470.

Mirrlees, James A. 1971. "An Exploration in the Theory of Optimal Income Taxation." *Review of Economic Studies* 38(2): 175–208.

Murray, Charles. 2006. "A Plan to Replace the Welfare State." University of Wisconsin–Madison Institute for Research on Poverty *Focus* 24(2): 1–3.

Nishimura, Yukihiro. 2003. "Optimal Non-linear Income Taxation for Reduction of Envy." *Journal of Public Economics* 87(2): 363–386.

Nozick, Robert. 1974. *Anarchy, State, and Utopia*. New York: Basic Books.

Parsons, Donald O. 1996. "Imperfect 'Tagging' in Social Insurance Programs." *Journal of Public Economics* 62(1–2): 183–207.

Polinsky, A. Mitchell, and Steven Shavell 1991. "A Note on Optimal Fines when Wealth Varies among Individuals." *American Economic Review* 81(3): 618–621.

Putnam, Robert D. 2000. *Bowling Alone: The Collapse and Revival of American Community*. New York: Simon and Schuster.

Rabin, Matthew. 1998. "Psychology and Economics." *Journal of Economic Literature* 36(1): 11–46.

Rawls, John. 1971. *A Theory of Justice*. Cambridge, MA: Harvard University Press.

Roemer, John E. 1998. *Equality of Opportunity*. Cambridge, MA: Harvard University Press.

Rothschild, Michael, and Joseph Stiglitz. 1976. "Equilibrium in Competitive Insurance Markets: An Essay on the Economics of Imperfect Information." *Quarterly Journal of Economics* 90(4): 629–649.

Rowe, Nicholas, and Frances Woolley. 1999. "The Efficiency Case for Universality." *Canadian Journal of Economics* 32(3): 613–629.

Saez, Emmanuel. 2002. "Optimal Income Transfer Programs: Intensive versus Extensive Labor Supply Responses." *Quarterly Journal of Economics* 117(3): 1039–1073.

Sen, Amartya. 1970. "The Impossibility of a Paretian Liberal." *Journal of Political Economy* 78(1): 152–157.

———. 1973. *On Economic Inequality*. Oxford: Oxford University Press.

———. 1999. *Commodities and Capabilities*. New York: Oxford University Press.

Stiglitz, Joseph E., and Andrew Weiss. 1981. "Credit Rationing in Markets with Imperfect Information." *American Economic Review* 71(3): 393–410.

Strotz, Robert H. 1956. "Myopia and Inconsistency in Dynamic Utility Maximization." *Review of Economic Studies* 23(3): 165–180.

Sullivan, James X. 2006. "Welfare Reform, Saving, and Vehicle Ownership: Do Asset Limits and Vehicle Exemptions Matter?" *Journal of Human Resources* 41(1): 72–105.

Tanguay, Georges, Gary Hunt, and Nicolas Marceau. 2005. "Food Prices and the Timing of Welfare Payments: A Canadian Study." *Canadian Public Policy* 31(2): 145–160.

Wright, Erik Olin. 2006. "Two Redistributive Proposals—Universal Basic Income and Stakeholder Grants." University of Wisconsin–Madison Institute
for Research on Poverty *Focus* 24(2): 5–7.

Ziliak, James P. 2003. "Income Transfers and Assets of the Poor." *Review of
Economics and Statistics* 85(1): 63–76.

9

Income Volatility and Certification Duration for WIC Children

Mark A. Prell
Economic Research Service

The U.S. Department of Agriculture administers 15 domestic food assistance programs, including the Special Supplemental Nutrition Program for Women, Infants, and Children (WIC). Policymakers establish program benefits and set criteria that determine who is eligible to receive benefits. WIC benefits include nutrition counseling, health referrals, and vouchers ("food instruments") that enable WIC clients to obtain particular sets of nutritious foods from authorized retailers. A common criterion for food assistance programs is a limit on income relative to the poverty line. The household income limit for WIC is 185 percent of poverty.[1]

People's incomes are not steady forever. Income volatility implies that, in any given month, the household income of a WIC client might exceed the guidelines for eligibility. At a recertification, WIC obtains updated information from the client. Recertification is an administrative tool by which WIC can ascertain whether a client has become ineligible. When a client is detected to be ineligible, WIC benefits are terminated. When a client is found to be eligible, the client may receive WIC benefits until the next recertification. The length of time between recertifications is known as certification duration.

I develop an economic model of an "optimal" certification duration that examines the policy tradeoff between recertification costs and benefit targeting—getting program benefits to those who are eligible to receive them. While the model has implications for food assistance programs in general, I use certifications for WIC children as a case study for simulations of optimal certification durations.

WIC benefits will be called *warranted* if the client is eligible in the same month that the client receives the program benefits—i.e., if the

259

client's current monthly income meets the monthly eligibility guidelines. If instead the client is ineligible in the current month because of income volatility since the application, the client's benefits will be called *unwarranted*. WIC will terminate the client's benefits at recertification once benefits are detected to be unwarranted.

A shorter recertification period fosters targeting of benefits to those clients who are eligible. Frequent recertifications detect and terminate unwarranted benefits more quickly. Because WIC benefits constitute a transfer payment from taxpayers to clients, it may seem that terminating payments to ineligibles is simply a zero-sum change. However, because of taxation, financing WIC benefits entails a marginal efficiency cost. Improved benefit targeting that reduces unwarranted benefits provides economic savings in terms of reduced excess burden (deadweight loss) from taxes. Thus there is a social gain to a shorter certification duration.

On the other hand, shortening the certification duration adds to recertification costs. Real resources involved with recertification include staff and equipment costs to WIC (and ultimately, to taxpayers) and a client's opportunity cost of time and out-of-pocket travel expenses.

The next section provides a static benefit-cost framework to analyze whether or not to conduct a single recertification. This artificially simple framework neglects recertification's critical intertemporal issues to focus first on valuation issues of what factors constitute economic benefits and costs for the problem. The third section develops the optimal certification duration model, which captures recertification's dynamic aspects. The fourth section uses the certification duration model to simulate sets of optimal certification duration for children in WIC. The structure of the certification duration model resembles "inspection" or "preparedness" models for maintenance and replacement of stochastically failing equipment, including work by Barlow and Proschan (1996); Jorgenson, McCall, and Radner (1967); and Radner and Jorgenson (1962). The simulations most closely resemble work in Greenfield and Persselin (2002).

The case study involves WIC children. There are five groups of WIC participants: 1) pregnant women, 2) breast-feeding women, 3) non-breast-feeding postpartum women, 4) infants (up to one year old), and 5) children (one through four years of age). Total food costs for WIC in fiscal 2005 were $3.6 billion.[2] The certification duration issue can be considered more salient for WIC children than for other WIC clients, since children make up half of the program's participants,[3] have the longest period for which they can be eligible—up to four years—and are recertified in WIC every six months, a time frame that potentially constitutes several recertifications over a full four-year participation period.

While WIC's actual certification duration for children is six months, the estimated optimal certification duration is 12 months in a baseline simulation that uses best-guess values for parameters. When the simulation is rerun for sensitivity analysis using alternative parameter values, the estimated optimal certification duration ranges from 7 months to 14 months.

STATIC BENEFIT-COST ANALYSIS

At a moment in time, under what conditions does conducting a recertification for a given client pass a benefit-cost test? Suppose the current month is just beginning, and the client has not yet received monthly WIC benefits worth M. While the client was eligible at application, some time has now passed. The client's eligibility status is unknown unless a recertification is conducted, which is the policy choice. Let P_{EI} measure the probability that the client, who was eligible at application, is now ineligible. In expectation, unwarranted and warranted benefits equal $P_{EI}M$ and $(1-P_{EI})M$, respectively. Let c_A and c_C represent recertification costs paid (if and only if a recertification is conducted) by the WIC agency and the client, respectively. The excess burden, or marginal efficiency cost, per dollar of taxes is given by ε.

Table 9.1 compares a policy of "Don't recertify" and a policy of "Recertify once" for the current month in isolation, without considering future possible months; the next section takes the future into account. For the policy of "Don't recertify" there are no recertification costs. Program benefits take on three values: 1) the client receives M dollars' worth of monthly WIC benefits (whether or not the client is currently eligible); 2) the taxpayer bears a cost of $-M$ and, in addition, an excess burden of $-\varepsilon M$, reflecting taxation's efficiency loss; and 3) the economic cost to society of WIC benefits, after taking into account the

Table 9.1 Static Benefit-Cost Analysis of Recertification

	Client's benefits and costs	Taxpayer's benefits and costs	Social benefits and costs
"Don't recertify" policy			
(1) Recertification costs	0	0	0
(2) Program benefits	$+M$	$-(1+\varepsilon)M$	$-\varepsilon M$
(3) E[net value] (3) = (1)+(2)	$+M$	$-(1+\varepsilon)M$	$-\varepsilon M$
"Recertify once" policy			
(4) Recertification costs	$-c_C$	$-(1+\varepsilon)c_A$	$-[(1+\varepsilon)\,c_A + c_C]$
(5) Program benefits if ineligible (probability P_{EI})	0	0	0
(6) Program benefits if eligible (probability $[1-P_{EI}]$)	$+M$	$-(1+\varepsilon)M$	$-\varepsilon M$
(7) E[net value] (7) = (4) + $[P_{EI}(5) + (1-P_{EI})(6)]$			$(1-P_{EI})\varepsilon M - [(1+\varepsilon)\,c_A + c_C]$
Benefit-cost test of "recertify once" policy vs. "don't recertify" policy			
(8) E[net value] (8) = (7) − (3)			$+P_{EI}\varepsilon M - [(1+\varepsilon)\,c_A + c_C]$

SOURCE: Author's analysis.

transfer-payment aspect of M, is $-\varepsilon M$ in row (3). Rows (4) through (7) examine the "Recertify once" policy. Recertification costs are shown in (4). In (5), if with probability P_{EI} the client is currently ineligible, WIC benefits are terminated. In (6), with probability $(1 - P_{EI})$ the client is currently eligible, and WIC benefits are paid. The expected net value in row (7) of the "Recertify once" policy shows terms that are the total of (4) and the probability-weighted values in (5) and (6).

Row (8) shows the net gain of adopting the "Recertify once" policy in place of the "Don't recertify" policy as the difference between (7) and (3):

$$(9.1) \quad E[NV] = P_{EI}\varepsilon M - [(1 + \varepsilon)c_A + c_C] .$$

Recertification passes a static benefit-cost test when the $E[NV]$ in Equation (9.1) is positive. In Equation (9.1), recertification saves neither warranted benefits nor their excess burden because the policy choice does not affect payments of warranted benefits. Under the "Recertify once" policy, WIC benefits are paid out so long as they are warranted, and warranted benefits (like unwarranted benefits) are also paid under the "Don't recertify" policy. Instead, (9.1) shows that the economic gain from recertification is $P_{EI}\varepsilon M$—the excess burden of financing WIC benefits, εM, with probability P_{EI} that those benefits are unwarranted. The link to unwarranted benefits can also be shown by rewriting that gain as $\varepsilon(P_{EI}M)$, where unwarranted benefits are $P_{EI}M$. Because the term εM recurs often in the optimal certification duration model, it will simply be designated m.

In the static benefit-cost analysis, a "Recertify once" policy tends to have a positive $E[NV]$ when, holding other factors constant, any one of the following four conditions occur: 1) "income volatility" is relatively high (in the sense of a high value for P_{EI}), 2) monthly benefits M are relatively high, 3) the excess burden of taxation ε is relatively high, or 4) the recertification costs for the agency and the client are relatively low. These same lessons can be expected to hold more generally for other food assistance programs.

OPTIMAL CERTIFICATION DURATION MODEL

The static benefit-cost analysis highlighted valuation issues, but it ignored intertemporal issues that matter for recertification policy. First, the static analysis treated P_{EI} as an exogenous constant, but $P_{EI}(t)$ can systematically depend on time. Second, if ineligibility is detected and benefits are terminated at some time, excess burden m is saved not only for the current month but also for future months that would have had payments if WIC benefits had continued until a future recertification. Thus, future flows of m and their expected discounted values will matter for optimal decision-making. Third, the static analysis did not model how decision-making for any one recertification affects outcomes of possible future recertifications. The optimal certification duration model takes into account these three issues, and this section considers each in turn.

Income Volatility and State Probability Paths

At the time of application and initial certification, time 0, the WIC agency determines that the client is eligible. The time of transition from eligibility to ineligibility is a random variable that can be called a time to "failure." The failure distribution $F(t)$ is the cumulative probability distribution showing the probability that the time to "failure"—ineligibility—is less than or equal to t:

$$(9.2) \quad F(t) = \int_0^t f(u)du = Prob\{time\ to\ failure \leq t\}$$

where $f(t)$ is the associated probability density for $F(t)$ given by $dF(t)/dt$. Although the client's current state—eligible or ineligible—is unknown, it is assumed that $F(t)$ is known to policymakers from past data on other clients that resemble the one being considered. A companion to the failure distribution is the reliability (or survivor) function $R(t)$, which is the probability a client is still eligible as of time t—or, equivalently, the probability that the time of transition to ineligibility is greater than t. The relationship between $R(t)$ and $F(t)$ is simply

$$(9.3) \quad R(t) = 1 - F(t) = Prob\{time\ to\ failure > t\}.$$

The hazard rate (also known as the "hazard function" or the "failure rate") $h(t)$ is the probability that the client will transition to ineligibility within an instantaneously small interval at time t, conditioned on having reached t as eligible (i.e., conditioned on not transitioning prior to t). The hazard rate can be expressed using the failure distribution or the reliability function:

$$(9.4) \quad h(t) = \frac{F'(t)}{1 - F(t)} = -\frac{R'(t)}{R(t)}.$$

Like previous work, the certification duration model adopts the common simplifying assumption that the reliability function for the eligible client to remain eligible is exponential:

$$(9.5) \quad R(t) = e^{-\lambda t}, t \geq 0.$$

The hazard rate of (9.5) for transition from E to I is a constant λ. The failure distribution is

$$(9.6) \quad F(t) = 1 - e^{-\lambda t}, \quad t \geq 0.$$

The expected duration of a continuous spell in E is $(1/\lambda)$ from the start of the spell.

The exponential distribution has been used in equipment maintenance and inspection models by Barlow and Proschan (1996); Jorgenson, McCall, and Radner (1967); and Radner and Jorgenson (1962). A key feature of the exponential distribution is its "memoryless" property, by which the reliability function for equipment that is inspected and found to be in good working order at some time is the same reliability function for the newly installed equipment as of time 0. The hazard rate to failure for a newly installed piece of equipment is λ, and at any point in the future—before or after inspection—the hazard rate is still λ. Inspection serves as a "regeneration" or "renewal" that returns the problem's stochastic characteristics to time 0.[4]

All models make simplifying assumptions. Despite the potential limitations of the exponential function, its advantage is that it provides the easiest dynamic structure for the optimal certification duration model. Moreover, in the next section, data are presented that show that the actual probability paths for some households' income dynamics are approximated well by the theoretical probability path predicted on the basis of the exponential distribution. Even if the assumption of an exponential distribution does not hold precisely in actual data, much can be learned about the trade-offs faced by program administrators by considering the optimal certification duration model. The more closely actual hazard rates are constants, the better the model's simulations will serve as first-order approximations.

A constant hazard rate is a strength of the exponential distribution (making difficult problems analytically tractable) as well as a potential limitation. More advanced models that allow for nonconstant hazard rates may build on the foundations provided by the optimal certification duration model developed here. When hazard rates depend on time, the model's solution would almost certainly involve a set of sequential recertification periods of differing lengths. A second limitation of the exponential distribution, and one shared by many distributions, is that its cumulative probability of transition approaches 1.0. It would be of interest to generalize the model by allowing some fraction of WIC clients to have zero probability of "failure," i.e., of ever having enough income to become ineligible. That complexity is not attempted here.

A complexity that is incorporated into the certification duration model, generalizing the models of the equipment maintenance literature, is permitting transitions not only from I to E but also from E to I. It is natural for analysis of optimal equipment maintenance to adopt the assumption that a transition into "failed" is irreversible: machines do not spontaneously fix themselves. The optimal certification duration model relaxes the assumption that failure is an "absorbing" state, with no return possible, because income volatility can move a household from eligibility to ineligibility and, at some random time later, back into eligibility. Such a possibility is captured by a "two-state transition process" or "alternating renewal process." Boskin and Nold (1975) considered it when examining the states of "participation" and "nonparticipation" in modeling the AFDC program. Lancaster (1990) considered it for the states of employment and unemployment.

In the next section, titled "Application: WIC Children's Certification Duration," data are presented that show that the actual two-state probability paths for some households' income dynamics are approximated well by the theoretical probability path predicted on the basis of the exponential distribution.

Let $G(t)$ represent the failure distribution for transition from I to E. $G(t)$ pertains to a formerly eligible, currently ineligible client who reenters E because of an income decrease, where

(9.7) $G(t) = 1 - e^{-\mu t}, \quad t > 0$.

A (formerly eligible) client who is ineligible at any given time exhibits the hazard rate μ for the conditional probability of transitioning from I back to E.[5] The expected duration of a continuous spell in I is $(1/\mu)$ from the start of the spell.

Just as inspection returned stochastic properties back to time 0 in equipment maintenance models that used a one-way transition assumption, so too does recertification serve as a regeneration point under two-way transitions between E and I. Let the probability that a client occupies a given state E or I at a given time t be a "state probability," given by $\pi_E(t)$ and $\pi_I(t)$, respectively. Generalizing a numerical example from Howard (1960), state probabilities are either

(9.8)
$$\pi_E(t) = \pi_E(0)\left[\frac{\mu}{\lambda + \mu} + \frac{\lambda}{\lambda + \mu}e^{-(\lambda+\mu)t}\right] + \pi_I(0)\left[\frac{\mu}{\lambda + \mu} - \frac{\mu}{\lambda + \mu}e^{-(\lambda+\mu)t}\right]$$

or

(9.9)
$$\pi_I(t) = \pi_E(0)\left[\frac{\lambda}{\lambda + \mu} - \frac{\lambda}{\lambda + \mu}e^{-(\lambda+\mu)t}\right] + \pi_I(0)\left[\frac{\lambda}{\lambda + \mu} + \frac{\mu}{\lambda + \mu}e^{-(\lambda+\mu)t}\right],$$

where the probabilities $\pi_E(0)$ and $\pi_I(0)$ represent the probability that the client is in E or I at whatever "initial" time 0 is considered. Suppose the initial time of the problem is taken to be the time of application (and initial certification) of the client. At application, the WIC agency knows that $\pi_E(0) = 1$ and $\pi_I(0) = 0$. For the eligible client, (9.8) and (9.9) each reduce to a set of *conditional* state probabilities, i.e., to state probabilities (for E or I) conditioned on initial eligibility at time 0, which can be written as $P_{EE}(t)$ and $P_{EI}(t)$:[6]

(9.10) $P_{EE}(t) = \dfrac{\mu}{\lambda + \mu} + \dfrac{\lambda}{\lambda + \mu}e^{-(\lambda+\mu)t}$;

$$(9.11) \quad P_{EI}(t) = \frac{\lambda}{\lambda + \mu} - \frac{\lambda}{\lambda + \mu} e^{-(\lambda + \mu)t}.$$

Not surprisingly, the stochastic time profiles $P_{EE}(t)$ and $P_{EI}(t)$ sum to 1 at all t: a client (who is eligible at time zero) is either in state E or state I at any given time.[7] These state probability paths approach steady-state values monotonically: $P_{EE}(t)$ is downward-sloping for all t, while $P_{EI}(t)$ is upward-sloping. What those behaviors mean, in practice, is that the probability of detecting that a client is ineligible at time t strictly increases as more time passes.

Consider next a recertification after some amount of time T has passed since application or the last recertification. Because of the memoryless property, the recertification serves as a "regeneration" of the two-state stochastic process of transitioning between states E and I. The stochastic time profiles $P_{EE}(t)$ and $P_{EI}(t)$ hold for an eligible client at time 0 by using $\pi_E(0) = 1$ and $\pi_I(0) = 0$ in (9.8) and (9.9). Similarly, at recertification at T, $\pi_E(T) = 1$ and $\pi_I(T) = 0$ for the client who is found, because of the process of recertification itself, to be eligible at T. Using those values in (9.8) and (9.9) again results in the same stochastic profiles at T as were found at time 0. That is, viewed from time T, the same $P_{EE}(t)$ and $P_{EI}(t)$ time paths are obtained that were derived at initial time 0 (so long as t is interpreted as "duration time from the last recertification" rather than calendar time). In short, recertification can serve as a new initial time.[8] The same result holds at each successive recertification—at 2T, 3T, and so forth after time 0.

A Single Optimal Recertification

The central role of discounting in a dynamic certification duration model is considered in the context of the optimal timing of a single recertification at time T, to be chosen by WIC. The per-certification cost is given by c equaling $[(1 + \varepsilon) c_A + c_C]$, as in the static benefit-cost test. The present value of c at time 0, with ρ as the instantaneous social discount rate, is $D(T)$:

$$(9.12) \quad D(T) = e^{-\rho T} c.$$

A delay in recertification lowers $D(T)$ through postponement of the recertification cost c.

Let $U(T)$ measure the expected discounted excess burden of unwarranted benefits that cumulate up to recertification time T:

$$(9.13) \quad U(T) = m \int_0^T e^{-\rho t} P_{EI}(t) \, dt = m \int_0^T e^{-\rho t} \left[\frac{\lambda}{\lambda + \mu} - \frac{\lambda}{\lambda + \mu} e^{-(\lambda + \mu)t} \right] dt.$$

$U(T)$ has three components. The excess burden component m (where m is εM) measures the flow of potential savings of excess burden from financing WIC benefits. The state probability path $P_{EI}(t)$ registers for each instant the likelihood that the excess burden from unwarranted benefits occurs at that moment. Each instant's flow is discounted by ρ to initial time. The cumulative aspect of $U(T)$ means that these expected discounted flows are added up by integration between 0 and T.

Upon evaluation of (4.2), $U(T)$ is given by

$$(9.14)$$

$$U(T) = \left(\frac{\lambda}{\lambda + \mu} \right) m \left[\left(\frac{1}{\rho} \right) \left(1 - e^{-\rho T} \right) - \left(\frac{1}{\rho + \lambda + \mu} \right) \left(1 - e^{-(\rho + \lambda + \mu)T} \right) \right].$$

The present value of an infinite stream of m is m/ρ. Importantly, the value of $U(T)$ in the limit takes on a smaller value, as follows:

$$(9.15) \quad U_\infty = \lim_{T \to \infty} U(T) = \left(\frac{\lambda}{\rho + \lambda + \mu} \right) \left(\frac{m}{\rho} \right).$$

Thus, if no inspection were ever to occur—i.e., if T were infinitely delayed—the expected excess burden of unwarranted benefits would be less than m/ρ because (in expectation) only a portion of the flow of excess burden m is paid to a client during times of ineligibility. The value that $U(T)$ approaches will be closer to (m/ρ) as λ is larger and μ is smaller relative to ρ, inasmuch as those income volatility parameters capture the rates at which clients have E-I and I-E transitions.

Expected discounted total cost for a single-recertification problem is given by

$$(9.16) \quad E[DC(T)] = U(T) + D(T) + e^{-\rho T} \left[P_{EI}(T)0 + P_{EE}(T)U_\infty \right].$$

In (9.16), a flow of excess burden from unwarranted benefits is accruing in expectation until time T, given by $U(T)$. At T, a recertification cost is paid (with certainty) for which the present value is $D(T)$. At recertification the client is found to be ineligible with probability $P_{EI}(T)$, in which case payments are terminated (meaning future payments equal 0) and the problem is over. Or, with probability $P_{EE}(T)$, the client is found to be eligible and the payment of program benefits forever begins. That is, if the client passes the problem's single recertification, the flow of m continues uninterrupted from T onward without limit. Discounting the two probability-weighted outcomes of recertification at T (of 0 and of U_∞) back to initial time 0, in order to express them in present value terms, completes (9.16).

Minimization of (9.16) results in the first-order condition

$$(9.17) \quad P_{EI}(T^*)m - \rho c + P_{EE}{}'(T^*)U_\infty - \rho P_{EE}(T^*)U_\infty = 0 .$$

The problem's second-order condition for minimization is

$$(9.18) \quad P_{EI}{}'(T^*)m + P_{EE}{}''(T^*)U_\infty - \rho P_{EE}{}'(T^*)U_\infty > 0 .$$

The optimality condition (9.17) can be reexpressed in terms of marginal gains and marginal losses from delayed recertification. To use a single state probability path and its derivative, note that $P_{EI}{}'(t) = -P_{EE}{}'(t)$, which follows from $P_{EI}(t) = [1 - P_{EE}(t)]$, so that (9.17) becomes

$$(9.19) \quad P_{EI}{}'(T^*)U_\infty + \rho c + \rho[1 - P_{EI}(T^*)]U_\infty = P_{EI}(T^*)m .$$

The first term shows a gain from delayed recertification: a slight delay in T^* increases the probability that ineligibility will be detected at the recertification, thereby saving U_∞. The second term captures an additional gain from delaying payment of the per-recertification cost c: that cost will be paid sooner or later, but if it is later then in effect the implicit interest earnings from delayed payment equal ρc. That is, if c were invested in the bank, earning instantaneous rate ρ until recertification, then proceeds from waiting until the next instant for recertification and earning ρ meanwhile on the invested capital of c is ρc. There is another gain associated with interest earnings. As of T, there is a probability $[1 - P_{EI}(T)]$ that the client is eligible and that at recertification the client will be due monthly benefits M forever, costing m forever, which is tantamount to a lump-sum cost (in present value as of T) of

U_∞. A slight delay in recertification means that that lump-sum value is not paid yet. The lump-sum value can be invested in the bank to accrue interest, resulting in the third term. The term on the right-hand side is the instantaneous cost of delayed recertification. That cost results from *not* terminating the stream of m for a client who is already ineligible (with probability $P_{EI}[T]$). The optimal T^* in (9.19) balances these four terms.

Making use of (9.15) to express U_∞ in (9.19) as a function of m (and the parameters λ, μ, and ρ) and then dividing (9.19) throughout by m reveals an important feature of the problem. At the optimum, the only dependence T^* has on c and on m is through the term $(\rho c/m)$—i.e., through their relative values.

Optimal Periodic Recertifications

The single-recertification problem just considered resembles the tree-cutting problem of Fisher. Both problems assume that an action—whether recertification or tree harvesting—is taken once, whereupon the problem is over. In this section, the optimal certification duration model incorporates multiple stochastic cycles to recognize that a decision about any one recertification affects the likelihoods and outcomes of future recertifications.

Suppose WIC determined at time 0 that the optimal length of the first certification duration is T_1^*. For a client who is eligible at the first recertification, the problem as of T_1^* for the second certification duration, T_2^*, resembles precisely, in its stochastic specification, the problem as of time 0 for how long to specify the first certification duration (because of the memoryless property and the infinite-horizon feature of the model). Thus, the problem will yield the same solution, that $T_2^* = T_1^*$. Moreover, each certification duration will be the same optimal length. Although there are multiple cycles, the problem condenses to selecting a single optimal T^*, taking into account all possible future cycles. The problem will have recertifications at times T^*, $2T^*$, $3T^*$, and further multiples of T^*.

$S(T)$ and $M(T)$ refer to costs associated with a single cycle and with multiple cycles, respectively. $M(T)$ is derived from $S(T)$. The expected discounted cost of the (first) cycle from 0 to T is given by

$$(9.20) \quad E[S(T)] = U(T) + D(T) .$$

The within-cycle discounted cost of the second cycle from T to $2T$, or within any future cycle, is also $E[S(T)]$. Because $E[S(T)]$ appropriately discounts within-cycle costs only to the start of the cycle, the present value of a cycle's cost involves discounting that value back to time 0. Conditioned on the client being eligible at T, that value for the second cycle would be

(9.21) $\quad PV\{Cycle\ \#2\,|\,eligibility\ at\ T\} = e^{-\rho T} E[S(T)]$,

and more generally for future cycles $n = 2, 3, 4, \ldots$, the value is

(9.22) $\quad PV\{Cycle\ \#n\,|\,eligibility\ at\ (n-1)T\} = e^{-\rho(n-1)T} E[S(T)]$.

In (9.22) the present value is conditioned on the client being eligible at a given recertification. As of time 0, those outcomes are uncertain. For example, only with a probability $P_{EE}(T)$ will the client be found to be eligible at the first recertification. With probability $P_{EI}(T)$ the client is ineligible and benefits are terminated. The second cycle's (unconditioned) expected present value is

(9.23) $\quad EPV\{Cycle\ \#2\} = e^{-\rho T} \left[P_{EE}(T)E[S(T)] + P_{EI}(T)(0) \right]$.

The third cycle commences if the client passes the second recertification, and that is possible only if the client has already passed the first recertification with probability $P_{EE}(T)$:

(9.24) $\quad EPV\{Cycle\ \#3\} = P_{EE}(T)e^{-\rho T} \left[P_{EE}(T)E[S(T)] + P_{EI}(T)(0) \right]$.

The fourth cycle is reached on condition that the third cycle was begun, an event that requires passing two recertifications in a row with probability $P_{EE}(T)^2$. Most generally,

(9.25)
$EPV\{Cycle\ \#n\} = \left[P_{EE}(T) \right]^{n-2} e^{-\rho(n-1)T} \left[P_{EE}(T)E[S(T)] + P_{EI}(T)(0) \right]$,

where the term $[P_{EE}(T)]^{n-2}$ reflects the number of recertifications that must be passed with uninterrupted successes to reach the start of any given cycle n.[9]

$M(T)$ is the sum of the expected present value of each successive cycle:

$$(9.26) \quad M(T) = E[S(T)] + e^{-\rho T}\left[P_{EE}(T)E[S(T)] + P_{EI}(T)(0)\right]$$
$$+ P_{EE}(T)e^{-\rho 2T}\left[P_{EE}(T)E[S(T)] + P_{EI}(T)(0)\right]$$
$$+ [P_{EE}(T)]^2 e^{-\rho 3T}\left[P_{EE}(T)E[S(T)] + P_{EI}(T)(0)\right] + \cdots$$
$$= E[S(T)] + [e^{-\rho T}P_{EE}(T)]E[S(T)] + [e^{-\rho T}P_{EE}(T)]^2 E[S(T)]$$
$$+ [e^{-\rho T}P_{EE}(T)]^3 E[S(T)] + \cdots$$
$$= \frac{E[S(T)]}{1 - e^{-\rho T}P_{EE}(T)}.$$

The final line in (9.26) follows from viewing $M(T)$ as the infinite sum of terms that involve a geometric sequence. It is helpful to express $E[S(T)]$ by its two components, $U(T)$ and $D(T)$:

$$(9.27) \quad M(T) = \frac{U(T)}{1 - e^{-\rho T}P_{EE}(T)} + \frac{D(T)}{1 - e^{-\rho T}P_{EE}(T)}.$$

In (9.27) $M(T)$ is clearly the sum of two cost curves (in expected present value, across multiple stochastic cycles), one for excess burden of unwarranted benefits and one for recertification costs. These two curves are depicted in Figure 9.1, together with the "Total cost" curve given by $M(T)$. Optimal T^* is that value of T at which $M(T)$ is minimized.

In the simulation, $M(T)$ is calculated using the functions and parameters in (9.27), and then letting T increase in one-month increments. (An upper limit of 99 months was examined.) The optimal certification duration, at T^*, is identified as the last month in which the change $M(T^*) - M(T^* - 1)$ is negative: a month past T^* results in an increase in $M(T)$, so $M(T)$ is minimized at T^*.

Time Horizons

An infinite-horizon specification embodied in (9.16) and (9.26) is helpful for distilling the dynamic essence of the benefits and costs accrued from delaying recertification. It is appropriate to consider how

Figure 9.1 Cost Curves of Optimal Certification Duration Model

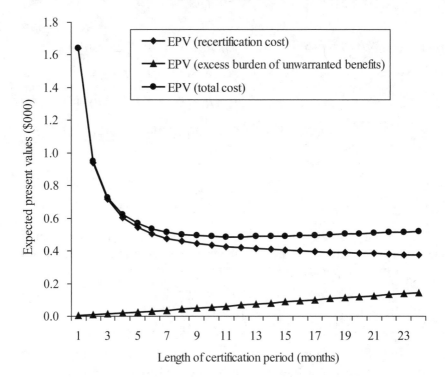

SOURCE: Author's analysis.

well an infinite-horizon specification can be used for conducting simulations of WIC children's optimal certification duration in the next section.

While in many cases it is less accurate to use an infinite-horizon rather than a finite-horizon specification, the infinite-horizon version is typically less complex. Its degree of accuracy depends, in part, on the length of the appropriate finite horizon and the social discount rate. The longer the finite horizon, the more accurate the infinite-horizon simplification will be. Accuracy is also better when the social discount rate is higher, which decreases the present value of any given future benefit or cost (values that are retained in the infinite-horizon specification but that might be cut off after a finite horizon).

The issue of an appropriate time horizon is pertinent for the case study on WIC children because the length of their participation is at most four years (up to age five). In the end, whether or not an infinite-horizon specification is a good approximation for WIC children depends in part on the numerical results of the simulation. If the so-called optimal certification duration T^* from the simulation is estimated at, say, seven or eight years, the use of the infinite-horizon clearly has a serious weakness: by neglecting the four-year maximum, the estimate T^* exceeds the upper limit of age-based eligibility. On the other hand, if the simulation's estimated T^* is, say, a few months, the estimate is short relative to a four-year maximum participation, and the difference between infinite- and finite-horizon specifications may be negligible. Even then, however, the simulation's optimal certification duration does fit best for a one-year-old, who has the longest potential participation. Accuracy diminishes when a child is older and thus closer to the upper limit on age requirements.

APPLICATION: WIC CHILDREN'S CERTIFICATION DURATION

This section uses the optimal certification duration model to simulate T^* for a case study of WIC children. Conducting any simulation exercise involves more than just specifying an economic model and assigning values for key parameters. While there has been some research done on certification activities for local WIC agencies (e.g., Macro International 1995) certification costs capturing the time involved, from both a WIC agency's and a client's perspective, have not been studied as much for WIC as for food stamps. And while some work has been carried out on dynamic income patterns and labor market behavior for families with WIC infants and children, the simulations need greater month-by-month detail than previous work has presented.[10] Information on the dollar cost of the WIC food package for children is incomplete. Of necessity, the simulations rest on assumptions used to develop a set of values for model parameters. A baseline simulation is conducted using best-guess values of parameters. To ascertain the effects of alternative assumptions, additional simulations are done as a sensitivity analysis using alternative parameter values. The simulations for optional certification durations are tentative, subject to refinement by improving the model or the estimates of parameters.

State Probability Paths of Households with Older Children

A longitudinal approach is needed that will allow the income trajectories of individual households to be followed over time in order to identify which months a household is eligible and which months a household is ineligible. The simulations draw on results by Newman (2006), who identified a set of households that were income-eligible for free or reduced-price meals in the National School Lunch Program (NSLP) at a particular moment (August at the start of the school year). Newman followed that set of households over time to examine, for the set as a whole, what percentage were not income-eligible in each successive month, yielding a state probability path $P_{EI}(t)$ for NSLP. There is a basis for using Newman's NSLP results for a simulation on WIC children: the income limit for reduced-price meals is the same—185 percent of poverty—as WIC's income limit. The income dynamics for households with older school-aged children are used to approximate the income dynamics for households with younger children of WIC age.[11]

It so happens that the Newman study contained three moments of eligibility, each for the month of August, but in three successive years, 1996 through 1998. The first three columns of Table 9.2 show Newman's results by year; the data make use of the seam-adjusted share figures reported in Newman (2006).

The table shows that in month 0 (August of each respective year), every household retained in the subsample is eligible, making 0.0 percent ineligible. Then, as the months of the school year pass, the percentage of households that are ineligible in a given month increases at a decreasing rate. The table also shows, in the fourth column, the monthly averages across the three years' state probability figures, which yields an average state probability path. The average path approaches a value that is taken to be a long-run or "steady state" value. The transitional nature of the average probability path is seen more readily in Figure 9.2, which depicts graphically the table's three-year average path (and a fitted path, described below).[12] In order to separate and estimate implicit exponential exit and reentry rates for eligibility, the steady-state

Table 9.2 State Probability Paths of Income Ineligibility, 1996–1998
(185 percent of poverty, households with school-aged children)

Month	1996	1997	1998	Average, 1996–1998	Fitted
0	0.0	0.0	0.0	0.0	0.0
1	13.7	11.8	7.2	10.9	6.6
2	12.9	13.1	11.1	12.4	11.5
3	17.6	21.1	17.0	18.6	15.1
4	19.5	18.4	16.8	18.2	17.7
5	20.3	19.8	19.0	19.7	19.7
6	22.1	23.8	20.0	22.0	21.1
7	23.0	21.6	18.8	21.1	22.1
8	22.2	22.0	20.6	21.6	22.9
9	23.1	23.5	23.8	23.5	23.5
10	25.9	25.3	22.5	24.6	23.9
11	23.3	23.2	23.6	23.4	24.2

SOURCE: Newman (2006), Tables 10–12 and author's analysis.

probability $\mu/(\lambda+\mu)$ toward which the state probability path approaches was set (by visual inspection) at 0.25. The rate of approach towards the steady-state probability was used to estimate the state probability path using OLS. From Equation 9.11, it follows that

$$(9.28) \quad \ln\left(1-\frac{P_{EI}(t)}{0.25}\right) = -\left(\lambda+\mu\right)t ,$$

where the average figures of column 4 are used for the data on $P_{EI}(t)$ in (9.28). The coefficient on time was estimated to be −0.309 (with the restriction of zero-intercept imposed), with an R-squared value of 0.85 for the equation. Based on the estimated coefficient, the estimated (monthly) value of λ was 7.725 percent, and μ was estimated at 23.175 percent. It is no accident that the estimated value of μ is precisely three times the estimated value of λ: that relationship is implied by the stipulation that the steady-state probability $\mu/(\lambda+\mu) = 0.25$, and it serves as the identification restriction by which the two structural parameters are obtained from the estimated coefficient on time. The fifth column of the table and its accompanying figure each show a "fitted" state probability path, based on the estimates of the two structural parameters.

Figure 9.2 Average and Fitted State Probability Paths of Income Ineligibility, 1996–1998

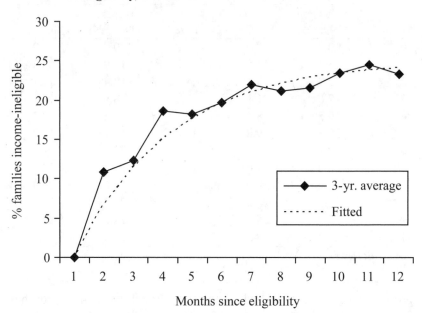

NOTE: Families with school-aged children become ineligible at 185% of the poverty line.

SOURCE: Newman (2006), Tables 10–12, and author's analysis. See Table 9.2 of this chapter for numerical values.

An R-squared value of 0.85 from (9.28) is considered here to be a good fit with the data. It is the empirical support for the claim (in the third section) that the actual probability paths for some households' income dynamics are approximated well by the theoretical probability path predicted on the basis of the exponential distribution.

Dollar Cost of WIC Children's Benefits

The simulations do not account for the dollar cost of WIC's nutrition counseling and health referrals: the cost of the WIC food package alone is used.

The simulation of the certification duration model requires a figure for monthly WIC benefits for children. The children's package contains such items as cereal, peanut butter, juice, cheese, milk, and eggs; participants have some choice regarding combinations of certain items. The cost of a WIC food package for a particular participant category is not routinely collected or estimated. The most comprehensive work in this area, by Davis and Leibtag (2005), examines the role of food prices, caseload composition, and cost-containment practices in affecting a state's WIC food package costs for 17 selected states under study. For purposes of defining a common cross-state food package standard by which to compare food package costs, Davis and Leibtag used the maximum quantity of food available in each food package. However, while WIC can provide a particular client with a prescription of foods up to the maximum set by federal regulation, WIC tries to tailor the amounts of a package's individual food items to the individual client to match preferences and avoid waste. The average prescriptions are typically below the maximum prescriptions. For example, in April 2004 the federal maximum prescription for milk was 24 quarts, but only 2.1 percent of children received the federal maximum. At the time, the average quantity of milk prescribed was 16.8 quarts (USDA 2006c). To better approximate the pattern of actual prescriptions, this chapter takes into account, by item, that the average quantity received by a child nationally may be below the federal maximum, resulting in a slight adjustment to the work by Davis and Leibtag. Table 9.3 shows the estimated value of the children's food package for each of the 17 selected states, based on prices reported by Information Resources Inc. for the market areas in the state; as Davis and Leibtag note, these prices may not be representative of prices in the entire state. The table shows $32.52 as the simple average across the 17 states. This figure is used as the baseline value for M.

WIC Recertification Costs

An estimate of agency recertification costs is derived using three factors: a figure for the hourly wage rate for direct staff time, a figure for the direct staff time (in hours) associated with recertification, and a percentage figure for an overhead rate. The cost figure that is derived is for 1998; that year is within the 1997–1999 range for which the WIC food package costs were derived and also within the 1996–1998 range of the Newman income volatility data.

Table 9.3 Estimated WIC Children's Food Package Cost by State, 1997–1999

State	Cost of WIC children's food package ($)
CA	34.71
CO	33.52
FL	33.15
GA	31.12
IA	30.36
IL	32.79
KS	32.64
MA	34.27
MI	31.60
MN	30.74
MO	31.25
NY	36.27
PA	32.18
TN	32.78
TX	31.24
WA	34.24
WI	30.04
Average	32.52

SOURCE: Davis and Leibtag (2005) and author's analysis.

Among the public health nutrition workforce in Full Time Equivalent positions, four-fifths (81 percent) of employees are employed in WIC programs (USDA 2003). Across the 2,200 local agencies and 10,000 WIC service sites, caseload and staffing vary. Some local agencies have one or two staff while others have more than 350 (USDA 2006a, p. 14) Various staff have administrative, nutrition counseling, and medical skills. Tasks involved with certification (as opposed to providing WIC benefits in the form of nutritional counseling or breastfeeding promotion) include determining identity, state of residency, and income eligibility; measuring height and weight; drawing blood and doing analysis; and determining nutritional risk. At the local level, WIC uses a variety of approaches and different combinations of professionals, paraprofessionals, and WIC's "competent professional authorities" to conduct the various certification tasks.[13] The simulations use Bureau of Labor Statistics (BLS) data to estimate a 1998 figure for total hourly compensation across "health care and social assistance employees" in state and local government to proxy what weighted-average combination of employees' wages and times may affect certification cost in any particular locality.[14]

The National Compensation Survey of the BLS reports that the cost per hour worked (in terms of wages and salaries) for health care and social assistance employees in state and local government averaged $23.53 in the second quarter of 2006, representing 65.9 percent of total compensation (BLS 2008).[15] Because the BLS recently shifted from the Standard Industrial Classification (SIC) system to the North American Industry Classification System (NAICS), the time series for NAICS figures begins only in 2004; thus, an NAICS figure for 1998 is not available. However, the SIC figure from BLS for 1998 for wages and salaries of "all workers" in state and local government is $19.19 per hour, representing 70.3 percent of total compensation. Thus, the total compensation in 1998 for all workers was $27.30. An adjustment of this figure downward, to better estimate total compensation of health care and social assistance employees who staff WIC, results in a estimate of $25.40 in total compensation per hour for 1998.[16] This figure is used as an approximation of a weighted-average wage rate across staff involved with WIC certifications.

Among the documents the Office of Management and Budget (OMB) provides for guidance and reference is a general guide to benefit-cost analysis that states the following:

> When calculating labor costs, the OMB recommends using prevailing wage rates and salaries. To arrive at fully burdened costs when estimating personnel costs for government employees, you must add overhead costs to salary and fringe-benefit costs. . . . Some examples of indirect costs include rent, utilities, insurance, indirect labor, and other expenses typically charged to the organization as a whole. . . . For evaluation purposes, costs (both direct and indirect) should be included if they will change with the introduction of a proposed system (Federal CIO Council 1999, pp. 14–15).

It is sensible to account for indirect costs. A change in certification policy can have long-term and large-scale effects on the caseload and on the agency's overall staffing and capacity to service that caseload. If certification periods were changed nationally, states could change (at least in the long term) not only staffing but also office space, equipment, and the like, to support the new flow of recertifications. Therefore, it is suitable for the certification duration model to use a "burdened" or a "loaded" hourly labor cost rather than considering wage costs alone. The total compensation figure estimated for health care and social assistance employees in state and local government for 1998 was estimated to be $25.40. To cover all indirect costs as well, this paper applies an arbitrary overhead rate of 100 percent to the $25.40 total hourly compensation to obtain a loaded hourly labor cost of $50.80. A sensitivity analysis will adopt the extreme factor of 0, implicitly ignoring indirect costs altogether.

For the simulation, a figure of 1.5 hours was used for the staff time involved with a certification. This figure represents a composite of figures from six Web sites at the county or state level that inform potential WIC applicants of how long they need to plan for conducting a certification.[17] It is presumed that the 1.5-hour figure represents certification activity, as opposed to time spent in the provision of nonfood WIC benefits in the forms of health referrals, nutrition counseling, and breastfeeding promotion. Separate appointments at the WIC clinic are often made for these other activities.

Although the time for staff is assumed to be 1.5 hours for certification, the time for a client is assumed to be two hours to take into account travel time. About three-quarters of WIC households earn a wage or salary. Even those who have no labor income place a value on their time. An arbitrary figure of $6 an hour is used to estimate the value of time to the person—presumably the mother—who brings the WIC child to the program for certification.[18] An arbitrary figure of $5 per certification is used for out-of-pocket travel costs for the WIC child's mother.

Social Discount Rate

There is a literature on what the concept of the social discount rate means, or ought to mean, and how to measure it in terms of an observable private market discount rate. A range of 2 to 10 percent (in real terms) may encompass most estimates. The OMB annually provides federal agencies with updated discount rates, in support of Circular A-94 (OMB 1992), which provides guidance on benefit-cost analysis. As of January 2006, real discount rates for use in cost-effectiveness analysis (as opposed to other decisions) were reported as ranging from 2.5

percent for a three-year horizon up to 3.0 percent for a 30-year horizon (OMB 2006). The simulation uses a monthly discount rate of 0.002 for the baseline and an alternative figure of 0.004 for sensitivity analysis.

Excess Burden

OMB Circular A-94 gives a figure of 25 percent for ε, excess burden per dollar of taxes, although it also provides for the use of other figures. The 25 percent figure exceeds an estimate of 19.5 percent efficiency cost for combined local, state, and federal level taxes relative to a nondistortionary, revenue-neutral tax in a study by Jorgenson and Yun. Their study was reported to be one of the two studies with the broadest scope in a U.S. Government Accountability Office review of the compliance and efficiency cost of taxes (USGAO 2005). The simulation will use the 25 percent OMB figure to represent excess burden for the baseline, and an alternative figure of 19.5 percent.

Simulations of Optimal Certification Durations for WIC Children

Table 9.4 shows the results from the baseline simulation and sensitivity analysis. The figure of $112.25, the baseline model's figure for recertification costs c, is the sum of taxpayer and client costs. The estimated budgetary costs for recertification reflect $25.40 an hour for direct staff cost, a 100 percent overhead factor to obtain loaded labor costs, and an estimated time of 1.5 hours for a recertification, resulting in a total of $76.20 in budgetary terms. Taking into account an excess burden of taxation figure of 25 percent, the cost to the taxpayer of a recertification is $95.25. The cost to the client is estimated at $17, reflecting $12 worth of time costs ($6 an hour and two hours of time, including the time of the recertification and travel time) and $5 out-of-pocket travel costs. Social cost per recertification of $[(1+\varepsilon)c_A + c_C]$ totals $112.25 under the baseline.

The baseline figure for excess burden m is $8.13, equaling εM of $(0.25) \times (\$32.52)$.

Columns 3 and 4 show the solution to the baseline simulation as a pair of values, T^* and its associated $M(T^*)$, representing the optimal, cost-minimizing certification duration and the minimized value of total cost that results from using T^*. The baseline simulation results in T^* of

Table 9.4 Results of CD Model Simulations

	Recert. cost ($)	Excess burden εM ($)	Optimal T^* (end-of-month)	Optimal $M(T^*)$ ($)
Baseline model	112.25	8.13	12 months	486.28
Change from baseline: double M	112.25	16.26	9 months	540.90
Change from baseline: overhead factor of 0	64.63	8.13	9 months	304.09
Change from baseline: ε decreased to 19.5 percent	108.06	6.34	13 months	455.40
Change from baseline: ρ raised to 0.4 per month	112.25	8.13	16 months	442.10
Change from baseline: low income volatility	112.25	8.13	14 months	492.23
Change from baseline: high income volatility	112.25	8.13	7 months	474.58

SOURCE: Author's analysis.

12 months and $M(T^*)$ of \$486.28. This solution occurs in Figure 9.1, which is depicted using the baseline values. Other parameter values used in the sensitivity analysis would change the locations and shapes of the curves, resulting in new, numerically different solutions T^* and $M(T^*)$.

Sensitivity Analysis: Monthly Benefits

The first sensitivity analysis considers how an optimal certification duration might change if a different figure were used for monthly WIC benefits M and all other parameters were fixed at their baseline values. While the baseline figure for M was \$32.52 (the 17-state average), the WIC children's food package cost in New York was estimated to be \$36.27 in Table 9.3. Using the New York figure—the highest among the 17 states in the table—results in a value for m of \$9.0675 and for T^* of 11 months (not shown in Table 9.4), which is shorter than the baseline's 12. It makes sense that T^* is now shorter because it pays to recertify more frequently when the potential savings from terminating unwarranted benefits is greater.

The \$3.75 increase in M to the New York figure is about 10 percent of the baseline value. The increase did lower T^* by a month; however, such effects are not linear: increasing M by a steady amount does not lower T^* by one month in steady increments. The curve for recertification costs steepens sharply as certification duration is lowered, and that factor becomes increasingly difficult to overcome. Suppose instead that monthly benefits M were to double, to \$65.04—a change in children's WIC food package cost that far exceeds the \$3.75 increase (and is far outside the 17-state range). Table 9.4 shows that an increase in effective benefits of this magnitude results in a decrease in T^* to nine months, down by just three months from the baseline case.

A doubling of the effective benefit is not simply a sensitivity analysis that gauges a relationship between T^* and M. While no state is known to have a WIC food package cost as high as \$65.04 per package—i.e., per child—in every state there are WIC households in which two WIC children (ages one to four) reside. While WIC certifies and provides benefits at the level of the individual, a household with two WIC children can receive double the food package benefits received by a household with one WIC child. An imaginable alternative to existing certification policy is that the WIC certification period for a WIC household could depend on the number of children (and, more generally, the number of other WIC participants) in the household.

Sensitivity Analysis: Overhead Rate

In the baseline, an arbitrary overhead rate of 100 percent is applied to total compensation (per hour) as part of estimating the WIC agency's cost of recertification. If no overhead factor is applied, the budgetary cost per certification would drop by half, to \$38.10 [(\$25.40/hr)(1 ½ hr)]. As would be expected, T^* drops below the baseline figure of 12 months. The new T^* is nine months, equaling the T^* from the simulation that considered doubling M.

Drawing on the result in the previous section that T^* depends on the relative values of c and m through the term $(\rho c/m)$, it would be expected that dropping c by half would necessarily result in exactly the same estimated T^* as doubling m by doubling M. However, c has not quite fallen by half: c is the sum of both c_A and c_C, and c_C is unchanged (at \$17). In the end, though, the change in c is close enough to half to yield the same nine-month figure in both sensitivity analyses.

Sensitivity Analysis: Excess Burden

As the value for ε varies, everything else being equal, excess burden εM will vary in proportion but recertification costs $[(1+\varepsilon)c_A + c_C]$ will vary less than proportionately because the component of the recertification costs paid by the client is unaffected by variation in ε. When reducing ε from the OMB figure of 0.25 to the Jorgenson and Yun figure of 0.195, the reduction in percentage terms for excess burden from $8.13 to $6.34 is relatively large, while the reduction in recertification cost from $112.25 to $108.06 is relatively small, making the $(\rho c/m)$ necessarily rise. The resulting increase in $(\rho c/m)$ drives T^* to increase from the baseline's 12-month T^* to a new T^* of 13 months. With lower values for both excess burden and recertification costs, the new $M(T^*)$ drops from the baseline (to $455.40).

Sensitivity Analysis: Discount Rate

Doubling the social discount rate from the baseline figure of 0.2 percent per month to 0.4 percent per month increases T^* from 12 months in the baseline to 16 months. $M(T^*)$ drops from $486.28 to $442.10 when future values are discounted more.

Sensitivity Analysis: Income Volatility

The pair of income volatility parameters (λ, μ) in the baseline simulation are (0.07725, 0.23175), derived from an ordinary least squares (OLS) best fit of the Newman data. If instead the parameters are selected to provide upper and lower bounds to the three-year average figures of the state probability path $P_{EI}(t)$, different estimates for T^* would result. Retaining the stipulation that the state probability path has a steady state at 0.25 (which is $\lambda/(\lambda+\mu)$ in the model) means that μ will be three times the value of λ for any selected λ. Thus, this sensitivity analysis is not being conducted as an exercise in which one parameter is varied and all others are held constant. Income volatility is examined here through the joint variation of λ and μ.

Figure 9.3 Average State Probability Path of Income Ineligibility, Framed by Low and High Paths, 1996–1998

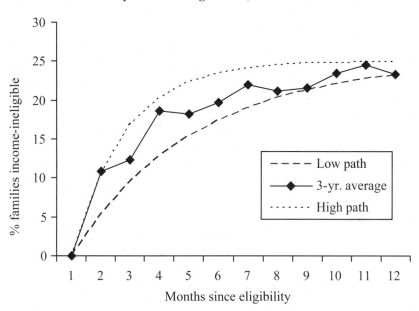

NOTE: Families with school-aged children become ineligible at 185% of the poverty line.
SOURCE: Table 9.2 and author's analysis.

Figure 9.3 shows two smooth state probability paths, a low path and a high path, that sandwich the three-year average state probability path of the Newman data. The low path is generated by $\lambda = 0.06$ (and μ of 0.18), while the high path is generated by $\lambda = 0.14$ (and μ of 0.42). The low path is associated with low income volatility (i.e., low parameter values for the two income volatility parameters) as well as low values of $P_{EI}(t)$ at any given t along the path. Correspondingly, the high path is associated with high income volatility and high values of $P_{EI}(t)$.

Table 9.4 shows the results for a scenario that uses the baseline parameters except for income volatility, for which low values are used. T^* increases from 12 months at baseline to 14 months with low income volatility. Under high income volatility, T^* is seven months.

CONCLUSION

The optimal certification duration model shows in algebraic and graphical terms two policy trade-offs faced by program administration. On the one hand, there is economic savings to be had from detecting ineligible clients and terminating unwarranted benefits, thus saving the excess burden of taxation that is used to finance the benefits. Recertification is an administrative tool by which to determine whether a client is currently eligible. More frequent recertifications can reduce the excess burden of unwarranted benefits. At the same time, though, more frequent recertifications entail economic costs paid by WIC (ultimately, taxpayers) and by clients. In optimal decision-making, the costs of staff and equipment, of time and travel, are balanced against the costs of the excess burden of unwarranted benefits.

The optimal certification duration model takes into account the probabilistic nature of income dynamics and the time-dependency of probability paths of exit from eligibility and reentry into eligibility. It discounts future benefits and costs. It recognizes that there are repercussions to the likelihood and outcomes of future recertifications from conducting any given recertification.

Despite its strengths, the optimal certification duration model is a simplified rendition of the recertification problem that made use of workable functional forms (the exponential distribution) and an infinite-horizon specification. There is another limitation of the model that merits recognizing. The model focuses on the trade-off between a pair of program goals—specifically, benefits targeting and recertification costs. Another program goal that was set aside by the model is client access, which refers to sustaining participation by eligibles. Each recertification is a burden on the client, entailing monetary and time costs. Frequent recertifications may act as a barrier or a disincentive to program participation, potentially decreasing participation by some of the very clients whom the program was established to support. Thus, a longer certification duration may provide a social value in terms of improved client access. If so, then the certification durations estimated in the simulations may be interpreted as lower bounds of those that would be obtained from a fuller model that includes client access.

In one respect, introducing client access into the model is easy: simply define a "cost of client access" function, say $A(T)$, that would be a positive function of T, and add it to get a new total cost curve and a new cost-minimizing T^*. However, to conduct a simulation would now require figures for $A(T)$, figures that in turn require knowledge of clients' behavior—knowing by how much participation falls as T varies—and a figure for the social value of participation by eligibles.

The best-guess values of key parameters resulted in a baseline simulation of 12 months for the optimal certification duration T^*. From the theoretical model, it could be expected that an increase in WIC benefits or higher income volatility would lower T^*, while increases in agency or client recertification costs, excess burden per dollar of taxes or lower income volatility would increase T^*. A reason for conducting numerical simulations is to gauge the sensitivity in numerical terms of changes in T^* to changes in parameters. T^* varied from 7 to 14 months, depending on the simulation. Because some WIC households have more than one child receiving benefits, the model suggests that optimal T^* could depend on the amount of WIC benefits any one household is receiving rather than on using a common certification duration for all WIC children.

An economic model can help clarify why different voices in the political process have different recommendations. The optimal certification duration model shows that there are many factors that affect certification durations. Different recommendations on certification durations would naturally follow from different notions of the size or strength of these factors that are in the model, as well as from different assessments of how important are the factors—such as client access—that have been left out of the model. Data and economic analysis can serve to quantify factors that may otherwise be impressionistic. The contribution of an economic model serves to help provide a common framework for analysis and discussion.

Every model has strengths and limitations; no model is complete. The theoretical and simulation results here are not presented as definitive, but as a first exploration of an issue of importance to policymakers, to program clients, and to the many other stakeholders with interests in the operations and effects of USDA food assistance programs.

Notes

I would like to acknowledge that this work benefited from comments by Dean Jolliffe, James Ziliak, Peter Gottschalk, Michael LeBlanc, David Smallwood, and Margaret Andrews. The views expressed here are those of the author and not necessarily those of the Economic Research Service or the U.S. Department of Agriculture.

1. To be eligible for WIC, a client must also be considered by a health professional to be at nutritional risk. Few applicants do not meet that criterion. Here I focus on income as if it were the sole determinant of WIC eligibility.
2. Total food cost and average monthly food cost per participant can be found at http://www.fns.usda.gov/pd/wisummary.htm (USDA 2008a, accessed April 18, 2008).
3. For fiscal 2005, the annual participation figures were 1,966,249 women, 2,047,118 infants, and 4,009,248 children (USDA 2008b).
4. As noted by Jorgenson, McCall, and Radner, "For the exponential distribution of time to failure . . . inspection, like replacement, serves as a point of regeneration of the investment process. This property of the exponential distribution, often referred to as the Markovian property or "lack of memory," is not shared by any other distribution of time to failure" (p. 90).
5. The parameter μ is a transition rate of reentry for clients who had previously exited from eligibility, as opposed to a hazard rate of initial entry for the general population of ineligibles. Formerly eligible clients constitute a group that can be expected to exhibit (a) lower income than the general ineligible population and (b) a higher rate at which eligibility is (re)entered.
6. The certification duration model makes repeated use of (9.10) and (9.11) and for brevity calls them "state probabilities" even though they are properly understood as "conditional" in contrast to (9.8) and (9.9).
7. There is another pair of probability paths (not shown) for the probabilities that the client is either eligible or ineligible at time t, given that the client is ineligible at time zero; these two paths are not used here.
8. It is this feature of the model that would be absent if hazard rates were non-constant.
9. Intuition suggests that the exponent on the $[P_{EE}(T)]$ term in Equation (9.25) should be $n - 1$ rather than $n - 2$. However, counting the number of passed recertifications to reach the nth cycle differs from the usual count of "successful trials" in statistical theory. WIC is examining the optimal certification duration for a client who has just been determined to be eligible at the initial application, thus removing one $P_{EE}(T)$ (for the initial application) from consideration and changing the exponent by 1.
10. Work in this area includes Bitler, Currie, and Scholz (2003); Gordon, Lewis, and Radbill (1997); Klerman and Leibowitz (1990); and Ver Ploeg and Betson (2003).
11. It is known from earlier studies that income is volatile for women surrounding the

birth event, raising the question of how well income dynamics match for households with WIC children and households with school-aged children. However, research findings suggest that many mothers who had been employed before pregnancy return to work within the first year after giving birth. Klerman and Leibowitz (1990) find that over one-third of mothers were at work within three months following birth, and three-quarters within two years. The simulations here presume that the volatility surrounding the birth event is sufficiently resolved by the end of the first year that the birth event does not substantially affect income dynamics of households with WIC children (ages one to four).

12. One small difference in labels is noted: the first month in the table is month 0, while in the figure it is month 1.

13. A recent study on WIC staffing states that "little specific information exists about the actual performance of duties throughout the various classifications within the nutrition workforce, or specifically the WIC workforce" (USDA 2006b, p. 31). The same study notes that "Some clinics attempt to get both anthropometric and blood work from other providers, while some clinics do their own anthropometrics and use blood work obtained elsewhere" (p. 21).

14. A weighted-average approach would draw upon such information as a 1999–2000 survey of staffing and annual salaries reported by the USDA (2003), in which the range between the median low salary and the median high salary for various positions was $18,804–$25,251 for nutrition assistant, $20,736–$29,163 for nutrition technician, $26,352–$39,000 for nutritionist, and $29,661–$43,496 for clinical nutritionist; five other job titles and salaries were reported, too. One difficulty with constructing weighted-average wage rate is that positions with these titles have nonuniform duties across local WIC agencies. Another is the absence of information on the time each contributes to a certification.

15. A check on the correspondence between the hourly wage of an actual WIC staff position and the BLS figure is provided by a job-vacancy notice posted in summer 2006 by Rice County, Minnesota, seeking a WIC professional—a public health nurse or nutrition professional (Rice County 2006). The job activities included "all phases of the WIC certification process, including hematological screening." The stated hourly salary range was $19.31–$26.71, for which the midpoint is $23.01, which differs from the BLS figure by about one half-dollar.

16. Quarterly data for 2005 are available for both "health care and social assistance employees" and for "all occupations" (both series in the state and local government sector). Total compensation was computed for each of four quarters of 2005 for the two groups using "cost per hour worked" and "percent of total compensation." The annual average of the quarterly figures is $35.92 for "all occupations" and $33.42 for "health care and social assistance." In 2005, "health care and social assistance" workers received (on average) 93.0 percent of the total compensation paid to "all occupations." Applying the 93.0 percent figure to the total compensation for "all workers" in 1998 of $27.30 yields a figure of $25.40 for "health care and social assistance employees" in that year.

17. The six Web sites were selected based only on convenience, rather than for constituting a nationally representative sample. The reported figures were "about"

30 minutes in Minnesota (MDH 2008); 1–2 hours in Michigan (MDCH 2008); 1–2 hours in Fairfax County, Virginia (FCHD 2008); "at least" 1½ hours in Clinton County, New York (CCHD 2008); "at least" 1½ hours in Utah County, Utah (UCHD 2006); and 1½–2 hours in St. Charles County, Missouri (SCCDPH 2008).

18. Of those households with WIC children, median annual income (all sources) was $15,325 for households with an adult male present and $8,520 for households without an adult male present in 1998 (USDA 2001, p. 76, Exhibit 3-22). The simulations take the $8,520 figure as the annual income (all sources) of a mother with a WIC child with or without an adult male present. The assumption of $6 per hour is consistent with annual earnings of $6,000 and 1,000 hours of annual work.

References

Barlow, Richard E., and Frank Proschan. 1996. *Mathematical Theory of Reliability*. Classics in Applied Mathematics 17. Philadelphia: Society for Industrial and Applied Mathematics.

Bitler, Marianne P., Janet Currie, and John Karl Scholz. 2003. "WIC Eligibility and Participation." *Journal of Human Resources* 38(Supplement): 1139–1179.

Boskin, Michael J., and Frederick C. Nold. 1975. "A Markov Model of Turnover in Aid to Families with Dependent Children." *Journal of Human Resources* 10(4): 467–481.

Clinton County Health Department (CCHD). 2008. *The Clinton County Women, Infants, and Children's Program (WIC)*. Plattsburgh, NY: Clinton County Health Department. http://www.clintoncountygov.com/Departments/Health/wic.html (accessed April 17, 2008).

Davis, David E., and Ephraim S. Leibtag. 2005. *Interstate Variation in WIC Food Package Costs: The Role of Food Prices, Caseload Composition, and Cost-Containment Practices*. Food Assistance and Nutrition Research Report No. 41. Washington DC: U.S. Department of Agriculture (USDA), Economic Research Service.

Fairfax County Health Department (FCHD). 2008. *Special Supplemental Nutrition Program for Women, Infants, and Children*. Fairfax, VA: Fairfax County Health Department. http://www.fairfaxcounty.gov/hd/wic/ (accessed April 17, 2008).

Federal CIO Council. 1999. *ROI and the Value Puzzle*. Washington, DC: Federal Chief Information Officers Council, Capital Planning and IT Investment Committee.

Gordon, Anne, Kimball Lewis, and Larry Radbill. 1997. *Income Variability among Families with Pregnant Women, Infants, or Young Children*. Report to the U.S. Department of Agriculture. Princeton, NJ: Mathematica Policy Research.

Greenfield, Victoria A., and David M. Persselin. 2002. *An Economic Framework for Evaluating Military Aircraft Replacement.* Project Air Force. Santa Monica, CA: RAND.

Howard, Ronald A. 1960. *Dynamic Programming and Markov Processes.* Cambridge, MA: MIT Press.

Jorgenson, Dale W., John J. McCall, and Roy Radner. 1967. *Optimal Replacement Policy.* Studies in Mathematical and Managerial Economics 8. Amsterdam: North-Holland.

Klerman, Jacob Alex, and Arleen Leibowitz. 1990. "Child Care and Women's Return to Work after Childbirth." *American Economic Review* 80(2): 284–288.

Lancaster, Tony. 1990. *The Econometric Analysis of Transition Data.* Cambridge: Cambridge University Press.

Macro International. 1995. *The WIC Dynamics Study.* Vol. I. Final Report. Prepared for the U.S. Department of Agriculture. Calverton, MD: Macro International.

Michigan Department of Community Health (MDCH). 2008. *Frequently Asked Questions about WIC.* Lansing, MI: Michigan Department of Community Health. http://www.michigan.gov/mdch/0,1607,7-132-2942_4910_4922-13973--,00.html (accessed July 7, 2008).

Minnesota Department of Health (MDH). 2008. *What Happens at Your WIC Certification Appointment?* St. Paul, MN: Minnesota Department of Health. http://www.health.state.mn.us/divs/fh/wic/aboutwic/wicappt.html (accessed April 17, 2008).

Newman, Constance. 2006. *The Income Volatility See-Saw: Implications for School Lunch.* Economic Research Report No. 23. Washington, DC: U.S. Department of Agriculture (USDA), Economic Research Service.

Office of Management and Budget (OMB). 1992. *Circular No. A-94 (Revised): Guidelines and Discount Rates for Benefit-Cost Analysis of Federal Programs.* Washington, DC: OMB.

———. 2006. *Circular No. A-94, Appendix C: Discount Rates for Cost-Effectiveness, Lease Purchase, and Related Analyses.* Washington, DC: OMB.

Radner, Roy, and Dale Weldeau Jorgenson. 1962. "Optimal Replacement and Inspection of Stochastically Failing Equipment." In *Studies in Applied Probability and Management Science*, Kenneth J. Arrow, Samuel Karlin, and Herbert Scarf, eds. Stanford, CA: Stanford University Press, pp. 184–206.

Rice County. 2006. *Human Resources.* Faribault, MN: Rice County. http://www.co.rice.mn.us/personnel/jobs.php (accessed April 17, 2008).

St. Charles County Division of Public Health (SCCDPH). 2008. *When*

You Come In for Your WIC Certification Appointment. St. Charles, MO: St. Charles County Division of Public Health. http://www.scchealth.org/docs/ph/ph_docs/phphs/wiccert.html (accessed April 17, 2008).

U.S. Bureau of Labor Statistics (BLS). 2008. *National Compensation Survey.* http://www.bls.gov/ncs/home.htm#data (accessed April 17, 2008).

U.S. Department of Agriculture (USDA). 2001. *National Survey of WIC Participants: Final Report.* Alexandria, VA: USDA, Food and Nutrition Service.

———. 2003. *Survey of the Public Health Nutrition Workforce: 1999–2000.* Nutrition Assistance Program Report Series. Alexandria, VA: USDA, Food and Nutrition Service.

———. 2006a. *WIC Staffing Data Collection Project.* Report No. WIC-05-WS. Alexandria, VA: USDA, Food and Nutrition Service.

———. 2006b. *WIC Participant and Program Characteristics 2004.* Report No. WIC-04-PC. Alexandria, VA: USDA, Food and Nutrition Service.

———. 2006c. *WIC Participant and Program Characteristics 2004. Addendum: Food Package Analysis.* Report No. WIC-04-PC. Alexandria, VA: USDA, Food and Nutrition Service. http://www.fns.usda.gov/oane/MENU/Published/WIC/FILES/PC2004FPAnalysis.pdf (accessed July 7, 2008).

———. 2008a. *WIC Program Participation and Costs.* Alexandria, VA: USDA, Food and Nutrition Service. http://www.fns.usda.gov/pd/wisummary.htm (accessed April 17, 2008).

———. 2008b. *Program Data: WIC Program. Monthly Data—National Level: FY 2005 through April 2008.* Alexandria, VA: USDA, Food and Nutrition Service. http://www.fns.usda.gov/pd/37WIC_Monthly.htm (accessed July 3, 2008).

U.S. Government Accountability Office (USGAO). 2005. *Tax Policy: Summary of Estimates of the Costs of the Federal Tax System.* Report to Congressional Requesters. GAO-05-878. Washington, DC: USGAO.

Utah County Health Department (UCHD). 2006. *Health: Women, Infants, Children.* Provo, UT: UCHD. http://www.co.utah.ut.us/Dept/HealthWIC/Index.asp (accessed April 17, 2008).

Ver Ploeg, Michele, and David M. Betson, eds. 2003. *Estimating Eligibility and Participation for the WIC Program.* Final Report. Washington, DC: National Academies Press.

The Authors

Robin Boadway is the Sir Edward Peacock Professor of Economic Theory in the Department of Economics at Queen's University.

Brian Cadena is a graduate student in the Department of Economics at the University of Michigan.

Katherine Cuff is assistant professor in the Department of Economics at McMaster University.

Sheldon Danziger is the Henry J. Meyer Distinguished University Professor of Public Policy and codirector of the National Poverty Center at the University of Michigan.

Marilyn Edelhoch is the director of research and evaluation at the South Carolina Department of Social Services.

Craig Gundersen is associate professor of agricultural and consumer economics at the University of Illinois.

Dean Jolliffe is an economist at the Economic Research Service in the U.S. Department of Agriculture.

Benjamin J. Keys is a graduate student in the Department of Economics at the University of Michigan.

Nicolas Marceau is a professor in the Department of Economics at the Université du Québec à Montréal and is director of the Centre Interuniversitaire sur le Risque, les Politiques 'Economiques et l'Emploi.

Robert Moffitt is the Krieger-Eisenhower Professor of Economics in the Department of Economics at Johns Hopkins University.

Constance Newman is an economist at the Economic Research Service in the U.S. Department of Agriculture.

Mark Prell is branch chief of the Food Assistance Branch in the Economic Research Service's Food Economics Division in the U.S. Department of Agriculture.

David C. Ribar is a professor in the Department of Economics at the University of North Carolina–Greensboro.

Kristin Seefeldt is a research investigator and assistant director of the National Poverty Center at the University of Michigan.

James P. Ziliak is the Carol Martin Gatton Endowed Chair in Microeconomics in the Department of Economics at the University of Kentucky and is director of the University of Kentucky Center for Poverty Research.

Index

The italic letters *f, n,* and *t* following a page number indicate that the subject information of the heading is within a figure, note, or table, respectively, on that page.

About the Institute

The W.E. Upjohn Institute for Employment Research is a nonprofit research organization devoted to finding and promoting solutions to employment-related problems at the national, state, and local levels. It is an activity of the W.E. Upjohn Unemployment Trustee Corporation, which was established in 1932 to administer a fund set aside by Dr. W.E. Upjohn, founder of The Upjohn Company, to seek ways to counteract the loss of employment income during economic downturns.

The Institute is funded largely by income from the W.E. Upjohn Unemployment Trust, supplemented by outside grants, contracts, and sales of publications. Activities of the Institute comprise the following elements: 1) a research program conducted by a resident staff of professional social scientists; 2) a competitive grant program, which expands and complements the internal research program by providing financial support to researchers outside the Institute; 3) a publications program, which provides the major vehicle for disseminating the research of staff and grantees, as well as other selected works in the field; and 4) an Employment Management Services division, which manages most of the publicly funded employment and training programs in the local area.

The broad objectives of the Institute's research, grant, and publication programs are to 1) promote scholarship and experimentation on issues of public and private employment and unemployment policy, and 2) make knowledge and scholarship relevant and useful to policymakers in their pursuit of solutions to employment and unemployment problems.

Current areas of concentration for these programs include causes, consequences, and measures to alleviate unemployment; social insurance and income maintenance programs; compensation; workforce quality; work arrangements; family labor issues; labor-management relations; and regional economic development and local labor markets.